'DEEP AS THE SEA is no ordinary
biography, nor just another war
book. It is the chronicle of a man
through childhood, marriage, as a
father, a diplomat, as a wartime
serving officer and, finally, as a sailor
at peace.
It is freshly written, the war
descriptions are instant and alive,
and it retains a personal touch.'
SUNDAY TIMES

Also by Joy Packer

Novels

NOR THE MOON BY NIGHT
THE HIGH ROOF
THE GLASS BARRIER
THE MAN IN THE MEWS
VALLEY OF THE VINES
LEOPARD IN THE FOLD
VERONICA
BOOMERANG

Autobiography

PACK AND FOLLOW
GREY MISTRESS
APES AND IVORY
HOME FROM SEA

and published by Corgi Books

Joy Packer

Deep as the Sea

CORGI BOOKS
A DIVISION OF TRANSWORLD PUBLISHERS LTD

DEEP AS THE SEA

A CORGI BOOK 0 552 10488 4

Originally published in Great Britain by
Eyre Methuen Ltd.

PRINTING HISTORY
Eyre Methuen edition published 1976
Corgi edition published 1977

This book is set in Intertype 10 on 11 pt Times

Corgi Books are published by
Transworld Publishers Ltd,
Century House, 61–63 Uxbridge Road,
Ealing, London W5 5SA
Made and printed in Great Britain by
Cox & Wyman Ltd., London, Reading and Fakenham

*For our four grandsons
Ron, Chris, Tony and Will Packer*

CONTENTS

Part Four: SAILOR AT WAR

Part Five: SAILOR IN PEACE
1947–1962

PREFACE

From a letter to her Publishers, in London, written by Joy Packer in the Cape Peninsula, January 1974.

WHEN last I was in London we discussed a novel but after my return to South Africa a curious accident threw me in quite another direction. So here goes!

During 37 years of marriage, constantly interrupted by the Royal Navy's demands, Bertie and I depended on our letters to keep us together. They were a lifeline woven of ideas, confidences and the sharing of our separate experiences, some dramatic and important, some funny, some not.

My letters to Bertie, like my War diaries, vanished with so much else in World War Two. His to me I somehow managed to preserve with a few documents. They were kept in a locked cupboard and were never intended to be disturbed. But last September a leaking pipe in the cupboard forced me to open it and take out the mildewed papers to dry in my sunny study. For days I tried to forget them. Then I picked up a random letter to see if it was dry enough to put away again. It was addressed to 'Miss Joy Petersen' and dated 1924. An irresistible compulsion to read it shocked me out of an 11-year 'block'.

There were other things. A midshipman's log and a few letters to his father written from HMAS *Australia* in the Pacific at the outbreak of World War One and some from HMS *Warspite* before and after the Battle of Jutland in 1916. I had to read them and, having begun, couldn't stop. Every word opened new windows on a life outside a woman's comprehension – the cramped, communal, yet lonely life of a sailor, his involvement with his ship and shipmates, and the need to shake himself free of that 'tin box' and become part of the land again – of the scent of the seasons and growing things – and of a home and family, even though it might not be his own.

7

Suddenly I realized that here in my hands I held the very essence of a fighting man's life in peace and war, from the arrogance of the teenage officer to the tolerance of high command.

That is why I want to write a sort of biography of Bertie, but 'different' because it has been very humanly and unconsciously written for me already. I want to use extracts from those long-ago letters and papers because they reflect much more than one man's philosophy of life. They reflect many of the great events of the past half century, not in retrospect with the problems resolved and analysed, but vital and immediate with the guns hot from recent action or the wailing of the Turkish people mourning the death of Kemal Ataturk still echoing in the writer's ears.

He said 'a man was made to fight and love' and the fighting and the loving are in those faded letters.

Of course there is a certain amount of interference from me to clarify situations. Let's call it 'narrator's privilege' . . .

Part One: A Man Was Made to Fight and Love
1894 to 1925

1.
'The Royal Navy, my lad?
Takes your life and gives
you the world.'

HMS *St Vincent*	Shropshire, Osborne, Dartmouth
HMAS *Australia*	Home Waters
1894 to 1915	Atlantic, Indian, Pacific Oceans,
	1914 Outbreak of World War One

HERBERT ANNESLEY PACKER was born on 9 October 1894 at 'The Mount', Cressage in Shropshire, the house of his parents, Dr. and Mrs. William Packer. He was their fourth and last child. Three girls, Dorothy, Winifred and Marion, had arrived in rapid succession followed with equal haste by Bertie. He was an excellent example of his mother's persistence and determination.

'The Mount' was a spacious home furnished with austerity and some beautiful but sturdy antiques. The grounds were large with a tennis court and croquet lawn and fields for horses to graze, for Dr. Packer made his wide country rounds with a horse and trap. The view from the hilltop was wide unspoilt countryside, across the pretty village of Cressage and the Severn River to green meadows, the wooded hump of the Wrekin and the blue Welsh hills beyond.

Dr. Packer was born and educated in Cheltenham, qualified in London and after his marriage to Edith Mary

Rutter settled in Shropshire where, apart from an extensive country practice, he was medical visitor to Salop Private Asylums and made important contributions to *The Lancet* and *British Medical Journal*. His greatest interest was the human mind in sickness or in health.

Mrs. Packer had studied music in Dresden and was cultured and intellectual with a slightly acid wit. Her continental outlook was inevitably limited by her husband's work and the atmosphere of an inland county steeped in the long turbulent history of England. Her children inherited her facility for languages and were encouraged to read the original French and German classics on her bookshelves. They were taught by living-in foreign governesses till the girls were old enough to go to Cheltenham College and later Lausanne University.

At the age of seven Bertie spent several months in the Rhineland with relations of his sisters' German governess. He was a pupil at the village school.

There was no naval tradition in the Packer family. But there was the cook's brother, a petty officer who came on leave to Cressage from time to time and brought with him a briny aura of distant lands and peoples, of pirates, battles and adventure. Bertie's imagination was fired as he hung on the words of this spell-binder from afar. 'I'm going into the Navy one day,' he announced.

The cook's brother laughed and gave him a hearty slap on his shoulder. 'The Royal Navy, my lad? Takes your life and gives you the world. It's a bloody hard master but I wouldn't change places with any man.'

Bertie Packer entered the Royal Naval College, Osborne, on 15 September 1907. He was not quite 13.

Queen Victoria had died at Osborne, her Isle of Wight home, in 1901. After her death Edward VII presented it to the nation and part of the estate was converted into a Royal Naval College which flourished until 1921 when it was closed. Meanwhile cadets were being transferred to Dartmouth. Thus Bertie received his education at both Osborne and Dartmouth.

His first taste of the ceremonial pageantry for which Great Britain is famed was the coronation of King George V in the summer of 1911 at Westminster Abbey. Two of the new King's sons were also naval cadets, Edward in the term above young Packer and Albert in the term below. Both were destined for the throne.

Cadets and naval detachments lined the streets of London round Trafalgar Square on the coronation route.

'Weren't you lucky!' I said many years later. 'Such a great occasion and a ringside view.'

'All I saw of the procession was the rump of a guardsman's horse. I was directly behind it and there isn't a thing I couldn't tell you about that beast's tail. We'd had nothing to drink since the night before for obvious reasons, and I envied that uninhibited horse.'

There were many things the cadets learned over and above the normal school curriculum in both work and play. They studied the use of nautical instruments and weapons of war, the rituals of naval life ashore and afloat, the arts of fencing, markmanship, unarmed combat, swimming, sailing and rowing; and Bertie was ordered to learn the flute and the piccolo, all of which he enjoyed.

In 1912 he was awarded the King's dirk and gold medal, the highest honour a cadet could receive on leaving Dartmouth and a tribute to outstanding qualities of leadership.

Midshipman Packer was 17. He was appointed to his first ship, HMS *St. Vincent* in the Home Fleet. There he was issued with an impressively bound volume of strong blank paper.

S. 519
JOURNAL
FOR USE OF JUNIOR OFFICERS AFLOAT

The fly-leaf informed the owners that 'The Journal is to be kept during the whole of a midshipman's sea time' and that it would be regularly inspected and signed by the Captain. 'Midshipmen should understand that the main object of keeping the Journal is to train (a) the power of observation

11

(b) the power of expression (c) the habit of orderliness.' The Journal was to be illustrated with maps, sketches and diagrams of all things of interest or importance 'on their Station, in their Fleet or in their ship'.

Bertie's first entry in the LOG OF H. A. PACKER. MIDSHIPMAN RN was:

[*St. Vincent* 6 May 1912 Weymouth Bay] *I joined the ship at 6.30 p.m. Found the Fleet drawn up for review. All ships dressed for Anniversary of Accession. There are six lines of ships, total number 136. The great feature of this review is the conjunction with the Fleet of the Naval Aviation Corps consisting of three naval aeroplanes, one hydroplane and two aeroplanes. ...*
8 May *At 8.30 a.m the Royal Yacht,* Victoria and Albert, *approached. All the ships saluted with a Royal Salute of 21 guns.*

That was a great year for demonstrations of might. There was a Grand Parliamentary Review followed by Fleet manoeuvres and a mock war between the 'Red Fleet' and the 'Blue Fleet'. Military forces were landed and evacuated to see for themselves that Britain was the world's greatest sea power and intended to remain so.

A year later the British-built battle-cruiser HMAS *Australia* was launched, and Royal Navy officers and men were invited to volunteer to be lent to the Royal Australian Navy for the commission. Applicants with relatives in Australia would be favourably considered.

'It's a chance to circumnavigate the globe,' said Midshipman Teddy Billyard-Leake, whose father owned sheep and cattle stations in New South Wales. 'Not to be missed.' He was a lavish young man with bright ideas and he lent Bertie one of his maternal uncles. 'Just claim him as a relative. He won't mind.'

So a new page was opened in the Journal.

[*Australia*, 28 June 1913, Portsmouth] *All 14 midshipmen joined today. We slung our hammocks, finding as is usual*

*that a battleship is built for fighting and little space allowed
for personal belongings. The King accompanied by Edward,
Prince of Wales and the Commander-in-Chief came on
board to inspect the Flagship. His Majesty conferred on
Rear-Admiral Patey the K.C.V.O. He wishes it made known
that he was greatly pleased with the extreme smartness of
the ship especially after only one week in commission.*

By 15 August the *Australia* was under the Southern
Cross. 'After Quarters the ship was swung for deviation in
order to correct the compass from the Northern to the
Southern Hemisphere.' Two days later they sighted Table
Mountain, were joined by the cruiser HMAS *Sydney* and
sailed into Table Bay, passing 'The *Balmoral Castle* bound
for England with a cargo of ostrich feathers worth
£1,000,000'.

Cape Town fêted the Australian Squadron with the hospitality for which the Mother City of South Africa was
famous and Bertie fell in love with the Cape. The ten-day
visit was concluded by the *Australia* and *Sydney* sailing
round the Peninsula to Simon's Town. 'We took on board
with us some 100 guests, the chief residents of Cape Town.'
One of these fortunate guests was Dr. Julius Petersen, a
kind jolly man who had two sons, Fred and Norman, a
little younger than Bertie, studying medicine at the London
Hospital, and a small daughter aged eight whose name was
Joy.

The *Australia* crossed the Indian Ocean to her home port,
Sydney, on the Pacific coast of Australia, where she received
a rapturous welcome. As she steamed slowly past the
crowded Heads up harbour, in single line ahead of the rest
of the Australian Fleet, the whole of New South Wales,
from the Governor General to the youngest schoolchild, saluted this splendid new asset to the Royal Australian Navy.
Her subsequent visits to all the ports and islands of the continent was in the nature of a royal progress.

Bertie wrote home enthusiastically about this young new
country and its islands. Fishing for trout in the Huon River

in Tasmania, a fortnight's leave riding and shooting in the Blue Mountains where Mr. and Mrs. Billyard-Leake entertained a number of midshipmen and girls at their 20,000-acre station, Clifton, 'gum tree parkland, all wired against rabbits. ... The parrots were so pretty, getting up in coveys quite like partridges, kangaroos are protected here so not to be shot. We went to a picnic race-meeting, only about 200 people there, all the squatters within a 50-mile radius. We all had a splendid time, the old man and his missus being excellent hosts. When we got back the five senior snotties (midshipmen) had been made Acting Subs and are putting on no end of dog.'

By June 1914 Bertie was made Assistant Navigator to Commander C. D. Longstaff. 'We'll be very busy as it will be all sea time now. The Gunroom is awfully smart after our refit. We inveigled some nimble-fingered maidens into making new curtains and cushion covers for the Gunroom and old man Billyard-Leake has presented it with an upright piano we call Joanna.'

On 29 June he wrote to his father from Palm Island.

'... so pleased to get such fat budgets with family news ... there's a buzz going round the ship that there's another critical situation in Europe ... we heard by wireless that HMAS *Torch* landed a party at Malakula and lost four men, two being eaten by cannibals. Poor Sir George, our pet parrot, also met an untimely end. Thinking the electric fan some kind of joywheel he leapt gracefully on to it. We still spend odd moments picking him off the bulkheads and the deck above.'

That day Austria-Hungary declared War on Serbia after the assassination of the Archduke Francis Ferdinand and his Archduchess; Russia, Serbia's protector, mobilized; on 4 August Russia and France were at War with Germany and Austria-Hungary, and the German invasion of Belgium began. By midnight Britain, Belgium's guarantor, had declared War on Germany.

The Journal was headed.

[War Routine – Passage from Sydney North on War Duty,

Tuesday, 4 August 1914] *At 9 p.m. weighed anchor. Speeded on our way by cheering crowds, cathedral bells, bugles and bands. Darkened ship and when clear of the Heads went to Night Defence. Loaded with Common Shell. Full charges. Orders to fire at once if searchlights trained on target. Two prize crews have been told off.*

From now on Bertie's letters home arrived at irregular intervals in unstamped envelopes marked *On Active Service. From HM Ship.* On 22 August Japan entered the War against Germany and proved a valuable naval asset to the Allies. Admiral Patey, flying his flag in the *Australia*, with a squadron of Australians, British and Japanese ships, took care of the middle Pacific, occupying German possessions and hunting down German raiders. Samoa surrendered unconditionally and Bertie's knowledge of German came in useful. 'It's rather lucky being Acting German Interpreter as one gets behind the scenes a bit. I have to translate the demand for surrender, ultimatums etc.'

Rabaul, German New Guinea and the Bismarck Archipelago were taken over and Wireless Transmission Stations were located and put out of action.

These excitements were followed by the 'long monotonous job of convoying Australasian troops across this devilish big ocean' during which time the junior officers continued with their instructions and exams. Bertie no longer addressed letters to 'The Mount' at Cressage as his father had retired and the family home was now at 'Brieryfield' in the pretty village of Grinshill a few miles away. Dr. Packer was an officer of the 1st Shropshire Rifle Volunteers and at the outbreak of War had joined the Territorials, serving as Medical Officer at Prees Camp where he was promoted to Lieutenant-Colonel. The three sisters were all in War jobs, Dorothy in censorship and interpreter for the interrogation of German prisoners, Winifred in a 'hush-hush' unit in London and Marion in the Red Cross nearer home.

15

At Sea, HMAS *Australia*, *7 November 1914*

My dear Pa,

We are now properly cleared for action, every bit of wood-work gone, all doors, lockers, cupboards, even our sea-chests and Joanna, the piano. The Mess is just a barn, one table and a few chairs. I wonder if I'll see my belongings again. They are roving somewhere in the South Pacific. It's wonderful how everyone has settled down to months at sea. It certainly makes a ship a warship and not a species of hotel. In the evenings those not on watch have sing-songs. With no Joanna our band is a violin (Billyard-Leake), man-dolins, flute and piccolo (me – I borrow the band's). We gather round and make a noise in the Gunroom and Ward-room.

I did my Seamanship exam last week and got a First. Also a First in my Oral and Prelim. Navigation.

The ship is alive with cockroaches, all the food, our clothes and I even found one in my pipe yesterday. Of course we are on salt grub – bacon and beans and tinned meat. . . ;

They were patrolling the Suva-Sydney trade routes when the disastrous Battle of Coronel scored a victory for the German Fleet. Bertie wrote home:

'Much to everybody's disgust we were out of it. We regard the *Scharnhorst* etc., as *our* meat and *we* should have been there.' On 10 November, however, there was jubilation as the *Sydney* sank the *Emden* in the Indian Ocean after that famous raider had 'played havoc with British trade. It is calculated she sank some 20 ships before she finally met her fate off Cocos Island. In all cases her Captain had treated captured crews and survivors with great consideration. In fact everybody recognizes him as being the best type of German Naval Officer and a thorough sportsman.'

On 10 December Admiral Sturdee's Squadron sank the *Scharnhorst, Gneisenau* and *Leipsic* off the Falkland Islands and the balance was restored. Soon afterwards the *Australia* was ordered to Jamaica through the Magellan Straits.

[Thursday, 31 December] *2.30 a.m. Picked up Cape Pillar and into Magellan Straits. These Straits are most intricate with hundreds of straits leading off the Main Channel to long fjords and stretches of water. High rocky hills rise from the water's edge, bleak and rugged. Tho' it is midsummer snow caps the hills and when the mist rolls back the blue of glaciers relieves the unbroken snow blanket on the higher peaks. The sun is seldom seen in these parts, but we are a fairweather ship and we saw him now and again. We rounded the Southernmost point of Patagonia at noon. . . .*

On 6 January 1915 off the Falkland Isles at sunset 'smoke was sighted ahead and we gave chase. "A" Turret fired a Common Shell half a mile to the right of the ship which hove her to successfully'.

The ship turned out to be the *SS Eleanor Woermann* of Hamburg, and Bertie was sent over with the boarding party. 'While Lieutenant-Commander Allen interviewed the Captain I fell the crew in and mustered them, 84 Germans, 11 Monrovians and three Krooboys. Meanwhile the signal came that the ship was to be scuttled. The Admiral had to scuttle her as we could not spare men or time to take her to Jamaica and put her through Prize Court Proceedings. A scuttling party was sent over, who took off the Condenser Doors. The officers and crew went to the *Australia* in lifeboats.

'While waiting I picked up a few keepsakes – pillow cases, bath towels, a West African gong, an accordion, some knives and forks and a champagne pail. I was clumsy and will know how to do it better next time. Lieutenant Williams had the thing off pat. Took a black blanket from a bunk, a screw-driver from his pocket and slid along the dark side of the ship with the huge bundle over his shoulder. A barometer, two clocks, and masses of sugar dishes, tea pots and Lord knows what else.

'We got back on board at midnight. "X" Turret put a couple of shells into her, and the 4-inch a couple of lyddite. She went up in a burst of flame and steam and then began to settle by the stern. An impressive but melancholy sight as we

17

saw her in the searchlights gradually sinking, the flames dancing along the decks, the waves lapping her sides creeping higher, and then, without a sound, her bow rose up, her stern sank and she slid out of sight in a tumult of seething water. Then came comic relief. Where a big ship had been, a small steamboat rode proudly on the waves lifted clean out of her crutches. One thing which struck me about a sinking ship was the spars breaking away below the surface and shooting up as much as 20 feet into the air.

'It was a pity to have to do it, as she was luxuriously fitted and a fine strong ship.'

The *Australia* with her many prisoners on board did not go direct to Jamaica but to Plymouth where she arrived at the end of January.

Meanwhile Dr. Packer received a courteous note from the Australian High Commissioner written in his own hand.

Commonwealth Offices, 72 Victoria Street, Westminster,
23 January 1915

Dear Sir,
From certain information I have obtained you should not be surprised if your son, Acting Sub-Lieutenant H. A. Packer, were to arrive home for a few days' leave in the imminent future. It is also probable that he will then be appointed to some ship other than HMAS *Australia*. I must beg that you will consider this information as confidential and personal and I regret that I am not able to be more explicit. *I am yours faithfully (signed) Frank Haworth North.*

Bertie's midshipman's log ended on Friday, 29 January 1915 when he made his final entry.

Home after 1¾ years.

2

*'We had a very happy ship . . .
but also our bits of trouble.'*

HMS *Warspite*   Home Waters
1915 to 1918   Battle of Jutland
                            Surrender of German Fleet

ON 22 February 1915, Bertie was 'standing by' the not-quite-completed new battleship, HMS *Warspite* at Devonport. He was Acting Sub-Lieutenant training to be a Gunnery Specialist and he had much to learn about the complex anatomy of his new ship, the seventh of her famous name, her first ancestor having been built at the command of Elizabeth I and launched in 1596.

The *Warspite* was to become the great sea-love of Bertie's life and together they weathered her stormiest passages. She had one serious and very feminine fault, a tendency to become unmanageable. This was forgiven by all who served in her for she had high courage and where there was danger to her country and her country's Allies her great 15-inch guns roared their flame and fury.

A true fighting ship is a living thing with a character all her own. She is the life and soul of those who share her fortunes and misfortunes and who become part of her. Her story has been told by the official naval historian, Captain S. W. Roskill,* an old shipmate of Bertie's, who had many talks to him about the 'Old Lady' so dear to both their hearts. Of her first commission in 1915 he quotes Bertie as saying 'We had a very happy ship indeed but also our bits of trouble ... they seemed to make no difference'. The same could be said of a good marriage. The *Warspite* was true to

---

* HMS *Warspite The Story of a Famous Battleship* (Collins, 1957).

her motto, *'Belli dura despicio'* ('I despise the hardships of war') and she and her ship's company lived up to it in two World Wars.

She was commissioned on 8 March, then did her acceptance trials and experienced a few 'bits of trouble'. Bertie wrote to his father, 'We gave our sister quite a nudge. It was very rough and I was between decks talking to Commander (G.), when suddenly there was a shock. The ship bent and jumped like an india-rubber thing, engines full steam astern and our cable going out with a run and a rattle. I thought we'd caught a mine. Commander (G.), who'd been blown up once, didn't seem a bit worried but merely said 'Ah—' and told a bugler to sound off Collision Stations. I ran forward to my station for Close W-Tight Doors and found the whole place thick with steam and water swishing in for'd so I got the cell prisoners who are down for'd up out of it. Our bow was split like a pea-pod and we could only make about ten knots home against a bad head sea. Not too nice in a possible submarine area ... We worked day and night shoring up etc., and got in all right.'

So back they limped to Devonport. While the damage was repaired the young officers found digs ashore and continued studying their ship.

21 March 1915

My dear Guv'nor,
I am going to be very busy when we get aboard again. I am Officer of Quarters in 'X' Turret. There is a Lieutenant in charge of the control and I have to do the drilling, repairing of breakdowns etc., as in the *Australia.* Of course the Turrets are absolutely different. I am Assistant T (Torpedo Officer) and responsible for the whole ventilation of the ship and as there are 951 ventilating shafts I'll need a course of mental training to remember them all. Also I'll be Sub of the Mess when we go to sea with 18 snotties and three or four clerks.

All the officers I've met so far are awfully nice and all

brain-waves. Most of them have been in action with Beatty or in destroyers.

On 11 April they were on their maiden voyage with the new commission and on 13 April, arrived at Scapa to join Admiral Jellicoe's Grand Fleet.

[16 April 1915] . . . The ship is making visible progress now, thank goodness. Our Padré joined yesterday and seems to be a sportsman. He comes from Oxford and is a Rugger International.

The Gunroom seem an awfully good lot and it's rather interesting comparing notes. One lot were in the *Hampshire* in China and took the *Emden* wounded to Colombo. The other lot in the *Cornwall* in the Falkland scrap. The clerk has been bombarding off the Belgian coast. We have six Public School entries, very different from the Dartmouth snotties in many ways. Ignorant of the Navy and worried at having to work all day after a midnight till 4 a.m. watch. But they are learning and seem keen.

It's wonderful the difference all oil makes as regards the cleanliness of decks and so on. At sea in a coalship like the *Australia* there's a steady stream of 'stokers' (unburned coal) from the funnels which gets everywhere. We have none of this.

The Padré has helped us get up a band consisting up-to-date of the usual piano, one violin, two cellos, two flutes and two piccolos. We tried some of Haydn's Trios the other day without piano. It reminded me of our efforts in the schoolroom at Cressage. Have we still got those things we used to play – *Poet and Peasant, Tancredi* etc.? If so, I wish you'd send them.

With regard to the Mess, we're very comfortable. The only thing I forgot was a waste-paper basket. Of course it makes it much easier running the Mess with snotties who are so junior and therefore inclined to take what they are given.

The Army and Navy Stores are running a Laundry Ship up here with other stocks on board as well. Also we have a Hospital Ship with two dentists. I went to one the other day and while on board a lunatic patient burst away from his escort and leapt overboard. A doctor went in after him and tho' only in the water about five minutes the man was drowned. Not surprising as the temperature is about 34° to 36° F.

They tried to have me for income tax today as you warned would happen, but as I showed them my pay was £137 per annum and you allowed me £20 per annum the total of £157, had to pay no tax. I shall very nearly be worse off when I'm a Lieutenant.

We are looking awfully smart now and today with Mrs. Austen Chamberlain's gift, a 16 foot silk white ensign flying at the ensign staff we were the envy of all eyes.

I had a letter from Haworth North saying he's got me £13 Interpreter pay due to me from the Commonwealth of Australia. Pretty generous on the part of the 'wallabies', I think!

The Australians in the Dardanelles have been doing awfully well but they've got a devilish tough oyster to open as far as I can see.

The new expression among the sailors is *'Gott Strafe'*. Today I was passing the P.O. of the Quarterdeck on which holy place some flatfoot in the sideparty had left a greasy footprint.

Conversation.

Petty Officer to Able Seaman: 'Ere! What bloomin' son o' 'Am done this 'ere?'

A.S.: 'Jumper Collins in the Soide Party, 'ee done it.'

P.O.: 'Gawd straffy the Soide Party!'

(Exit in search of Jumper.)

I'm sure the Kaiser would turn down his moustache in righteous indignation at the rank blasphemy.

I dined with the Captain E. M. Philpotts last Friday and very nice too. He really is the best skipper in the Navy, and the Commander H. T. Walwyn too. We are undoubtedly very lucky and have a very happy ship. . . .

In that summer of 1915 the *Warspite* was working up efficiency, exercising in and out of Scapa Flow and sailing on manoeuvres with the Grand Fleet. In November she and

22

several of her sister ships joined the new 5th Battle Squadron under the command of Rear-Admiral Evan-Thomas at Scapa.

Scapa Flow is to all naval appendages a cold barren part of the Orkneys in which warships spend an immense amount of time preparing for battle. It is the secret place which few naval wives know. In Ludovic Kennedy's excellent book *Pursuit: The sinking of the Bismarck*,* I found my first real description of it. 'Scapa was ideal for guarding the approaches from the North Sea to the Atlantic, a sweep of water ... ringed almost entirely by islands, a natural refuge for war-weary ships ... the islands were heather and grass, seabirds and sheep and across the bare face of the Flow tempests blew, often for days on end. There were no shops, restaurants or girls, just a couple of canteens ... a hall for film-shows, and the occasional concert-party, football fields ... and yet in summertime when the Flow sparkled blue in morning sun and the hills of Hoy were touched with purple and green, at night time too when the Northern Lights wove pale patterns over the sleeping ships, the place had a rare beauty.'

Long afterwards when my book *Grey Mistress* was published a number of Bertie's old shipmates wrote and gave me new glimpses of a young man of 20. One wrote: 'I served under your husband when I commissioned HMS *Warspite* at Devonport in 1915. He was then Assistant Gunnery Officer and I was a Gunlayer 19 years of age. ... He was tough, strict and fair. ...' Another had joined the *Warspite* in 1917. 'I was a snottie, though older than most as I was a Public School entry, and though your husband was a Lieutenant, there was a bond of friendship between us. ... He had a rather sardonic air and could be pretty fierce if he was angry! On one occasion he said to me 'You are to go this afternoon to play for the ship against the Q.E. ...' 'Oh, Sir,' said I, 'I'm afraid I can't. I am playing golf with the

---

Padré.' He was furious!! 'What the devil do you mean?' he said. 'You've been chosen to play Rugger for the ship.' I said, 'I am greatly honoured, Sir, but I'm not used to backing out of my obligations.' He scowled at me. Then he laughed and said, 'Fair enough. If I square the Padré you'll play?' 'Of course,' I said. After the game, W. J. A. Davies (later Captain of England) told me I had the makings of a first class three-quarter. He took me in hand and the sequel was that I got an England cap! So it was largely due to Bertie. Did you know any of his contemporaries? Billyard-Leake, a flamboyant Australian. . . .'

In July the *Warspite* was in Rosyth 'near an absolutely beautiful river', where Bertie was able to get ashore sometimes and cycle four miles to fish for sea-trout. 'This place is chock-a-block with Highland Regiments. They look very fine. Brown as berries, marching along, bagpipes playing, fit for anything.' To his joy, 'flamboyant' Teddy Billyard-Leake joined the ship.

Soon afterwards, back at Scapa Flow, the whole Grand Fleet assembled and the 'Sailor King', George V, inspected his naval might. Bertie wrote to his father: 'The King steamed round the ships in a destroyer. Everyone fell in along the ship's side facing outboard with arm extended Navy fashion and cheered him as he passed. Just like in peacetime. We had a marchpast of 85 per cent of each ship's company. . . .

'I had a letter from Henry MacWilliam in Germany. He says that Rhodes (in my term, who is also a prisoner) got into trouble. He insisted on discussing the Crippen–Miss le Neve case with the German sentry all the way from the coast to Heidelberg. The German sentry both failed in sense of the ridiculous and knowledge of English. He thought Rhodes was pulling his leg and so reported him – without any serious consequences. MacWilliam also said "Please write to Rhodes. He's only had two letters since he's been here, one an LCC summons and the other a Dover Police Court summons." Poor old LCC. They have no sense of the ridiculous either. . . .'

In December the *Warspite* had a brush with the enemy –

'a misadventure' – and had to go into Devonport Dockyard, her home port, much to the satisfaction of the ship's company. She was back with the Fleet before Christmas, sailing 'in the worst blow I've ever been in – head sea, water coming in solid green lumps right over my unfortunate Turret, and spray right up to the Bridge. You simply could not walk against it unless you had something to pull yourself along by. Christmas Day was a splendid show and the Captain lunched with us in the Gunroom and was in great form.' The inevitable Fancy Dress Ball was followed by 'the great ceremony of the brewing of the punch and a right noble brew too. Then "Auld Lang Syne" and so toe bedde.'

HMS *Warspite*'s pantomime ushered in the New Year of 1916 with much hilarity. And at church on board in the grey ice cold northern winter the ardent prayers of eager warriors rose heavenwards, imploring the Old Testament God of Wrath to offer them a chance to get at the foe and smite him hip and thigh.

The New Year of 1916 began disastrously with the final failure of the long Gallipoli campaign, and on Easter Sunday a German-incited rebellion in Ireland did nothing to improve matters while, across the North Sea, British Intelligence reported unusual activity in Heligoland. The German High Seas Fleet, under Vice-Admiral Scheer, aimed to lure the Grand Fleet over the minefields outside the German ports into nests of U-boats, and in Scapa the Commander-in-Chief, Admiral Jellicoe, intended to bring the High Seas Fleet to action and annihilate it.

The scene was being set for the greatest naval engagement of all time, the highly controversial Battle of Jutland which raged round the North Sea Jutland Bank off the Danish coast during the calm summer day of 31 May to 1 June.

HMS *Warspite* and her sisters *Barham, Valiant* and *Malaya* comprised the 5th Battle Squadron under the Command of Rear-Admiral Evan-Thomas, part of the Grand Fleet gathering in the North Sea on that long hazy summer day darkened by the smoke and gunfire of 252 warships, 64 of them capital ships.

The 5th Battle Squadron in Beatty's section of the Fleet was where Bertie always wanted to be – right 'in the thick of it'. Winston Churchill has said in *The World Crisis* that at one stage '... the *Warspite* and *Malaya* fought the whole of the finest squadron in the German Fleet.'

Captain S. W. Roskill in HMS *Warspite* has written an account of the whole battle with its many manoeuvres, misunderstandings and separate engagements, and of that critical stage in particular. Beatty from his Flagship HMS *Lion* had signalled Admiral Evan-Thomas to turn and follow him to the north with the 5th Battle Squadron. Captain Roskill quotes the diary of Commander Walwyn, the *Warspite*'s Second-in-Command. ' "... Very soon after the turn ... I suddenly saw on the starboard quarter the whole of the High Seas Fleet ... masts, funnels, and an endless ripple of orange flashes down the line ... the noise of their shells was deafening ... I felt one or two very heavy shakes...." ' An officer who had an excellent front-row view from the cruiser *Southampton* wrote: 'The 5th Battle Squadron were a brave sight. They were receiving the concentrated fire of some 12 German heavy ships but it did not seem to be worrying them. I saw several shells hit the *Warspite*....' Commander Walwyn noted: ' "I distinctly saw two of our salvos hit the leading German battleship. Sheets of yellow flame went over her mastheads and she looked red fore and aft like a burning haystack...." '

But the *Warspite* too was receiving shell after shell, which was why, at 6.15 that evening, she saved the crippled cruiser *Warrior* by what appeared to be a sacrificial manoeuvre, circling round and round her, thereby drawing the fire of the High Seas Fleet upon herself. In fact her helm had jammed, she had become unmanageable and was behaving like a cat chasing its own tail. Captain Roskill wrote: '*Warspite*'s Sub-Lieutenant (Bertie Packer) was officer of "A" Turret at the time, and he has remembered those exciting minutes vividly. "In the end my Turret was the only one left in action. The direction had gone, the transmitting station had gone and I fired about 12 rounds at the enemy in local control. I was mentioned in despatches and specially promoted to Lieutenant – but *not* for hitting the target!" . . . Meanwhile the three remaining ships of the 5th Battle Squadron had slipped into the Grand Fleet's battle line and were trying to shield their comrade with their fire.'

The *Warspite* was struggling to resume her place in the battle line, but Admiral Evan-Thomas decided that the severely damaged battleship would be a liability rather than an asset and ordered her back to Rosyth. It was 8.30 p.m. when she began her hazardous return to port.

During the ensuing night the German High Seas Fleet and their Scouting Force used the hours of darkness to slip back into their home ports. At daybreak Admiral Jellicoe's Grand Fleet sought them in vain and finally set course for Scapa while the grey North Sea settled over many fine ships and those who had served in them.

Both sides claimed Jutland as a victory, the British because the High Seas Fleet were virtually imprisoned in their own ports for the rest of the War and the Germans because they had inflicted severe losses on the Grand Fleet.

The *Warspite* was attacked by shoals of U-boats on her way to safety but somehow survived and on 1 June at 8.30 a.m. she passed under the Forth Bridge amid wild cheers from troops lined ashore. By 3 that afternoon she was in Rosyth Dockyard where her wounds received attention.

The morning papers of 1 June 1916 carried pages about the Battle of Jutland, some news good, much bad. The *Warspite* was reported sunk. But in 'Brieryfield', a few hours later, Dr. Packer opened a telegram very different from what the family feared.

'SAFE BERTIE'

This was followed by a note.

HMS *Warspite*, c/o GPO, Saturday, 2 June 1916

My dear Pa,
At last a chance of writing you a very slight enlargement on my telegram.

Since last Tuesday life has been crowded with incident which I'm not permitted to write about.

Personally I'm fit as a flea but only uncomfortable owing to a total lack of water to wash in or clothes to change into, but these are trifles.

I think your knowledge of the happenings will soon be pleasantly increased. The first communiqué was not optimistic, the second better, and we await the third with confidence and optimism. . . .

Bertie and the ship of his heart had been blooded together in the greatest naval victory since Trafalgar.

From then on Germany depended on her U-boats to starve Britain and sink her convoys. In February 1917 she proclaimed *Unrestricted Submarine Warfare. All merchant vessels, neutral or not, would be sunk without warning.* America was enraged to find her own ships being torpedoed off her own coast. In April Russia, in the throes of Revolution, collapsed and signed a separate Armistice with Germany. But the United States more than restored the balance by declaring War on Germany on 16 April. Her immense resources and manpower supplied the blood-transfusion to the War-weary Allies.

On 14 October Bertie wrote home from Scapa: 'Of course by far the greatest topic here is the mutiny in the German Navy. We all wonder how far it went. It's very cheering news!' On 14 January 1918 he posted his last letter from HMS *Warspite*, again from Scapa.

. . . Yes this is a proper Gunnery Course I've put in for which will qualify me as a specialist with additional pay of 2/6 a day. So I'll be a plutocrat after all!

We are coated all over with ice and it's blowing half a gale. Mooring ship with everything frozen up was a nasty job and it's impossible to keep warm on watch. However, the prospect of a drop of leave gets the blood circulating and I've not got frost-bitten tho' two of my men did, their feet and hands swelling up like pumpkins.

Bertie qualified as a Gunnery Specialist and became a

'plutocrat', but he was envious of his friend Billyard-Leake who was in the famous Zeebrugge operation of 22 April which, with the Ostend action, effectively closed the Straits of Dover to the enemy. 'What price Master Billyard-Leake at Zeebrugge?' he wrote home 'Lucky young tiger, he deserves full marks. It's put new heart into the Navy from cook's mate to Commander-in-Chief, I'll lay on that. It proves what *can* be done if one has a dart at it. Billyard-Leake was wounded in the leg but the shrapnel's been cut out and he's toddling round on crutches.'

In August Bertie was temporarily appointed to HMS *Marlborough* and on 10 November the last shot of the War at sea was fired by a German U-boat torpedoing the veteran battleship *Britannia* off Cape Trafalgar. Germany's destroyer and submarine flotillas had remained loyal to the last.

Next day the Armistice was signed. And on 21 November 1918 HMS *Marlborough* was at Rosyth and Bertie witnessed the most moving sight of World War One, the surrender of Germany's High Seas Fleet, a formidable array of battleships, cruisers, destroyers and submarines.

They steamed slowly between the long lines of British warships and anchored below the Forth Bridge where, in the wintry sunset, the German flag was hauled down for the last time.

Yet that was not the end. In the summer of 1919 the interned and disarmed ships lay in Scapa Flow awaiting the Allied decisions about their disposal. When the final peace terms were signed Germany's naval might was reduced to next to nothing and her still impressive ships were to be divided between the victorious Allies.

But at 10 o'clock on that bright midsummer morning on 21 June 1919, by pre-arranged signal, the skeleton crews opened the sea-cocks and all the vessels of the once proud adversary sank beneath the waters of the Flow.

3
'I didn't enjoy seeing you off.'

HMS *Dublin*   South Atlantic
1922 to 1924

AFTER a West Indian training cruise there were other ships, cruises and courses. With peace restored Lieutenant Packer made the most of the lighter side of life.

In 1922 he was appointed Gunnery Officer of HMS *Dublin*, a cruiser in the South Atlantic Fleet based on Simon's Town. The girls of the Cape Peninsula loved the Royal Navy, and the squadron returned the compliment.

In the summer of 1923, he was invited to dinner by Mr. and Mrs. Fritz Spilhaus and their daughter, Freda, my close friend, who lived near my home, 'Tees Lodge', on the lower slopes of Table Mountain. Freda rang me up one summer afternoon.

'Can you and Fred come to dinner next Saturday? Mother's getting up a party before the dance at Wynberg Club. Some naval officers are coming.'

I was 18, a University student and all I knew of the Navy was that my brother, Fred, towards the end of the War, had been probationer surgeon in a destroyer. After the War, he resumed his studies at the London Hospital and had recently returned to Cape Town to go into partnership with a well-known ear, nose and throat surgeon. My younger brother, Norman, also a surgeon, was still gaining experience in hospitals in England.

'I'm sure Fred would love it, Freda,' I said, 'but I think I'd better be out of it—'

'Nonsense, Philip Glover, the Flag Lieutenant, looks like a Spanish matador and is the Navy tennis champion. His partner, who won the Navy doubles with him, is in the *Dublin*. His name's Packer but we call him Uncle.'

'Why Uncle? Sounds a bit old and dull.'

Freda's voice bubbled with amusement.

'He's pretty old – 28 – but not dull, and being Uncle gives him all sorts of privileges. You wait and see. I met him in Norway last year when I was staying with friends there. He was in a visiting warship, the *Téméraire*. He said his feeling for me was strictly avuncular, but it slips occasionally and then he's rather naughty. Well, we'll expect you and Fred at 7.30 on Saturday.'

Fred, who was kind and exuberant and could make any woman from eight to 80 feel attractive, jollied me out of my shyness; Freda was merry and poised, her parents charming as always, and the Flag Lieutenant told me that blondes called Joy should write their names in the Visitors' Book at Admiralty House as soon as possible – tomorrow, in fact. Freda's cousin, a dancing sort of girl called Cecil Barry, used her seductive green eyes to entrance my brother, and there were several other guests. A gramophone played background music softly. The 'naughty Uncle' was adrift.

Suddenly a roar in the drive and some fearful explosions heralded his arrival. Mrs. Spilhaus went into the hall.

'Oh, good!' I heard her say. 'We'd almost given you up.'

'I'm terribly sorry. My old palfrey went lame at Plumstead and I had some trouble getting him under way again. Dirty work. May I wash my hands?'

A very odd thing happened to me then. *I knew that voice.* I'd known it always. Deep, with light and shade and a hint of laughter.

Freda greeted him as he came into the room.

'Hullo, Unkie. That horse of yours – that awful motorbike! Always breaking down. Have a cocktail ... Joy and Fred Petersen, this is Lieutenant Packer—'

He was tallish, darkish, with blue eyes that narrowed and crinkled at the corners. His smile and his nose were crooked and he had a weathered look. You felt he'd be master of most situations. I was glad to find him next to me at dinner. He made me feel safe. Pretty too, because the blue humorous eyes told me so. He was a stranger, yet he wasn't.

Mrs. Spilhaus said: 'Uncle, it looks as if you've got yourself a new niece. Your youngest yet.'

'That's dangerous. The youngest is always the most beloved, I'm told.'

Next day my mother telephoned my favourite aunt. I overheard mother's end of the conversation.

'I can't go with you to the cinema tomorrow, Etha. I'm taking Joy to call at Admiralty House in Simon's Town. . . . Yes, I know it's silly while she's still at University, but she met a naval officer last night. . . . What has that to do with it? Everything, my dear. She says he's quite unusual and has a wonderful voice, and he'll be there. . . . Yes, she's crazy about his voice. They get that way at her age. . . . Oh, no, Etha! It's *not* the beginning of the end. What a thing to say!'

To begin with he joined Gardens Tennis Club in Cape Town instead of Wynberg, which was a great deal nearer Simon's Town, the naval base of HMS *Dublin*. He partnered my brother Fred in the first team in the League matches. Of course, if there was a Navy match anytime, he partnered Philip Glover.

In the circumstances 'Uncle's palfrey' – that terrible motorbike was often parked in 'Tees Lodge' drive, and after a homely supper, he'd play a rubber of bridge with my parents. Sometimes the Flag Lieutenant, who seemed to have a good deal of 'business' in Cape Town, made up a fourth, or Fred took a hand if he had no better fish to fry. I watched, got bored, and decided it was a good move to learn this game in self-defence. Mother began my instruction.

When the swimming and tennis season was over and the winter storms hit the Cape, the *Dublin* departed on a west coast cruise. Fred, sorry for my long face, ruffled my hair and laughed.

'High time your war-horse galloped off to sea, my babe. Cheer up!'

The ship sailed in the afternoon while I attended a social anthropology lecture on the tribal customs of the Andaman Islanders. My mind was elsewhere, for early that same morning a young sailor had arrived at 'Tees Lodge' bearing a note and a package for me. He had a fresh sun-tanned face with a knowing beam all over it.

'From Lieutenant Packer,' he said, and waited for me to open the package.

My heart was jumping about as I drew the little ivory figurine from its bed of cotton wool and tissue paper.

'Oh, no, he loves this! His little Japanese girl—'

I had seen and admired the charming little ivory girl in his cabin many times. She'd kept odd company with a coconut Fijian head with a small pipe in its grinning mouth.

'There's a note too,' said the sailor. 'Any answer, Miss?'

I nodded. 'Please have a cup of tea or coffee while I write one. I'll tell Cookie.'

So Cookie took his tea on to the stoep and Mummy joined him for a 'cuppa' while I scribbled my first note to Lieutenant H. A. Packer. His to me – also the first – threw me into a whirl.

HMS *Dublin, Friday morning.*

Joy dearest,

A simple sailor with a beautiful smile – look at him and watch it spread slowly across his face – is bringing you my little Japanese lady to look after you.

She was quite alone and very home-sick when I found her in a little store in Sierra Leone. I asked her if she would run away with me and she just gave me a gentle look and put her little hand in mine.

I told her last night she must leave me to go and stay with the dearest girl in the world with the kindest heart and the prettiest smile and the naughtiest look, and would she look after her and keep her very nearly true.

She said she'd try for my sake, but she's jealous. So don't let her feel neglected.

Write to me lots and lots. Saldanha and Walvis will find me, but don't wait to write, just do so when you feel you like me a bit better than anyone else.

Uncle.

I called the little Japanese lady *Sayonara*, which in her own language means 'Goodbye', and I loved her dearly. At Walvis Bay in South West Africa he'd heard from me.

Joy, most beautiful of nieces,
I wanted to say 'most beloved of nieces' but a wily old war-horse can't go and give himself away like that.

We came up here from Saldanha at full speed rattling and crashing – it's fine! When we are at sea I keep watch every morning from 4.0 a.m. till 8.0 a.m. I think everything out then. One is up in the fresh air in the dark, all alone, and not much to do and one's brain is ever so clear. So if one morning you wake at about 5.0 a.m. and find an ear burning like the fiery furnace you'll know it's me thinking about you.

Today I sailed over to the Whaling Station where they were cutting up and boiling down whales at full speed. There's only one smell I know worse than putrefying whale corpses and that's human beings burnt alive. However, we don't talk about the War nowadays. ... A whale's anatomy is now an open book to me. It's remarkably human and that's why it interests me. Human anatomy and above all human mentality is the most interesting study there is because in my line of country where you are continually meeting new people under every conceivable variety of condition you've got a continual supply of 'models'. I study them the whole time I'm talking to them.

I'm afraid you're different. I can't even try because when I'm with you, my dear – steady, my lad, you're writing to your niece!

Are you playing lots of tennis and getting new freckles I haven't seen? Tell me all about yourself – everything – because you know I'll understand. Somebody has taught you how to write a letter and somebody has taught me how to appreciate it – so remember that. ...

In the summer our friend, Freda Spilhaus, and Captain

34

D'Urban Cloete, the South African *aide-de-camp* to the Governor General, Prince Arthur of Connaught, were married.

A week before the wedding Mr. and Mrs. Lochner de Villiers, the most hospitable of couples, gave a dinner party for the prospective bride and bridegroom and their attendants and a few special friends. I was one of the six bridesmaids; 'Uncle' was to be an usher. The historic de Villiers homestead of 'Klein Constantia' had never looked more enchanting with its yellow-wood rafters and floors, teak shutters, silver candelabra and a rose bowl overflowing with perfect blooms. Violet shadows of oak leaves were painted on moonlit gables and, below the wistaria pergola, honeysuckle poured its scent over a white balustrade on the path to the swimming-pool. Ethereal mountains curved round the old house and the vineyards stretched down the long valley to the twinkling lights of False Bay.

We were all immortal that night – young forever as we danced or strolled with our partners – partners for an evening, for a while, and, in the case of Freda and me, for a lifetime.

In November, Lieutenant Packer told my parents that he and I wanted to marry. They were sympathetic but adamant that their daughter was too young, impressionable and inexperienced to know her own mind. Moreover, she was undomesticated and impractical. Life in the Navy was precarious for a woman – no real security. Anyway they were taking her to Europe for a holiday, Christmas in Switzerland, then Monte Carlo and London.

'Next year, when she's 19 we'll talk about it again if you both feel the same way about each other.'

So my parents and I sailed for Southampton on a bright summer afternoon with just enough southeaster to set the white horses romping in the bay.

HMS *Dublin, Sunday, 18 November 1923*

. . . When you sailed today I was on the Upper Road to see

35

you go and my palfrey and I bade you goodbye and wished you God-speed together.

I didn't enjoy seeing you off and am not going to do that again. '*Ça coute trop chèr*' as you'll soon be saying to Madame la Modiste. . . . *Thursday* Fred and I played tennis at Rondebosch yesterday. Then we swam, dined and played bridge with the de Villiers at 'Klein Constantia'.

The honeysuckle on the way from the house to the swimming-pool was smelling away and redoubled its efforts when it saw me coming. It made my heart jump. It was our night, that one; you said it should be, and it was.

You know I've knocked about a good deal and I've never found a family as happy as yours. Of course you realize it's your mother and father, the kindest people imaginable. I love seeing them together. That afternoon when we were sitting on the grass bank they were walking arm in arm on the tennis court, so content. And they've been married 30 years. Let's be like that. . . .

My younger brother Norman, who was a surgical registrar in a big Manchester hospital, joined us for Christmas in Switzerland and we had fun and falls learning winter sports.

On 11 December my 'Dublin Uncle' wrote from 'Tees Lodge' where he was spending a few days with Fred while waiting to take passage to Portsmouth in a naval cruiser.

. . . I came back here from Freda and D'Urban's last night. Fred was out playing bridge but Cookie, looking very coy in a snappy kimono, let me in and doubtless remembering your instructions on parting – 'Mr. Packer take whisky and soda? What time Mr. Packer like breakfast?' – took a lot of trouble about me and has even darned my socks! Fred has put me in his room. He reckoned I wouldn't be able to sleep if he put me in yours. I reckon he's right. The house is pathetic in its loneliness and wonders where you have gone.

I get promoted the day after tomorrow – Lieutenant-Commander H. A. Packer after that please. I'm very touchy about my rank. This is the last letter you'll get for about three weeks and then if you're not careful you'll get me.

Joy dear, d'you know what the Captain told a man he had staying with him on board as his guest? He told him that I was the one officer here he'd pick out as likely to get on in the Navy if I stuck to it. It sounds like blowing my own trumpet but as I seem to matter a bit to you I thought I could tell you and you'd be interested. I wouldn't tell anybody else. I'd hate to. . . .

But the Captain's guest had met my Aunt Etha and repeated the Captain's remark. She immediately wrote and reported it to my mother. It underlined one basic fact. Bertie Packer would stick to the Navy. It was his vocation. My parents sighed, for they still disapproved of a life of inevitable partings and regretted the meagre pay of a naval officer without private means.

4
'A Man was made to fight and love.'

HMS *Excellent*	South of France
1924	Portsmouth

TOWARDS the end of January Norman left us in Switzerland. Daddy, Mummy and I went to Monte Carlo where Bertie planned to join us. But the course of true love was impeded by a pair of rusty nail-scissors when he carelessly cut a toe-nail and finished up with a badly poisoned leg in a nursing home in London.

50 Beaumont Street, London W1, Monday, 21 January 1924

... Too silly, the village doctor wrote this morning telling me to write him details and symptoms so that he could 'calm' my mother. She oughtn't to bother about me. When I was a kid and got anything the matter she'd turn me out into the fields after breakfast and not let me into the house till supper time. I had a wonderful three months of whooping cough like that and never enjoyed anything so much except for odd moments of whooping my soul out.

Two of my sisters visited me yesterday. The one is a perfect dear (Marion) and the other (Winifred) is too clever. She's secretary to an MP and knows a damn sight more about it than he does.

I've been reading a lot of Nursing Home trash. In every book the husband and wife come to blows and don't understand each other. What an outlook if one believed it!

The only book I've enjoyed since being in bed is a country book and the farmer says to his young lady: 'When we'm married, Mary, the first 'ard word you'll ever 'ear from me will be in answer to your'n.'

At last the poisoned leg cleared up, and one splendid day

at the end of January, I walked down the hillside to Monte Carlo Station.

The month that followed was wonderful. We danced and played tennis and discovered the mountain villages and little fishing harbours of this glorious coast. We discovered each other too – within tantalizing limits.

On my 19th birthday we went to a jeweller's shop in one of the little streets on the hillside above the sea.

'I don't need a present,' I told my lover. 'I have *Sayonara* already.'

'*Sayonara* means goodbye. This will be the opposite.'

'She'll be jealous – our little ivory lady.'

'She'll be glad. She's going to have us both.'

His birthday present was a very narrow eternity ring of diamond chips. It fitted the little finger of my right hand rather loosely and the third finger of my left hand perfectly.

It was noon when we got back to the hotel and Daddy and Mummy were on the terrace. We told them that when we returned to London at the end of the month we would like to get married quietly right away and then we'd find a small flat in Portsmouth or Southsea, somewhere near HMS *Excellent*, the Gunnery School to which Bertie had been appointed.

'It's not a ship,' Bertie explained. 'It's a big shore establishment, rather lovely, on a sort of island attached to Portsmouth. Whale Island. It's a shore job – two years and good leave. It would be a wonderful start for us.'

'You've only known each other a few months. Marriage is for life – you mustn't rush into it. . . .'

Why did we give in?

Mine was an exceptionally united family. We wanted their blessing. We also badly needed the £300 a year they would allow me if we waited. My future husband's pay after tax deduction was £516 a year. For a bachelor the Navy was fine. But a wife then was an unrecognized appendage granted no marriage or travel allowance and no free medical attention (unlike the Army, where families were accepted as reasonable encumbrances). Today's Navy has changed and is allowed the obvious perquisites our generation was denied.

So I sailed for home with my parents and Bertie went to Shropshire for the tail end of his leave. His father had for some years been slowly paralysed by Parkinson's Disease for which there was as yet no cure. After nearly three years abroad it must have been a sad homecoming, even for the tough philosopher he was.

'Brieryfield', Grinshill, Salop, 4 March 1924

. . . I arrived home to find nothing but snow, all looking very beautiful but rather wet to walk on and in.

Much to my surprise I found my youngest sister – my favourite one – at home. Last night over the fire I couldn't keep it in any longer so I had to tell Marion all about you. She took it very calmly. . . . I found my father just about the same, quite helpless now. He sits in his chair absolutely still, eyes not moving and tries to talk. He can at times and is very clear-headed. My mother is very much altered – looking at least ten years older but simply brim full of grit – won't give in and won't go away for a change. She was very pleased to see me. I knew that when she produced some beautiful old claret for dinner last night. . . .

Our habit of writing our thoughts and feelings to each other was established during the following months. It assuaged the need for one another which was the recurrent fever of our lives – a sort of soul malaria induced by the demands of an inexorable Service.

In the summer Bertie spent three weeks at Bisley Camp in Surrey where he lived in a tent, ate in the Army Mess and shot for the Naval rifle and revolver teams in his charge.

Army Rifle Association, Bisley, 12 July 1924

. . . Such wonderful weather here. You'd love it. Nothing can beat England when you get real sunshine because it doesn't go brown and dry and dusty but is so green and smells lovely.

I'm so proud of you getting that article in the *Argus*. You get better and better so go on with journalism. The German friends you met on board sound delicious. The lady especially. Her saying Englishmen make love like butchers may, I'm afraid, have a tiny grain of truth in it. A woman once told me the same. She was a woman of many lovers and very catholic in her tastes but she said that nobody could make love like a German – not even a Frenchman. The Germans, she said, are robust in their love-making but tender and passionate too; the French, she said, were too effeminate altho' very subtle. *Auf Wiedersehen, liebchen.*

The 'woman of many lovers' was French. I never knew her name or, to my knowledge, met her. Had I done so, I would surely have hated her with great ferocity. As it was, I always felt a strong affinity for her and even a touch of gratitude.

The Bisley Rifle Meeting ended; the Navy team did well, and Bertie went to London to play in the Navy tennis championships. He won the doubles with Commander Woodhouse. His usual partner Philip Glover was still at Simon's Town.

He stayed in London with his sister Marion, who worked for Glaxo's which was destined to reach great eminence during World War Two when it developed penicillin and streptomycin.

7 Dover Mansions, Brixton, SW2, Sunday morning, 20 July 1924

... I am writing this in my sister's flat. She met me at Bisley after the Rifle Meeting to see the Prince of Wales presenting the prizes. He looked very smart and charming, speaks well, but he is nervous with his hands.

My eldest sister is to be married in September. When I go home for her wedding I'll tell my mother about us. She would hate to have it sprung on her suddenly. She'd feel

41

very hurt, tho' she wouldn't say a word. She never has. She has always let me do exactly as I liked since I've been at sea – before that, exactly what *she* liked. Which shows she is a woman of sense and is not narrow-minded.

What a different family we are to yours. We've all been absolutely independent – all fond of each other, but not more so than if we were very good griends. I was always trying to make a real friend of my father – but he would never let me. Perhaps he was doing the same and I wouldn't let him.

I see you've been reading *Peter Jackson*. I read it when it came out and liked it immensely – chiefly because of the War bits. No person who was not in it could realize what the War was like. A man was made to fight and love. They are the two big things in his life. A good fighter makes a good lover because if he can fight hard he can love hard.

Do you remember the film *La Bataille*? It made you unhappy, didn't it? But I know this, my beloved Joy, if ever we had another war and I had to go off and fight you'd be a real sailor's wife then. Just like the little Japanese woman was. That chin of yours would come in handy then. There's nothing of the weakling about you. Dependent you are, thank God. That is because you are so essentially a woman. But a weakling, no!

5
'*A great love that's going to grow for the rest of our lives . . .*'

HMS *Excellent*   Portsmouth
1924 to 1925

ON 15 August, my parents gave way and our engagement was announced. I slipped the little eternity ring from the small finger of my right hand to the third on my left and sent Bertie a cable. His reply came fast rate. Just one word 'SPLENDID'.

No airmail or trans-ocean telephone then. His letter followed by sea.

HMS *Excellent, Portsmouth, 15 August 1924*

Joy, my darling,
I'm the happiest man in the world – madly and gladly happy in spite of missing you more than ever. And oh, so proud . . . I got your cable just before dinner and, well laugh at me, I simply couldn't eat any dinner. Hold that against me for the rest of my life! Your cable was sent at 3.15 today and I got it at 7.30 p.m. So close, just four hours away but 6,000 miles all the same.

D'you know what pleased me most? It was taking me at my word.

I gave you an absolutely free hand to announce our engagement when you liked. I remember doing it on our last day, walking towards Buckingham Palace.

This is a great love, my Joy, that's going to grow for the rest of our lives and pull us through the bad bits because I know it can. You are giving your happiness into my hands and should they fail I'd want to be dead. . . .

Darling, I was frightfully bucked about my confidential

43

report but it's all been driven out of my mind and I wouldn't tell you all that was in it or you'd think I was a swankpot. But it was full of 'exceptionals' and the Captain said 'he has a very strong personality which exerts a very good influence on his Messmates, he is even-tempered and of a buoyant disposition' and lots of other tripe and tommyrot. . . .

Tuesday Listen, Joy dear, don't let's wait till May to get married. Let's make it February and go to Monte Carlo for our honeymoon!

Friday, 12 September 1924

. . . Your cable arrived this morning to say February was the month. I've never been so happy about anything. Only five months, *liebchen,* looking forward to something very tangible and somebody very beloved.

Today I have enjoyed myself so much. It has been soft and sunny – the occasional summer day one gets in September. This afternoon I took an armchair on to the lawn and read a story in *Blackwood's Magazine.* An old farmer, in giving advice to a youngster, says, 'If you can't do nobody no good, doant do 'em no 'arm.'

That's fine. I like that.

Later In my mother's letter to me she said how pleased she was about us so I expect she'll write to you herself.

Though it's very different from the way you all love your mother – I love mine too. Don't think I don't, but being away so much and she having been a very busy person all her life and a very undemonstrative one, naturally enough doesn't show it so much. She can't. But she's a wonderful woman and used to be very much a woman of the world, that's why I think it's so splendid of her to retire from everything she loved in the way of recreation and devote herself to looking after my father who is just as crotchety as a permanent invalid can be.

From his letters I had already come to know his many friends in Portsmouth, but now I began to feel the genuine and practical kindness and welcome waiting for me for his sake. Old shipmates from HMAS *Australia* were to become our lifelong friends.

Teddy Billyard-Leake was now married and was Flag Lieutenant to the Commander-in-Chief, Portsmouth. Commander 'Cuddie' Longstaff, the Navigator who had taken Bertie ashore with him as Assistant Navigator in remote Pacific Islands, was retired and lived in Southsea with his charming wife, Hillie, in a beautiful house of great hospitality. Wyn Macintosh of Sydney and her New Zealander Surgeon Captain husband had promised to lend us their little daughter Margaret as my bridesmaid.

Bertie's eldest sister, Dorothy, was married on 25 September, at Grinshill, and he went home for the wedding and to give her away, deputizing for their father.

Grinshill, Friday, 26 September 1924

... All is peace again after yesterday's turmoil of kissings, cakes and conversation.

The wedding went off splendidly.

Dr. Norman Capon, the husband, comes from Liverpool, so I gave a lunch at the Village Pub to him and his friends. Very cheery. We quite woke up the place. He's a dear. I think Dorothy is lucky and so is he. He is very charming with a most attractive face, manners and smile and I'm sure will be a huge success as a children's specialist. He was in the Royal Army Camel Corps in the Desert during the War.

In the bar of the pub where we foregathered was a curious-looking stranger, obviously on a walking tour, with a dog and no coat. I thought he was what they call here 'weak in th' yed'. I was laughing and chatting to everybody and he suddenly turned to me and said, 'I can see things – yes I can see things not so far off. There's happiness for you – so much happiness! Today is a wedding day. By your smile it is not long till you too are wed. You may not believe me, but I can see—' and then relapsed into muttering 'I can see, I can see!' I asked who he was but nobody knew and he certainly didn't know who I was. It gave me quite a jump.

My father is very visibly worse. He can only just speak

45

now. It's all rather dreadful, a kind of living death. My mother keeps going but doesn't look any younger. She was anxious to hear all about you. Already she's planning all sorts of things as best she can – about getting to London somehow to meet you and what she can do for you. She's very excited about us really, but doesn't show it. But then, where sentiment is concerned, we're a very Spartan family.

I dare say you've noticed it.

Tomorrow being Saturday, I'm off back to Portsmouth. I have to drive past our old home. 'The Mount', at Cressage about 16 miles away, so am going there for lunch. It always gives me little twinges when I go back there. I was 19 when we sold the place, and being in the country I knew every tree, where there were holes in the hedges one could crawl through, where the trout in the brook lived, where I could shoot a rabbit or wood-pigeon or wait in the winter for the wild duck to pass over.

His sister's wedding intensified his planning for ours.

HMS *Excellent, Friday, 3 October 1924*

... I've had such a brain-wave I can't keep it in, so I've dashed up in the dinner hour to tell you.

We'll have the reception after our wedding here. It's a splendid place for it and no trouble whatever. We've got everything, rooms, waiters and a very good Messman who will do the catering, and it's only about $\frac{1}{4}$ mile from St. Mark's Church where we'll be married.

It's never been done before and we shall be the privileged pair to start it!

His letter was continued during a weekend at Windsor with his great friend and term-mate, Philip Rhodes. It was a large house-party. (Philip was invalided out of the Navy after the War during which he spent four years as a prisoner of war in Germany. He was now a highly successful jobber on the Stock Exchange.)

... People are dears to me and I often wonder why. All the party were anxious to do everything they could, to lend houses or cars or waiters or things for our wedding. It's the same with friends in Portsmouth. I'm damned if I deserve it.

We had one quaint problem. It seemed to my older relatives absurd that I should call my future husband 'Uncle' or 'Unkie', as was my habit. Then what? Bertie had many nicknames – a good sign. A man without a nickname is a man without a friend. But to his parents and mine he was Bertie. I resolved to call him Bertie on all formal occasions. As he grew more senior the switch to Bertie inevitably became more of a habit, but never when we wrote to each other.

In his last letter to me before I left 'Tees Lodge' for England he had a momentary qualm.

... I expect you'll hate leaving and will be very miserable saying goodbye to all your friends. Don't be unhappy. Remember your man is waiting for you and living for you. ...

A happy voyage, *liebchen*. All my love goes with you on Friday. ... Give my love to Cookie before you go. Don't forget.

When we reached Madeira, letters came on board for me. Only one was sad. Bertie's father had died.

Grinshill, 2 December 1924

... My heart is full to overflowing. The funeral was today – everything naturally very gloomy, and then, when things were becoming insupportable, your letter arrived. Providence knows that you want to be sympathetic and understanding always, and so it allowed your letter to come on this of all days and cheer me up enormously.

I arrived here last night. Fortunately Marion was here when Father died. It must have been horrible for her. It's away in the country, this house, and in winter the wind moans and whistles round it as it's doing now. But she rose to the occasion, firmly and quietly arranged everything and

47

collected the family, so today we were all here. That is enough of what is past and done with.

I've been talking to mother and got her thoroughly interested in you and our wedding plans and she's bucking up already.

Anyhow, if it does seem quaint to cure funerals by weddings it works!

I believe the world is a wonderful place, and in everybody more good than bad if you look for it. I believe that perfect love, understanding and trust is possible between a man and a woman and that it can last.

That's my creed.

Let's think big and act big, jealous always of each other, but not guilty of petty jealousies, stupid little things that can blow up into the Lord alone knows what magnitude.

That's the logical way – the 'big' way of looking at it, but all the time you jolly well know I'd fight like 40,000 dyspeptic wild cats to keep you – and it isn't easy at long range!

Bertie's mother made the stupendous effort of coming to London to stay with Marion in order to meet us. Winifred (the high-brow sister) was there too. Dorothy and Norman Capon could not get away from Liverpool so my meeting with them had to wait till our wedding day.

Strangely enough, Bertie had 'urgent business' at the Admiralty that week and the weekend was his own. Ours.

His mother looked so frail and tiny that she made me feel protective, but the astringent gleam behind her spectacles permitted none of that. Mummy and she revelled in concerts together and Daddy won her heart with his jokes and chuckle and the masterful way in which he whisked her on to an escalator in the tube before she had time to think and protest.

Philip Rhodes came from Windsor to dine with us. He was splendid at making us all feel at our ease, a big generous man with a velvet voice, very witty and perceptive, always a step ahead of the game.

Back in his cabin on board HMS *Excellent*, Bertie wrote to me.

... I have been house hunting and have found the very thing we want! Half a converted house. It's light and airy and looks out to sea. From your bedroom, which has a French four-poster bed and a French window with a little balcony, you can see the Isle of Wight. It has an adjoining dressing-room and a spare-room.

It has a beautiful sitting-room, big and comfortable with a gas fire and a bow window. A few lovely antiques and rugs. A plain dining-room. A telephone. A kitchen and one bathroom which are not too bad. A maid's room. The entrance is bad. A narrow staircase with a hideous wallpaper and carpet. The neighbourhood jolly good.

If they accept my price of £16 per month I want to take it straight away for fear we miss it. Are you willing for me to do so?

I was very willing and at once went to Southsea to see it. Surviving the shock of the staircase wallpaper, I was delighted. I loved the view of the English Channel with its many moods and the salty breath of the wind when it came our way. There was also a patch of garden with a lilac tree.

A week later Bertie posted his last letter to Miss Joy Petersen, in London.

HMS *Excellent, Portsmouth, Tuesday evening, 17 February 1925*

Very best beloved,
Somehow I can't believe we are to be married on Friday. Do you know that this is the last letter you will have from your fiancé? That again is unbelievable to me as I sit here at my desk in my room where for so long I have sat and thought of you as I write – more beautiful thoughts than I have ever known in my life.

So sweetheart if this be a love-letter know that it is not the last – there never will be a last for to the very end you will know that were I able, I should still write another, for the love and the spirit would be there, and only the hand would be weak.

Part Two: Husband and Father
1925 to 1936

6
'He's not one to be pushed around.
He's deep as the sea.'

HMS *Excellent*   Portsmouth Scotland and
HMS *Warspite*   Malta
1925 to 1926

My wedding was dreamlike to me. So many smiling unknown faces and figures that were to become the well-
known companions and friends of many commissions at
home and abroad.

We returned from our honeymoon in Monte Carlo and
settled into 'Greystones'. Bertie discovered that, as he had
foreseen, his bride was a chameleon, quickly taking her
colour from her surroundings.

Spring came with bluebells and primroses and at Easter
we drove 'Tommy Clyno', our little car, to Shropshire
through ancient Oxford, the weathered Cotswold villages,
the Vale of Evesham, feathery pink with apple blossom, and
down to the green banks of the Severn.

My mother-in-law welcomed us to 'Brieryfield'. I called
her 'mother', as her son did, and practised calling him
'Bertie' in her presence, but when he took me for walks up
Grinshill, I slipped back into 'Unkie' which was natural for
us both. The earth-scented spring was chill and keen on the
hill top, and we looked across a lonely mysterious landscape,

here blandly open, there interlaced with winding lanes and hedgerows, or shadowed by the long blue guardian mount of Salop, the Wrekin, all of them linked by the winding river.

Mother's garden was tame and pretty after the wild hill and smelt of lavender and roses. She'd made me lavender sachets for my linen cupboard, and dried rose petals spiced with other aromatic ingredients 'for a *pot-pourri* bowl.'

That summer of 1925 was tremendous fun. We enjoyed every moment of it. Tennis, dances, Goodwood, Wimbledon, rifle meetings, friends to stay for weekends, including Freda and D'Urban Cloete, who were on holiday in England.

'When we get back to the farm,' Freda confided to me, 'we want to start a baby.'

'Boy or girl?'

'We don't mind.'

'I'd mind. I'd want a boy.'

In January 1926, we had to decide whether or not to renew the lease of 'Greystones'. Bertie had done a great deal of foreign service and we had hoped that his next appointment would be a ship in the Home Fleet. One evening he came in without his usual eager buoyancy. No two steps at a time. It was dark and the damp of a sea-fog followed him up the narrow stairs.

'It's the *Warspite*,' he said, his cheek cold against my hair.

'Why not? You love the *Warspite*.'

'She's to refit here in Portsmouth. Then to the Mediterranean – to Malta.'

'When does she sail?'

'Somewhere around April.'

'Peter's due in July. I can go to Malta.'

'You'd be alone. We'd be on the long summer cruise. No medical services for naval wives. It's hot as hell in Malta in July. I've thought about it all day. Asked married chaps about it – the ones who know Malta.'

'You think I should go home – and leave you?'

'We'd have to be apart anyway because of the cruise. I'd

go crazy leaving you in Malta without me – feeling rotten, no one I can trust to take care of you.'

'Do you know who your Captain will be?'

'Humphrey Walwyn.'

'Your magnificent Commander at Jutland?'

'The same.'

'If it had to happen, let's be glad it's the *Warspite* and Captain Walwyn.'

On a cold day at the end of February, he took me to see the *Warspite* in dry dock.

The big battleship looked grotesque to me, out of her natural element, cluttered with wire hawsers and tangled ropes, and stained with red lead as if she were bleeding from innumerable wounds. He helped me clamber into a 15-inch gun turret with its memories of Jutland and his brave gun's crew. It's vast complexity amazed me and I could imagine the mighty roar and flash of this deadly mechanism. The dockyard mateys at work on the huge disabled hulk looked like 'Lilliputians' scrambling over the tethered body of some mighty beached leviathan.

We spent our last few days together with Hillie and Cuddie Longstaff. They even invited Jon, our young wire-haired Fox Terrier, a wedding present from Philip Glover. Jon would now have to become a sea-going dog.

My welcome home was as wonderful as we had known it would be, from my parents and brothers to Cookie, her sister, Teena, and Arend, the chauffeur. Best of all, my German Nannie who'd waited for my arrival 21 years ago now awaited Peter's. She had married when I was a school-girl but was still my bossy old friend and mentor. Her sympathy at present was entirely with the unborn child about to be pitchforked into our extraordinary mode of life. But she knew and esteemed his father with whom she'd often conducted long conversations in German. Dresden, so well known to his mother, was her birthplace.

'If you marry him,' she'd warned me severely, 'you'll have to lead *his* life and put up with it. He's not one

53

to be pushed around. He's deep as the sea. Don't you forget it!'

His first letter to Mrs. H. A. Packer, 'Tees Lodge', Hope Street, was written from the ship nearest to his heart HMS *Warspite*, but he was being 'pushed around' and was far from happy.

HMS *Warspite, Portsmouth, Tuesday, 30 March 1926*

... It had been decided that all of us should be transferred from *Warspite* to *Valiant* on arrival in Malta. That was bad enough, but Commander-in-Chief Med. cabled to say he did not agree with the principle of it and it was not for the good of the Service that *Warspite* officers should leave the ship. That is obviously true. But apparently I will be one of three exceptions. We are to go to *Valiant* without the others but with Captain Walwyn. The Gunnery Officer of the *Queen Elizabeth* will take my place here. He is two years senior to me and it will give him a chance of promotion. *Warspite* will be Fleet Flagship.

So I shall soon be in the happy state of having lost everything. First of all my darling, then my ship, then my ship's company, then my officers and in their place get a ship due for a refit.

To cap it all, Jonnie-dog has gone sick. At present of course the ship is horrid for him, hammering and riveting and hundreds of workmen. You know how he used to get in a crowd. He's like that – nervy.

Tomorrow I start ammunitioning and have a beast of a week ahead. We work 5.30 a.m. to 8.0 p.m. every day till we sail.

From here we go to the Clyde. We shall be in the Clyde when the Coal Strike crisis arrives. I fancy it will come to nothing.

I'll thank God to leave England. I hate it now you've gone. It hurts. There's no place here I haven't been with you and that's the devil of it.

... There was a big crowd on 'Farewell Jetty' to see us off, all the sailors' wives and sweethearts waving handkerchiefs and the sailors fallen in on deck and not allowed to wave back.

I had the morning watch, 4.0 to 8.0. It was a glorious sunny morning as we passed Eddystone and Land's End and it's been a glorious day. The kind one seldom finds in England. Blue blue sea, a fresh little wind and a blazing sun.

I'm quite happy, darling, living on hard work and looking forward. The Captain is a good one. Very sound.

Sunday at Rothesay It's icy cold, kills the 'joy of spring' feeling all right.

Write and tell me all about everything. I ache for news of you. Last night I dreamt of little Peter and you. You just wandered into my cabin and popped Peter into Jon's basket and said, 'Oh, here's Peter and here's the newspaper cutting about him. I had him this morning!' I woke up before I could say or do anything.

They are clamouring at my door for me to hurry up and shift and go away boat-pulling. ...

7
'All this never knowing what next makes life worth living.'

HMS *Warspite*	The Clyde
1926	General Strike

HMS *Warspite, Rothesay, 26 April 1926*

... THE Captain last night had all the officers and ship's company aft on the Quarterdeck and, as is customary on commissioning, addressed them. You would have appreciated it. His choice of words and method of putting things was excellent. What's more, his elocution was too.

It went down well.

I'm working hard and taking a pride in it. I'd hate to turn over a dud show to my successor, but it's poor comfort to know one shortly starts all over again. I don't really mind. Be happy too sweetheart and please do what your Dad tells you – he's so wise at babies. It's a wonderful world for both of us and we'll be together again soon with Peter too.

Thursday night, 29 April 1926

... We got under way at 4.45 a.m. today and have just got in. We've been dashing about at 24 knots doing trials. At that speed one gets tremendous vibration aft here from the propellers. Jonnie hates it, but I think he is settling down. I find the Sick Berth Steward is a doggy man. His father looks after a kennel of foxhounds.

D'you know, it's five weeks tomorrow since you left – seems like 50,000 years.

Friday night Tonight is the night which decides whether there will be a Coal Strike or not. If there is I doubt if we'll leave till it's over.

Saturday 1 May The Coal Strike has happened but how seriously I don't know. On Monday some sort of Universal

56

Strike is starting so we have orders to sail at 4.30 a.m. for Greenock – up the Clyde from here. I've been organizing a landing party – all told about 450 strong. All this never knowing what next makes life worth living. One does things and gets on with them. Meanwhile my only fear is that you will think I'm in danger or something of that sort. If so, you're making a mistake. This isn't one of your Rand Strikes.

When we sail for the Mediterranean we don't know. Just shows that plans far ahead in the Navy are not worth much. That is what we decided long ago. It's why you are going to send me a cable as soon as you are fit to bring Peter to see me and when I cable 'Come' you will do so – just as fast as you can. I wish that day were nearer.

Greenock, 3 May 1926

... What a day we've had! At 7 o'clock this morning we arrived here and were met by a staff officer with orders to land seven parties of various strengths – 350 in all – to guard oil tanks and pipe lines and torpedo-factories about ten miles up river. So we crashed up the Clyde in a tug and arrived alongside a small cruiser, the *Comus*, lying in the middle of Glasgow at Prince's Docks. My own party of two platoons of sailors and two of marines have to guard the Docks – a big place, much bigger than Cape Town Docks. All the food ships are coming in here and being discharged by Volunteer Workers whom we protect. It's all fairly peaceful really, an odd bottle or two over the rail and a few words of abuse.

We have a warehouse full of flax and sulphur to live in. It was a sweat organizing the feeding, washing and sleeping arrangements. It's all working like clockwork now. It's all great fun when looked at in the right spirit. I brought a hammock luckily and sleep in that when there's time. The sailors do 12 hours' patrol in the 24 – strenuous when one has taken off the time to march out and in, and for meals and cleaning up the Mess Shed.

Last night there was a bit of a set-to, but the Police didn't

57

need our assistance. I watched about 500 men, women and kids being chased by three policemen. The 500 were chasing a Volunteer Worker, who was running like mad to find the Police, so they went round and round Glasgow all chasing each other.

The policemen are mostly Highlanders, the biggest men I've ever seen, not one under 6 foot 3. There's a lot of hooliganism including a female gang called the 'Redskins'. The dear things caught a policeman some time ago, hit him over the head and stripped him naked. It's all right, darling, they can't run fast enough to catch me!

The strikers surround every gate with Peaceful Pickets – they are allowed to by law – and they are the most amazingly Peaceful Pickets. Just stand and spit.

The Volunteer Workers all seem to be medical students or unemployed. A good lot. We stay here indefinitely.

I'm so glad I wasn't married during the War. We are never going to be apart again like this. . . .

Prince's Dock, Glasgow, Sunday, 9 May 1926

. . . The *Hood* relieves us tomorrow which means, I suppose, that we are shortly sailing for the Mediterranean.

We had a bit of fun last night. Our scouts reported half a dozen stealthy figures carrying 'something' approaching thro' a railway cutting.

We stalked them but they ran like the devil leaving full petrol tins behind. I fancy they had hoped to get thro' and burn down a warehouse or two. Today I've been organizing odd traps and ambushes against similar parties. Keeps the sailors amused.

Last night I dined on board the *Comus* with the Captain – a very good dinner and a pleasant change. . . .

At sea off Land's End, c/o GPO London, 13 May 1926

. . . As you can see we sailed all right yesterday. We ought to arrive at Gib. on Monday, and Malta today week.

The General Strike fizzled out and for once I was right – I

have thought it would all along. Of course the Coal Strike is not over, but the General Strike is, and I'm sure thro' the country, and thro' the world for that matter, Baldwin's firm constitutional attitude will have a great effect because of its success, and we shan't see any 'Direct Action' Strikes again for a long while. If it had been more protracted or if the Government had walked back an inch, or if the Government had given in, however gracefully, the lead given would, I am sure, have been followed in many other countries too.

That's enough about the Strike. It's a tiresome subject which will add to next year's income tax and which has done no one any good.

Sunday. Off Cape St. Vincent We turn the corner round the South of Spain tonight. I had the 4–8 a.m. watch, a beautiful morning which has turned into a wonderful day.

A list of Food Precautions has been stuck up all over the ship. No fresh milk can be drunk, or butter or cheese eaten if made from local milk (goat's). No lettuce or vegetables unless cooked. No fresh fruit unless it peels. The oranges luckily are wonderful. So I'm afraid you'll find things a bit rocky after Cookie's wonderful efforts. For God's sake, darling, get yourselves vaccinated and inoculated before you and Nannie leave with Peter. The place stinks of smallpox and typhoid. Everybody on board has been done.

Monday. At sea There has been all the voyage an 'end of term' feeling. It isn't as if we were all settling down for two years together. I'm getting all my Gunnery Papers ready for the turn-over. It will be a relief to get to Malta and be done with it.

I've got to 'declare' Jon but fancy I'll be able to land him all right. I gave Tommy Clyno's engine a run this evening – started at the first tick and ran like a silk engine.

Tuesday night A beautiful still sunny day again. We passed quite close to Algiers this evening and it looked so lovely, the white houses under hills not yet burnt by the sun but green and fresh.

Just as I was coming here to my cabin the ship's tortoise-shell cat sprang at Jonnie, spitting and cursing and looking like an infuriated tigress. I kicked the cat under the ear. Not very hard.

A signal from the Admiralty arrived today granting one week's leave to the *Warspite* on returning to England as a reward for their services in the Coal Strike.

Two years hence! Seems a pretty safe kind of offer to me at the moment. I hear we are not to leave the ship till Saturday.

Damn.

At sea off Bizerta At 2.30 tomorrow afternoon we get to the end of what has been quite a lengthy journey.

I kept my last Dog Watch on board here with Jonnie. That, as you know, is 6–8 p.m. It was very beautiful and calm and at 7.30 the sun set and the moon rose and I went goose-fleshy all over because it looked like South Africa. Even the coast with the mountains looked like the Cape in the moonlight and I spent a lovely two hours up on the bridge to which you once climbed. I wasn't a bit lonely because you were on watch with me.

A few of us go in the *Valiant*. I like Leicester Curzon-Howe and Hotham. Curzon-Howe is really very amusing. He says 'Thank God I'm a snob and most people loathe me' and really acts up to it. Also he has a dry sense of humour. He's the most outstanding character on board and one can really talk to him.

Hotham is a real good chap but a little too dogmatic. It isn't easy to have a conversation with him. It's more an exchange of bald statements. Stocker is a very nice chap but one sees little of him and he will keep dropping the three false teeth he has in front. . . .

The *Warspite* anchored in the magnificent Grand Harbour at Malta and my husband bade his fine ship and most of his shipmates goodbye.

To his distress, our dog, Jon, disappeared in the general turmoil.

After that *Warspite*'s activities no longer concerned us closely. What happened to the battleship *Valiant* was to rule our fate for the next few months. Or longer. Or less.

HMS *Valiant*   Malta and Mediterranean
1926

It would be difficult to imagine a more disheartening job than the one to which my husband now applied his energies. It was, however, as bad for Captain Walwyn and for the few other officers who were to be transferred to the *Valiant*.

At that time promotion was at its most dicey, especially from Lieutenant-Commander to Commander. In the Navy promotion is not automatic but highly selective. In those post-World War One years – and at various times since – only one in seven could hope to clear that hurdle which faced them in their early to mid thirties. The six who failed might be good officers but they were shouldered out by better ones or by unfortunate circumstances and for them there was no more future in the Service to which they were dedicated, a much reduced Navy upon which the 'axe' had already fallen ruthlessly.

The *Warspite*, after her refit and now Flagship of the Mediterranean Fleet, was a 'promotion job'. Bertie had gone ahead too fast in his career and was therefore considered 'young enough to wait'. The Gunnery Officer who took over from him was two years senior to him and nearing the dreaded 'last chance'. If you were 'passed over' those chilling words meant a few more years in drop-out jobs and a desperate search for civilian occupation.

The 'insecurity' my parents had stressed went deep indeed at that period. For officers, especially those with families, it was a load they carried with anxiety, but with a remarkable understanding of each others' predicament and an extraordinary lack of bitterness against the Service which was so often forced to treat them shabbily.

Bertie settled into the *Valiant*, reorganized the confusion in his office, put up the chintzes we had chosen together and his photographs so that he could 'see and talk to' me when he went to his desk to write the letters that kept us so closely together. The empty basket of his missing dog was just an added reminder of personal loneliness. He got to know the new officers in the Wardroom and the new ship's company.

Off again to a new start.

HMS *Valiant, Malta, 29 May 1926*

... At last a chance of writing to you.

We were out firing on Thursday and Friday, practice for the Great Competitive Firing next week. I won't bother you with that but I can assure you that with new Officers from three different ships and all the upset of the turn-over it's a business getting things on the top line. In addition, as we foresaw, the ship is in a terrible condition as she is due for a two year refit.

JON-DOG is back! I feel about ten years younger. Little swine. I'd notified the police and circulated photographs of him all over Malta and whilst at sea got a signal from the Commander-in-Chief's Flag Lieutenant.

Apparently Flags had been motoring through a village miles away and saw Jon, realized he was a thoroughbred and probably mine, collected him and took him to Admiralty House.

He's very thin, but perky and full of fleas as big as grasshoppers. After I'd scolded him he was ashamed and then sprang all over me. God knows what the little beast has been living on. I believe he's been living in sin. He has the set smirk of the successful seducer. I've told him it's got to stop. There's a strict law that dogs have to be quarantined for three months. I've heard nothing more about it and Jonnie's been ashore for a week on his own!

Wednesday Tomorrow at 9.30 a.m. we do our shoot for the Commander-in-Chief's Cup. It's the great thing of the year out here. In the circumstances, we haven't had a fair chance. Never mind, we'll have a good run for our money. We start as an outsider at about 40–1. I know Walwyn realizes the position. He's a wonderful man to work with – grasps the essentials of everything in a second and everyone likes him. I'm glad I'm here with him.

Later Whatever the result of the shoot – I think we will be second – we did not do well. The hydraulic machinery is in terrible condition and all sorts of mechanical defects arose. . . .

In June the *Valiant* went into dry dock for a two months' refit, a very different story from the two years' refit in her home port for which she had originally been scheduled. 'We are sizzling to death here in the dockyard,' Bertie wrote. 'But Mrs. Walwyn has very kindly asked me to stay with them for a few days and come and go as I like.'

Meanwhile he had found a suitable house for us at the top of Guarda Mangia on Piéta Hill, about 20 minutes' walk from the Grand Harbour where the battleships lay, most of them veterans of Jutland.

'Villa Diana' was part-furnished, stone floors, distempered walls, a marble staircase and a garden looking down upon Scaramanga Creek. Malta, in those days, lived on the Navy and, to a lesser degree, the Garrison. It was a British island fortress. Very gay, but glaring, hot and dusty in mid-summer, and plagued by tiny sandflies. The winter climate, though cold, was invigorating and bright. 'It's all burnt up now, like the veld before the rains,' wrote Bertie. 'But there is sunshine and a brilliant sea and there are the most beautiful evenings I have ever seen. Last night there was a moon so white and cool that I damned and blasted it for the memories it brought.'

At the end of June, Mrs. Walwyn sailed for England for her young son's summer holidays, and Charles Hotham, the *Valiant*'s Second-in-Command, and Bertie went to live ashore and 'look after the Captain' while the ship was still refitting.

Chez Captain Walwyn, 29 June 1926

. . . Mrs. Walwyn was due to leave at 9 p.m. for England last night. Hotham was out and we three – the Captain, Mrs. W. and I – had a wretched dinner, Mrs. W. with a bad attack of nerves at leaving. She wouldn't eat anything and the Captain trying to buck her up. Me too. Eventually a brandy and two aspirins did the trick and we popped her on board.

Then I had to cope with him. It may be ridiculous after being married 14 years, but he was just like a sulky child trying hard to behave. He was really miserable.

But he's not really too easy to amuse as he doesn't play tennis, billiards or bridge and can't swim 'cos it gives him ear-ache. Also he confided to me that he didn't know how to read a novel – only Gunnery and Service Text Books. So I'll get him something with plenty of rifles blazing and rattling sabres and foam-flecked horses. We've just got 100 books from the Times Book Club.

At 8 o'clock on Thursday morning, 15 July 1926, our son Peter was born at 'Tees Lodge'. The mid-winter light streamed pallidly through the window on to his cot. Later the sun shone and Mummy slipped a note into my hand. 'For Joy when Peter is born.' I stared at it.

'From Unkie! But how?'

'It was enclosed in a letter to me – some weeks ago – a welcome for Peter and a surprise for you.'

It was undated, written from HMS *Valiant*.

Dear Sweetheart,
When you read this it will be because our Peter has arrived.

How proud you'll be if you have the little chap you wanted and how proud of you I shall be! And if he's a little girl you know there's a naughty husband of yours who has a sneaking feeling he'd love a little Joy-Joy so that he can see her growing up into someone beautiful and sweet.

When your cable comes how happy I shall be. We're going to be so happy, you and I and the little one, and Jonnie will be taught to guard him and everyone will envy us.

You have given me another reason now to love you more

64

than ever. Lie happy and content with your baby – a bit of both of us.

That year, Mummy struck it lucky on the Stock Exchange and instantly decided to share her luck with her children. My allowance of £300 a year was doubled and all Nannie's expenses paid. Mummy and Daddy had, moreover, arrived at a delightful and entirely satisfactory conclusion. 'Tees Lodge' must always be a Packer 'home base'. Our life must be uncertain but at least 'Tees Lodge' could provide a sure refuge for any of us three. To me this did not seem surprising, so great was my faith in my home and parents. To Bertie it was something very warm and wonderful.

Of course, Mummy had simply fallen into the pit dug by nature for grandmothers. There was again a baby in the house.

9
'The Admiral will send for the Captain and bite his head off.'

HMS *Valiant*　　　　　　　Mediterranean and Aegean
1926 to 1927

My first attempt to pack and follow was farcical in its incompetence.

I still have a horrifying list of the paraphernalia we took with us.

The voyage was calm and we were lucky in having my cousin Maisie te Water and her family on board. Her husband Charles te Water, had been appointed South African High Commissioner in London by the Hertzog Government, a post which he held with distinction till the outbreak of World War Two in 1939.

We landed at Tilbury on a lovely autumn morning and were conveyed to the Haymarket Hotel by two disgruntled taxi drivers who rightly regarded the bulk and variety of our belongings as outrageous.

Mail was waiting for me.

HMS *Valiant, Malta, 16 August 1926*

... It feels funny not writing to you at 'Tees Lodge'. Damned exciting too....

I dined with Teddy Billyard-Leake at the Club last night. He's leaving the Service and is frightfully bucked as he's come into big money. By the time we'd finished dinner he was offering me jobs at anything from £2,000 a year to start with, rising rapidly to being the Archangel Gabriel. I wasn't very excited and told him I'd think about it if I didn't get promoted.

Oh, it's so hot – the ship is like an inferno – I must go on deck and breathe some air. Do come with me, darling.

There's a fine fat moon reflected in the water and the Grand Harbour is romantic with the lights and high old buildings and battlements round it. I'll be showing you before long.

Sunday evening I've had a busy time these last two days, working practically non-stop from 5.30 a.m. to 7.0 p.m. You see we go to sea with the Fleet tomorrow and have to be prepared to do everything they can in spite of things having been taken to bits and stuck together again – all wrong in many cases.

Very good for me and everyone else.

We are off to the Greek Islands tomorrow.

At Sea, Wednesday, 25 August 1926

. . . We've been having the devil of a time. Exercises day and night. A proper shake up.

The Captain is at present rather rattled. You see, we've a new Navigator who has never been Navigator of a battleship before and yesterday while the Captain was snatching a few minutes off the Bridge to have a bath the Navigator nearly rammed the *Barham*. In fact if the Captain hadn't arrived on the Bridge in time he would have. Now, of course, on arrival in harbour the Admiral will send for the Captain and bite his head off. Promotion being as congested as it is, one adverse report on a Captain – or anyone else – and his number is up.

It's a bad show because the fact induces the atmosphere of playing for safety all the time. It suggests 'I've got a good record, if I never do more than I have to, take no chances and have no accidents, I'll get by.'

That's damn bad, and the Captain is the last man living to adopt that attitude but one can see the temptation. Personally I can't do it and won't. It's a mug's game. If I see an opportunity of cutting out a line of my own, I will, and if it's a failure I'll stand by it, knowing, what's more, that you'd back me up. You're the last person in the world to encourage a man to go plodding along without a kick in him.

Incidentally, I write odd Service happenings like this to

you because I know you're interested, but never talk about them to other people. There's nothing more deadly than to meet a woman and find she has nothing to talk about except what's going on in the Fleet. One lives with it and wants to get away from it.

Thursday evening Things are very tense on board, the Captain worrying his head off about the near collision. I'm steering clear of him 'cos I know him when he's like that. His is a very up and down temperament. That's all there is to it.

Deuthero Cove, Greece, 9 September 1926

. . . *Friday night* Today we raced the best gig in the ship – the *Seaman's* – over a mile and beat them. Good show.

Incidentally there's been a bit of a scrap up the Yangtse River in China – a Commander, Lieutenant-Commander and two Lieutenants killed and one wounded. The Commander was my Gunnery lieutenant in the *Australia* before the War and took me thro' my Gunnery Course, both Lieutenants were Cadets in the Training Ship when I was there. The Lieutenant-Commander – Acheson – was in the *Dublin* with me, but before your time. You were then conquering wherever you went at the University, weren't you?

Sunday evening We had a tremendous day yesterday. The Captain, Commander, Engineer Commander, myself and two others got off at 6.0 a.m. in the picket boat to a place 15 miles away by water and nine by Ford car – wonderful, a whole day ashore after being cooped up on board. We walked hundreds of miles over mountains, shot two hares, six partridges and four pigeons and got back on board pleasantly worn out at 8.30. And there was your letter! Full of Peter and I loved that.

Thursday. Off Volos Sea, rocks, sky and jelly-fish – oh, 'the Isles of Greece where burning Sappho loved and sung'.

On Monday we started the Fleet Regatta and pulled in the Squadron Race and, after the devil of a tussle, won by two lengths over a mile course.

Stroke by stroke with the *Barham* all down the course, all

the ships cheering and shouting as we passed, then one big
spurt at the end, all out, not quite knowing where one was,
just determined to win, and win we did. Then back to the
ship and a cheering crowd of Officers and sailors to greet us.

Today we had the Fleet Races.

All the winners of the Squadron Races competing.

Just the same thing again – nothing in it – pulling neck
and neck and the final burst which put us over the line a
length ahead. We finished alongside the *Warspite* and the
Commander-in-Chief and everybody was there to give us a
round of applause. Personally I thought I was going to be
very sick over the side, but many years of sailoring and bad
habits have given me a certain control over my stummick.

The days till you come will be like months. These last
seven months without you have been the worst I've ever had
in my life. I cannot stand it again.

What a journey! Not only the taxi drivers but the porters
at Victoria and everywhere else were displeased with the size
and shape of our luggage. 'Should have gone goods,' they
said in England. 'Must be registered.' They naturally de-
manded enormous tips. The French porters showed no trace
of chivalry and fleeced us, and in Rome the Italians saw the
labels for Malta and flung the crates about in a fury. 'Malta
Inglesi? Pff! Malta Italiano!' We had to pay double for that!

As we left bellicose Rome, Nannie said, 'After all that
tipping everywhere what's left of the money you got in
London?'

'Not a bean.'

She emptied her purse which yielded a few shillings.

'There's our food – and the porters in Syracuse. You'll
have to borrow some money,' she said.

'Who on earth from?'

'Look for a kind face.'

So I went hunting. There were some kind faces but they
had been brought up on the principle of 'neither a borrower
nor a lender be' and when confronted with my anxiety to be
a borrower their expressions altered. At last I saw a long tin
case on a luggage rack. It had to be a naval officer's. This

one laughed when he heard our predicament. He took out his note-case.

'I know your husband and I'll have him courtmartialled if he doesn't pay me back in Malta.'

Commander Burroughs, who was decorated in World War Two for his gallant exploits in charge of the icy Russian convoys, came to our compartment to inspect Peter.

'I'm an expert,' he said. 'I have five at home, assorted sizes and sexes. Your husband will approve of this specimen.'

'He's no judge,' I said. 'I don't think he's ever seen a very young baby.'

'Then I'm up on him. And in a few minutes on Syracuse Station there's going to be the usual pandemonium, so I'll take Nannie and Peter straight to the *Maltana* – she's a cockroach-ridden old packet, no distance from the train – and while I get them installed you can get your gear from the guard's van and I'll be right back to deal with porters and so on.'

I fumbled in my bag and gratefully handed him Nannie's part of the ticket for the last lap of the long journey, the night passage to Valletta. Italian and English voices, a noisy throng and the thud of baggage dumped on the platform surged round me as the tall Commander, carrying Peter, piloted Nannie's sturdy figure towards the wharf where the *Maltana*'s lights swayed gently against a Madonna blue sky and a scattering of stars. The guard was hurling cases marked FRAGILE out of the van in a fine frenzy. I stood for a moment feeling exhausted and helpless. Then suddenly I saw the well-known and utterly unexpected figure coming towards me. Next moment I was in his arms.

'But how, Unkie, *how*?'

'The Commander-in-Chief's yacht brought some VIPs from Malta and offered me a passage. We landed a few minutes ago.'

When I think of Malta, I recall only the immense enjoyment that lit our lives like Mediterranean sunshine. In a way, perhaps, Nannie got more out of Malta itself than I did. She was blessed with the quality of gusto, was interested in everything from the story of the Island to its people and their customs and she made many firm friends. Most of our neighbours had young children, or infants, like Peter, and a squadron of prams sailed daily down steep Piéta hill and were pushed up again by lively dark urchins who received a penny for their labours.

'Villa Diana' was barely furnished, but to us it seemed perfection. Those were the days when families could live very well on very little. The two sisters who looked after us – Carrie, the cook, and Angela, who was as nice as her name, made our entertaining easy, and twice a week a swarthy young gardener, wearing a rose behind his ear, tended our long narrow slit of barren earth, aglow with larkspur to match the blue sky and the sparkling creek, and made melting eyes at Angela, who pretended not to notice.

'He's very handsome,' I said. But she laughed amiably. 'I don't want to marry and make 12 babies.'

'Must you make as many as that?'

'The priest, he say so.'

Jessie, who sold Nannie and me Maltese lace patterned with the Cross of the Knights, always rested a while in our hall for a cool drink and a chat and we feared that her tenth baby would be born on that hard stone floor. She wore the traditional black hooded *faldetta* which served many purposes, the robe concealing the figure of an expectant mother, the hood keeping out the glare. In World War Two the women made their *faldettas* into black-out curtains and after that the uniform female garb went out of fashion.

The Maltese language had an Arab base but Italian was the language of the courts and English of the waterfront. A strong political element favoured affiliation with Italy and a break with the Commonwealth, but the British supporters recognized that the Island's economy depended on the Services and the export of part of its surplus male population to British dockyards. The Governor was usually a high-ranking soldier, for the Island, only 90 miles in circumference, with its long history of Crusaders at war with the Infidel, was a military and naval fortress of vital strategic importance to Britain's seapower.

Today Britain's Navy is depleted, Malta is independent and the creeks where warships once lay have become anchorages for the yachts of the wealthy and the gypsies of the sea.

The Island was terraced, for every scrap of soil was precious and in days gone by ships that put into Malta were always expected to land a cargo of good earth. There were few trees except the orange and lemon groves but these were fragrant and heavy with fruit and flowers. The many churches had two towers, each with a clock face, one telling the right time and the other wrong – to cheat the devil.

I loved the bells. They sounded melodiously through the clear air; so did the bugles of warships lying in the many creeks that probed the Island like long fingers. We lived so close to the Navy that we could hear the rattle and clank of anchor chains and even orders given on deck! At nightfall the infinitely sad call of the 'Last Post' floated to our ears. Twice a day herds of goats shuffled up and down our hill towards the narrow staircase streets of Valletta, with much maa-ing and baa-ing and the shouts of the goatherd 'Halib! Halib!' ('Milk! Milk!'). We had to ignore it but the Maltese women poked their dark heads out of windows, let down a coin in a can on a cord and the goatherd took the coin, pulled down the hygienic 'bra' goats had, by law, to wear, and milked his animal into the can.

When the battleships went out shooting we heard the boom of the 15-inch guns and the bark of the 6-inch, and I'd hold my thumbs for the *Valiant* and her Gunnery Officer. For three months, except for exercises, shoots and 'days on', we led the normal life of a happy family, and our terrier, Jon, stayed home with us.

Then early in the New Year, the *Valiant* sailed with the Fleet for Greece. I stood on the mighty fortifications of the Barracca to see the ships go.

In my husband's first letter to me I understood that our brief period of being 'settled' was already drawing to its

72

close and that it was now my turn to pull my weight in
helping to organize the next move.

HMS *Valiant, At Sea, Wednesday, 12 January 1927*

... We set to right away doing exercises and things with the
Fleet and we've been at it ever since. Winston was in the
Warspite. ...

Winston Churchill, then Chancellor of the Exchequer,
was the guest of Admiral Sir Roger Keyes, the Commander-
in-Chief, and the *Warspite* was the Flagship. Winston loved
the Navy and was loved by it. I had met him at a dance in
Admiralty House, Valletta, and he had spent the supper
dance talking to me about South Africa and his adventures
there in the Boer War – so long ago.

Thursday evening We arrived at Phaleron Bay this morning.
It was a lovely fresh sunny day. Athens looked very attractive from the ship. Tomorrow I'm going ashore to play
tennis and practise for a match against the Club. We play,
I'm told, under the shadow of the Temple of Jupiter. It
ought to help one's overhead smashes having Jupiter behind
one. What fun to run about again!

The Captain sent for me this evening and read me a bit
out of a letter from Tottenham, Captain of Whale Island.
He said I should see most of *Valiant*'s refit out in Devonport, but that I am *not* going to recommission the ship.

So now we know. Get rid of the house, my darling, if you
can find a sub-let. My next job depends on the June promotions. I might get *Chatham* or *Whaley*, or the *Hood*, Atlantic Fleet. Dammit, it might be anything.

Saturday Have just heard we are probably sailing for
Plymouth on Monday, 14 February.

We had our tennis match today – teams of four a side –
four singles, then two doubles. I was captaining our side. We
won five matches to one.

73

10

'Commercial planes formation flying.
Before dawn!'
'So we saw the birth of the Luftwaffe.'

HMS *Valiant*	Plymouth, Germany
HMS *Queen Elizabeth*	Portsmouth, Malta
1927 to 1929	

I WENT ahead with Nannie and Peter to find digs in Plymouth. The Clyno, packing cases and Jon followed with Bertie in the *Valiant.*

By 22 February, we were in part of a converted house on Plymouth Hoe, badly furnished but with a beautiful view of the sea where, in 1588, Drake had seen the Spanish Armada on the horizon.

So on that cold winter evening Mrs. Walwyn and I stood together on the breakwater, to watch the *Valiant* enter harbour.

We loved the wild heather lands and when the soft West Country spring came we explored the rolling moors in the Clyno, but poor Jon was in quarantine kennels for six months.

Bertie was not very busy with the ship in dockyard hands so he brushed up his French and German and passed the Naval Interpreter's preliminary exams which entitled him to take three months in Germany and in France whenever he could best be spared. After that, if he passed the final qualifying tests, he would receive an interpreter's special allowance and was eligible for appointment as Naval Attaché.

So we planned to go to Munich. But first we spent a few days with Bertie's mother who firmly insisted that while we were in Germany, Nannie and Peter should stay with her at 'Brieryfield'.

Munich was a fine city with wonderful opera and while

Bertie swotted at German terms and grammar, I spent much of my time with my German second cousin, Reni, whose father was a general of the old school and whose mother was Daddy's niece and a close friend of my own mother.

The Alpine *Blumen* were a glory in the green Bavarian mountains and the woods and lakes were sheer enchantment. Thanks to Reni's current boyfriend, we were made honorary members of the University.

One of the members was a Lieutenant Franke who was thrilled to find that he and my husband had both been in the South Seas in 1914. He had been in command of a corvette while the *Australia* was patrolling near Rabaul.

'Just imagine! There we were, hiding in a little bay off the coast of New Guinea, and we sighted you just before dawn. You could have blown our little vessel to bits with one broadside. I didn't even dare to sound off "Action Stations" but shook the men awake as they slept in their hammocks and orders were given in whispers!'

Germany with her *Lufthansa* now led the world in civil aviation and it was in Munich that I took to the air for the first time. A 'complimentary flight' arranged by the Munich Director.

'It's a remarkable achievement,' said Bertie. 'They've damn well scooped the sky! But I noticed that those aircraft we were shown today could easily be converted into bombers, fighters or troop-carriers.'

When we left Munich to take the romantic Rhine route to Holland and across the Channel back to England, it was in the gossamer grey hour before daybreak with the last stars fading. A distant drumming throbbed in the sky and Bertie stopped the car. We got out and looked up. A flight of huge birds, V-shaped, winged overhead.

'Not birds, Joy-Joy. Commercial planes exercising formation flying. Before dawn, before anyone is awake.'

So we saw the birth of the *Luftwaffe*.

Bertie was due for a course at Whale Island and Hillie Longstaff had taken a flat for us in Portsmouth for three months. It was part of a Clock Tower at the apex of two busy streets. Peter loved the view which consisted entirely of traffic. There he spoke his first intelligible word and clearly knew what he was talking about.

'Car!' he said and pointed out of the window. Then his vocabulary advanced and he uttered the word that determined the course of our security for several months to follow. 'Nan-Nan', he said and bounced laughing in her arms.

One hot August evening Bertie brought us the news of his next and most vital appointment. He came into the nursery where Nannie was bathing Peter.

He stood looking at the pair of them, then patted Peter's head with a certain sad-happy look I knew well. He beckoned me to follow him.

When I went back I had Nannie's sundowner in my hand, the glass of medium dry sherry she enjoyed. Peter lay in his cot trying to keep his sleepy eyes wide open.

'What is it?' Nannie said, sharply. 'You look white as a sheet.'

'It's Malta again. In October. The Flagship *Queen Elizabeth*. She's a battleship like the *Warspite*. It could be a promotion job, Nan.'

She stared at me in disbelief. 'But you thought it would be the Home Fleet—'

'It was a wrong guess.'

We both knew that her husband intended to join her in England for Christmas and take her back to South Africa after visiting his family in Liverpool.

'We must go in September. Somehow we'll have to get along without you.'

Her head was bent and tears trickled into the work-hardened hands that had knitted so lovingly for all three of us. Her hands were the story of her life – no task too hard for them, the pain of swollen joints, disregarded with an irritable click of the tongue and the knitting needles, hands that gave without stint.

'Go to your husband now, Joy. Leave me with our child. . . .'

Next morning Nannie looked as if she hadn't slept a wink.

'You take Peter out this morning to do the shopping,' she told me. 'I'm going to write to my hubby.'

'To ask him to come sooner?'

'To ask him to come later. Next summer. He gets bronchitis. Christmas is a silly time for him to come to England.'

So once more it was Malta and Guarda Mangia and, happily, Angela and Carrie.

When I stood on the Barracca to watch the *Queen Elizabeth* go out for exercises, I took Peter with me, wide-eyed and excited. He was not yet two but he saluted the battleship flying the flag of the Commander-in-Chief, and the figure of his father up for'ard, and the sailors lined up on deck.

On Christmas Eve the church bells pealed for Midnight Mass and on Christmas Day the Island quivered with chimes and *carillons* from near and far. The New Year of 1928 was ushered in with gay processions and firecrackers.

But by early summer the little round Maltese doctor was too regular a caller at our house. Peter had developed chronic colitis and nothing we could give him agreed with his tummy.

Dr. Azzopardi said: 'The summer here will be bad for him. Take him home to England.'

'We have no home in England—'

Nannie interrupted fiercely. 'You have a home in South Africa. Your Mummy and Daddy will want you both. What's more, they'll help pay your passage.'

So when the *Queen Elizabeth* was to sail for the long summer cruise there were more partings. Bertie saw Nannie, Peter and me off for England where her patient husband met her. I sailed for Cape Town alone with Peter.

When we arrived my parents and brothers were shocked. Mummy said later, 'You are both transparent – a dragonfly and a mosquito!'

I recovered quickly, Peter less so in spite of all Daddy's care for his health.

Cookie's sister, Teena, now came more closely into our lives. The nursery was to be her special domain and its occupant her charge. As he could twist her round his little finger the arrangement suited him admirably.

Three months slipped away and it was September with almond blossom, wild flowers and young oak leaves unfurling.

'Mummy, I must confirm our passage back to Malta. The *Queen Elizabeth* will be there in October. I can't go on drifting.'

'Confirm yours if you must. But let Peter stay with us for a while longer. He's so much better already.'

Nannie was back with her husband in their pretty house in Sea Point. She pleaded with me to follow my parents' advice.

'Your child's health comes first, he'll get all the love and care in the world here.'

So there was no villa for a family in Malta this time. Bertie and I had rooms in Richard Saguna's hotel in Valletta. Even Jon was missing. He had been killed by a car. The hectic season had lost its zest for us.

Bertie turned over to his successor in the *Queen Elizabeth* and we left for England overland. Our train stopped at Rome on the afternoon of 1 July. We were both very tired and very tense. By now the promotions would be out, and among our friends in Malta there would be many of Bertie's seniority rejoicing or lamenting. Bertie's own fate was in the balance. Today he would be a Commander or 'passed over'.

It was sultry hot. There was a 20 minute wait.

'Let's get out of this stifling beastly train and walk along the platform,' I said.

As we did so we saw Thomas Cook's courier hurrying towards us, waving a telegram.

'Commander Packer, RN?'

Bertie took it and drew a deep breath before tearing it open. It was from the *Queen Elizabeth* and all it said was:

CONGRATULATIONS COMMANDER PACKER

78

11
'We'll meet again somewhere in China.'

Famille Française	Paris
RN Staff College	London
HMS *Kent*	China Station
1930 to 1932	

AFTER our return to England Bertie was sent to Paris to qualify as a Naval Interpreter in French. We lived in Montparnasse with our *famille Française* until Christmas when we went to my mother-in-law in Shropshire. Bertie passed First Class and was appointed to Greenwich Royal Naval Staff College.

It was 1931, the year of the Economic Depression which hit America, Britain and most of the world and forced Britain off the gold standard. It was a national crisis and a coalition government was formed to meet it.

London was much more expensive than a home port and we took a semi-basement flat in Earl's Court. Bertie had to live in at Greenwich but was free to come home for weekends. I wrote to my parents to ask them to bring Peter to us. For once they were unco-operative. Mummy wrote that her grandson was happily established in his pre-prep school. 'He is settled here and his health improves from month to month. You say the Greenwich appointment is only to the end of this year. Let us keep him till then when you'll know what next.'

Being alone in London was very different from a naval port with friends and sports clubs. I made up my mind to take a full-time job. How I got on to the London *Daily Express* as a 'news hound' and also covered various stories for the *Sunday Express* is told in my first book *Pack and*

Follow. The experience was invaluable and influenced the whole course of our lives.

The Editor was Canadian Beverley Baxter, one of the most enterprising journalists in Fleet Street, a writer and politician destined for the House of Commons. He took a gamble in giving me a chance. Like his controversial boss, Lord Beaverbrook, he always followed a 'hunch'. The dynamic quarrelsome team of 'Max and Bax' was famous in the world of newsprint and beyond it.

At the end of that turbulent year Bertie was appointed to HMS *Kent,* Flagship of the Commander-in-Chief of the China Station as Fleet Gunnery Officer. The *Kent,* a cruiser, was recommissioning in her home port, Chatham.

'It's not on to take Peter,' Bertie told me. 'China's full of tummy trouble from dysentery to cholera, and there's no chance of schooling in the gypsy life we'll be leading. Hong Kong in South China in winter, Wei Hai Wei in the north in summer, and cruises anywhere from Japan to Singapore in between times. I join her in Chatham in January and I want you with me till we sail. Then you must go home, darling, and we'll meet again somewhere in China.'

A fortnight later I stood on 'Farewell Jetty' at Chatham and watched HMS *Kent* sail for the Far East. It was a raw winter day and there was the usual little group of women, children, fluttering handkerchiefs and tears. She was a pretty ship, three-funnelled and slender, painted the pale tropical grey of the China Fleet. She looked like a model you'd find in a toyshop. Only the guns, turrets, catapult and aircraft, and the sailors lining the side, suggested menace. The Marine band played as she steamed slowly out of sight.

Bertie called her his 'Fair Maid of Kent'. I called her his Grey Mistress. Straight away she headed towards trouble.

The Sino–Japanese War of 1932 had reached Shanghai and was endangering lives and property in the Foreign Concessions and the International Settlement. Shanghai was the greatest international trading port in the Far East, but that spring the Whangpoo was choked with the warships of many nations guarding their nationals and investments, to say nothing of Japanese ships shelling the Chinese city of Chapei.

When I arrived in South Africa at the end of January, it was high summer. Autumn came all too soon, and before we could celebrate Peter's sixth birthday the Shanghai War was over. Daddy and Mummy and I were having tea in a sunny corner of the stoep and Peter was at school when the cable arrived.

'COME HONG KONG AS SOON AS POSSIBLE LOVE UNKIE.'

I handed it to Mum.

My mother's eyes were sad. 'These are lovely years you'll be missing – just when you and your child are getting to know each other so well. *He* needs you too.'

'We all three need each other. But I haven't really any choice. You understand that.'

'I do, darling – but Peter won't.'

'I'll be back home soon. In a few months.'

Months or years, I knew that every one of these partings inflicted irrevocable wounds on both of us. Children change, like the seasons, with every day that passes, and no power on earth can restore to a mother moods and phases of her child's life irretrievably lost.

The voyage to Hong Kong took over five weeks. A little Dutch cargo boat, with less than a handful of passengers, carried me across the Indian Ocean to tropical Batavia (now Djakarta). Then the Dutch Mail to Singapore. From there I changed to a Japanese ship. The last lap!

I woke at dawn on the morning of our arrival at Hong Kong. Passing slowly outside my porthole was the great patched sail of a sea-going junk. Everything looked wonderful in the windy sunshine – the green Chinese mainland, Hong Kong Peak rising from the sea terraced with buildings, fleets of trading and fishing junks and craft of every description going about their business, grey warships on anti-piracy patrol, great liners berthed at Kowloon, the busy little ferry plying back and forth between Hong Kong Island and Kowloon on the mainland. But I couldn't see Bertie's 'Fair

Maid of Kent'. Then suddenly there was a picket boat coming towards us and the figure of a naval officer in tropical whites.

The harsh Chinese language of the baggage coolies and the hawking and spitting known as the 'Chinese national anthem' reverberated everywhere.

The cabin door opened and a naval officer stood there, smiling. He was an old friend of ours.

'I'm awfully sorry, Joy. Bertie isn't here. The *Kent* sailed for Wei Hai Wei yesterday at short notice. He sent me a signal to meet you and put you on the first northbound coastal steamer.'

'How long will it take to get to Wei Hai Wei?'

'A few days. Six or seven if you don't run into fog. The Yellow Sea is very fog-ridden. Wei Hai Wei is a little dream Island – the China Fleet's summer base. You'll love it.'

The *Shuntien* was very small and her vital areas like the bridge were enclosed by pirate-proof grills. There was no fog, and one soft summer evening at sunset we dropped anchor between the 'little dream Island' and the blue mountains of the Shantung mainland.

This time the *Kent* was riding at anchor off shore and it was indeed my husband who came aboard to meet me.

No traffic except the rickshaw was permitted on the Island and we were conveyed to the only hotel by the human horses who smelt strongly of garlic and an aroma that was uniquely China. Among themselves they complain that Europeans stink of cheese.

In the fading light the white acacia trees dripped their petals like snowflakes in summer and the pomegranates glowed among their spiky leaves. The hotel, which was just one long wooden bungalow divided into 'horse-boxes' and extended by a number of ramshackle annexes, was on a green rise above the harbour. Lights swaying on the darkening water, bugles and the sounds of life aboard the warships were part of the dream to me.

'It's pretty primitive,' said Bertie, as the rickshaw coolies set my baggage in our bedroom. 'Just this room, the little veranda and you'll have a fit when you see the so-called bathroom.'

There was no plumbing, just an earthenware 'Soochow tub'. The sanitary system was a diffident man with black cotton gloves known as the 'foo-foo coolie' and when he paid his visits he also left an ewer of brackish water with which to fill the tub.

On the veranda was a small oak barrel of distilled water from the ship.

'Drinking water – or for washing your hair,' Bertie said.

The coolies had gone.

'Darling – everything's heaven. But it was awful you not being in Hong Kong when I arrived.'

'I'm going to mix you our summer China-sides drink. A gimlet.'

'What's that?'

'Gin, lime, ice, water and a touch of bitters. The ice is all right. It's from the ship.'

'Unkie, something's wrong. Tell me what it is.'

'We sail tomorrow morning for Hankow. It's one of the Treaty ports with a big British community. The Chinese Communists in the Yangtse basin are cutting up rough.'

'Gerry didn't warn me when he met me.'

'Gerry didn't know. Nor did we – till yesterday.'

'How long will you be gone?'

'Maybe a month—'

'Can I get to Hankow?'

'Back down to Shanghai, then 700 miles up the Yangtse? Cholera and Communists in Hankow, riots, our nationals in danger. It simply isn't on.'

By noon next day the harbour was empty save for the submarine depot ship *Medway*, with her submarines against her flanks, and a few sampans.

There were three other stranded wives on the Island, one from a destroyer and two from *Kent*. The *Medway* supplied us with fresh water twice a week and the little barrels were delivered by Tomato-Face, the chief sampan man who had a huge red face, several wives and many 'cheese-eyes'. One could ask after the 'cheese-eyes' (children) but not after the wives, for women were of no account and not a suitable subject for polite conversation. The two lesser sampan men were Tomollow-Fish and Yesterday-Fish.

The *Medway* and submarine officers were kind to us and invited us to play tennis and golf, or to the cinema on board on Sunday nights and to church on the Quarterdeck on Sunday mornings.

We each had our own washee-washee sew-sew amah who came daily to look after us. Mine was called Goo and she tapped into my room, her bound feet tiny and triangular like a buck's. She was very proud of her 'lily feet'. They were a sign of class. Peasants stumped around on 'big' feet. Her hair was sleek, lacquered and drawn back into a bun and her voice was a bird's 'Missie gottee washee-washee sew-sew for amah?' I had my own rickshaw coolie too – the fastest runner on the Island. Small wonder! He had no ears, for those had been chopped off and sent to his family before he escaped from the bandits who had captured him two years ago.

Most days a smiling individual aptly named Ugly came to my veranda, padding across the hotel garden, which was a sea of blue cornflowers. He sold me plants he had 'lifted' from the gardens he tended. He was also a seer who knew when warships were coming or going long before the official signals informed their own captains.

The naval store officer kept his supplies in a tiny disused temple with strange symbols and dragons on the tiled up-turned eaves. Admiralty House was a flimsy double-storied affair with a homely temporary air about it. After all, the Island was only leased to the British as a summer base, and, well – you never knew in China.

Manual labour needed on our tiny Island – two miles by two and a half – was done by a chain-gang of convicts from the mainland prison inside the old walled city of Wei Hai Wei across the harbour. They laughed and chattered as they worked.

Sometimes we sailed across to picnic in the lovely coves of the mainland or for walks up those blue Shantung mountains I could see across the bay from my veranda. There we met people like the scorpion hunter who turned up stones and found strange creatures which he slung into a bag to be used as aphrodisiacs. Tiger whiskers and imported rhinoceros horn were even more potent but such luxuries were for mandarins and war-lords.

Young girls gathered leaves in the mulberry woods to feed the silkworms which they nurtured in their bosoms at body heat till they were big enough to be placed in trays in semi-darkness where they munched the leaves like toothless ancients with a rhythmic muffled sound. Later we bought our lengths of Shantung silk or raw silk in shabby old Wei Hai Wei city between the mountains and the sea, and Wei Kong, the little tailor, in his long grey gown, came across to the Island and made them up for us.

There were no shops on the Island except Sin Jelly Belly the Naval Outfitter. He cashed cheques, too, made out to 'Jelly Belly'.

Then one day Ugly came hurrying to my veranda.

'Missie, Missie! Kent-ship, he come tomollow.'

'Ugly! How do you know?'

'Me savvy.' He grinned.

Next morning early, Tomato-Face shouted loudly from the little jetty.

'Kent-ship, he come!'

For the rest of that summer Wei Hai Wei was truly a dream Island.

But it was not long before Ugly sold me an exotic plant, probably from the Commander-in-Chief's garden, and said as I paid him.

'Kent-ship, he go welly soon.'

'Where to?'

'Tsingtao-side.'

'Tsingtao b'long far?'

He shrugged. 'Tsingtao b'long south – one night, one day.'

Bertie confirmed Ugly's information that evening.

'It's only a fortnight, darling.'

In the morning I hired Tomato-Face to take me to Wei Hai Wei city. The fresh breeze filled the sampan sail, red to match his big bland face. The Northern Chinese are sturdier and ruddier than those in the south.

He lolled in the stern, hand on the tiller.

'You takee me ship agent Wei Hai Wei city, Tomato-Face.'

'Missie wantchee go Tsingtao. No can do. No ship b'long plopper for Missie. Master, he savvy.'

So enquiries had already been made? I might have guessed.

There was nothing except the *Burma Maru* – a coolie ship, deck passengers only – and its last port of call had been cholera-stricken Darien.

I mentioned it to Bertie that evening.

'A coolie ship from a cholera port – *No!*'

The *Kent* sailed next day at noon. It was a Saturday and I lunched on board the cruiser, *Suffolk*, with the Captain, John Godfrey, a tall man with a brilliant, unconventional and labyrinthine mind.

After a gourmet's lunch, my host's eyes wandered to the open scuttle.

'Extraordinary craft ply the China Seas. Look at that thing coming into harbour! But hold your nose.'

'It must be the *Burma Maru*,' I said.

He fetched his binoculars. 'It *is* the *Burma Maru*. How did you know?'

'She's going to Tsingtao. And I've just decided to go with her.'

'I'll have to put you in irons,' he said gently. 'Bertie's an expert shot, fencer and bayonet fighter. If I let you sail in that, he'll be after my blood.'

Much against his will he took me on board the dilapidated vessel and arranged with the amiable Japanese Captain that I should have a deck-chair on the bridge. John supplied me with sandwiches, a water bottle and a bottle of champagne and made me swear to touch no other food or drink on board.

'I'll send Bertie a signal,' he said.

So, towards sunset, off we went. The crowded deck passengers were all instantly and noisily sick.

I went below. In the one and only cabin, dark and airless, I found three seasick European children. They were aged ten, eight and six. Ten and eight were girls.

'Where's your Mummy?' I asked.

'In Tsingtao. Daddy's a missionary up country, and we're boarders at school at Chin Wan Tao. Mummy will meet us and take us to the Mission for our holidays.'

'Have you had supper?'

'Not yet. We feel too sick.'

I took three coarse blankets from the bunks and three pillows and the children followed me on to the bridge. The Captain and helmsman looked surprised but good-humoured. The fresh air revived the children and later we four tucked into Captain Godfrey's sandwiches and drank some champagne. In the night a fog engulfed us and every few minutes the fog-horn blared. The ship rolled steadily and more and more deeply from side to side. The little boy curled up on my lap and his sisters came closer to my deck-chair. I wished we had lifebelts.

Next evening we steamed past the *Kent*'s anchorage outside Tsingtao, so near that Bertie took a snapshot of us as we waved a greeting.

When we landed I expected my husband to embrace me. He did not.

'Joy,' he said. 'We could smell that coolie ship a mile off. I expect you're used to it after 24 hours. I'm not and I don't care for it. There's a real bath in this hotel with hot and cold. Very relaxing after your Soochow tub in Wei Hai Wei.'

When I returned to our room he had gimlets ready.

'Unkie, are you really so furious? Aren't you glad I'm here?'

'You know damn well I always want you with me. So if I say *no*, it's for a sound reason. You know nothing about China. That stinkpot of a so-called ship isn't even in *Lloyd's Register*. If you'd run aground in that fog last night the pirates would have been on board fast. They're like bloody vultures in these waters. If you'd struck a typhoon that thing would have turned turtle. She came past us with a roll that gave me the horrors. China isn't England or Malta or South Africa. Don't do these things, Joy-Joy.'

The Chinese Mayor gave a banquet for the visiting warship. I was placed next to a cheerful official of the Central Government of Generalissimo Chiang Kai-shek. He instructed me in the use of chopsticks and insisted that I taste every course. Bird's nest soup, sharks' fins, boiled sea-slugs, Peking Duck and, believe it or not, bear's paws. I kicked at fillet of snake. The featherlight rice that was the basis of everything was delicious. Hot rice-wine, like hot dry sherry, was served in tiny china cups, and every time someone proposed a toast it was good manners to say *Banzai*, toss back the rice-wine and replace the cup on the table upside down.

We survived. But, oh, what a waste of the following day!

The last evening came and Bertie said:

'Now, how the hell do you get back? I can't stow you away.'

'Don't worry. I'll be all right. No coolie ship, I promise. Something'll turn up.' As, of course, it did.

12
'He is an officer whom all would follow.'

HMS *Kent*	Far East
1933 to 1936	

THE ships went on their various autumn cruises and we met again in Hong Kong before Christmas.

Bertie and I had suite 305–6 in the Peninsula Hotel at Kowloon on the mainland. Our view was across the harbour to the Peak. The winter season was bright and cold with tennis, sailing, golf, hunting at Fanling, and wonderful country walks. We explored sheltered coves where the sampan people lived, and saw the young rice piercing the flooded paddy-fields with a new-washed green even more radiant than an English pasture. The good earth was made productive by men, women, children and water buffaloes. The peasants were industrious and patience was written on their faces, for a true farmer must be a fatalist.

In January the *Kent* went south on her spring cruise and Bertie wrote to me from British North Borneo which was in a sad state owing to the world rubber slump.

At sea, Jesselton* to Saigon, 6 February 1933

. . . The country is pitiful. Just dead rubber estates left with a white caretaker at a reduced salary. So in the inevitable wooden bungalow Club a few sodden relics loll in rattan chairs in gloomy silence.

That's one side of it. The other is that our arrival was an *Event* – the first in two years.

---

* Jesselton is now Kota Kinabalu and British North Borneo is the State of Sabah, part of East Malaysia.

We did our stuff and they did theirs.

On Wednesday we became acquainted. On Thursday we had a tennis and a soccer match, Friday a cricket match and a dance on board and the Commander-in-Chief gave a dinner party. All the people came in from the jungle, many of them *'direkt von baum'*.

On Saturday six officers went to Beaufort for 24 hours – a planters' jungle settlement.

Some of us went down a jungle river at night, crocodile spearing. Not a sport but a business. Our host is known as the 'White Dyak'. For three years he lived as a Dyak wearing only a loin-cloth. Then he was a soldier, stock trader, tobacco grower, rubber planter, elephant hunter and now skin collector. Once he was a District Commissioner and went out in his police launch to bring in a Dyak wanted for murder. He got his man. On board the launch the man broke loose and ran amok. The escort promptly jumped over the side, the 'White Dyak' coming out of his cabin to see what was up had his skull split open by the murderer. But he hung on to his man and killed him. Now what to do? No good taking a dead body ten days down river in that heat! So he cut off the murderer's head as evidence. When the launch got to the nearest town a week later the police officer boarding her found the 'White Dyak' delirious, lying on deck, clasping the black Dyak's head to his chest and refusing to let go!

I had this story from the policeman who boarded the launch.

If we come here again you must certainly come. The place isn't particulary beautiful. Not enough birds, butterflies or flowers which are hidden in thick jungle, but the people and modes of life are well worth studying.

The climate is hot and steamy, but healthy enough. The planters, if normal and single, keep women. You can buy a Javanese for $30, a Tusun (local native) for $50, a Chinese girl of 15 for $300, or of 18 – if still a virgin – for $600. Their price is really in proportion to their virtue. A Javanese opens her quiver to the darts of all men the moment her white man's back is turned – for money, of course. They don't give way to love. The Tusun is very accomplished in her amours but fickle. The Chinese girl will not give herself to anyone of, or below, the status of her white man, but will do so at the imperative request of an important personage.

'For instance,' said my informant, a local doctor, 'if you came to my house and asked my housekeeper somewhat peremptorily to accommodate you, she would refuse courteously, but if the Commander-in-Chief did she would graciously accommodate him.'

I didn't tell the Commander-in-Chief!

The Chinese girls, apart from this nice respect for themselves and their white man, are housekeepers and mend his clothes and rule his houseboys. The other girls only do the one job.

So I'm thinking of buying a Chinese!

Well, that's all I can tell you about Borneo for the moment.

I received my mother's newsy letter in Hong Kong on my birthday, 11 February 1933. She had written it on 21 November 1932.

'It's a month since I heard from you. *I don't like the China Station at all.* Peter's little letter will show you how nicely he is learning to write. Our new cinema, the *Plaza*, was opened by the Administrator on Tuesday night. Daddy and I took a party. The official guest of honour was Amy Mollison (Johnson) who appeared on stage to say a few words. It was a wonderful feat to fly out here from England in five days all by herself! She was modest about her achievement and was given an absolute ovation. . . .'

'Five days from England to Cape Town,' I said to Bertie. 'Makes one think!'

'*Lufthansa* has pioneered civil aviation in Europe. Soon we'll follow suit with long distance Empire flights.'

When the *Kent* returned to Chatham early in 1934 to refit I was there in time to meet my husband.

We were in for a shock. The new Commander-in-Chief of the China Station had asked that Commander Packer, Fleet Gunnery Officer, be reappointed to his Flagship *Kent* as

Second-in-Command. We had been married nine years and I knew very well that this appointment was one in which his entire life would be devoted to his ship for the first six months of the commission. During that period a wife would be frowned upon.

Peter would soon be eight and his name was down for the Dragon School in Oxford and also for Bishop's (Diocesan College) Prep School in Cape Town. I must go home and see him settled as a Bishop's boarder before rejoining my husband in China. But I was determined that *somehow* the time wasted in travelling must be shortened. There was a chance. Imperial Airways was pioneering the Empire routes. London to Cape Town had just launched a 'fast ten-day flight', and a second 'ten-day flight' was being planned from London to Singapore via Cairo.

I had a proposition to put before the Director. He sat behind his huge desk and turned over the cuttings of my feature articles splashed in South African papers and various others.

'So you want to be the first woman passenger to cover our entire route as far as it goes – London to Cairo and Cape Town. Then – later – Cape to Cairo and on to Singapore. You'll get us good press and personal publicity in South Africa and you'll send me all possible suggestions for improving the comfort of passengers. You'll write your story so that we can use extracts for our publicity. And you want to travel for as near free as no matter?'

I could hardly breathe. He smiled suddenly.

'Well – let's go from there—'

So a fortnight later Bertie saw me off at Croydon in a Handley Page 42 (W) *Heracles,* a weird-looking biplane, now a museum piece.

Meanwhile in Chatham Bertie prepared his 'Fair Maid of Kent' for her second term as Flagship of the China Fleet, this time flying the flag of Admiral Sir Frederick Dreyer, a tall impressive Gunnery Officer of formidable repute, who had four sons in the Navy, two daughters married to naval officers and a gentle wife loved by all who knew her.

The Commander-in-Chief and Lady Dreyer were to sail for the Far East in comfort, and the Admiral would hoist his flag in Wei Hai Wei.

HMS *Kent, Chatham, 1 June 1934*

... Before I tell you what a big excitement I had today I must tell you that the Commander-in-Chief's visit went off very well. The ship – a week after commissioning – was really in good condition. The Captain (Ion Tower) is splendid. Doesn't fuss and leaves me to get on with it. The officers are good, the young one's inexperienced but keen and know how to talk to the men.

Tomorrow we have a big ship's company farewell At Home for wives, friends and relations, and on Sunday a Wardroom At Home for 200 members of the Association of Men of Kent.

Now for the *big* excitement.

Two letters arrived from you today, one from Khartoum and one from Juba. Darling, they gave me a kick like nothing else could. You gloss over your discomforts on this journey and make an adventure of everything. Your interest is unfailing, your letter full of humour and I travelled with you through the blistering heat.

Aden to Colombo, 1 July 1934

... The great heat of the Red Sea is over and we are bowling along before the S.W. Monsoon.

From the Red Sea till we left Aden the heat was terrific – shade temperature on deck 105° and not a breath of air. You can imagine what it was like inside our tin box. We had 24 cases of heat exhaustion and two of heat stroke. Fortunately none died, though one was touch and go, his temperature being 106! It was the young boys who collapsed. We are, of course, overcrowded with passengers and stores for China.

Later We've had a real gruelling. All hatches and scuttles closed and my beloved 'Maid of Kent' behaving like a blousy woman with the wind under her skirts on a boisterous March day.

A stream of folk persecute me with minor troubles from dawn to dusk and I try to impress on them that they must deal with these themselves. After all, the officer of the boys' division should be able to cope with the case he came to see me about yesterday. The boy in question forgot himself in his trousers – white ones. He had only one other pair and those were hanging up to dry after washing. What was to be done? What I mean is that a Lieutenant-Commander trained for 20 years to a high degree of practical and scientific knowledge should be able to deal with a comparatively simple accident of this sort. Nannie could!

I said 'Good God, cork the boy up and put him back in the bin.'

'Aye aye, Sir,' said the Lieutenant-Commander and saluted and went.

What happened I don't know!

At sea, Friday, 20 July 1934

. . . We are driving along up the China Seas – the S.W. Monsoon soft and caressing.

The men are still good as angels, if slightly tipsy angels on occasion. The ship is very dirty from continual steaming. We'll give her a new dress at Wei Hai Wei all ready to welcome the Commander-in-Chief.

Sunday afternoon Arrived Hong Kong 6.30 this morning. Several 'old flends' to see me. First of all Tomato-Face! I'm giving him a passage back to Wei Hai Wei. Then tailor Wei Kong – ditto. Ah Chang – ditto. Also Ah Lin who is to be our Number One at Wooden Bungalow *next* summer!

I've just organized 35 coolie women to chip and paint the ship's side where it's rough and rusty and they are working away like the devil.

It tugged at my heart to see the Peninsula as we came in and to know that there'd be no slim fair-haired darling sitting on the window ledge of 305 dangerously, waiting for me. I put that last comma in on purpose. I'd love to be waited for by you dangerously. I'm going to send you a cable tomorrow. You know my time with you will be very limited but I need you frightfully. As I've always foreseen this Second-in-Command job is a full-time one and you must be very tolerant of my inattentions and absences. You will, darling, won't you? You'll just save my life.

Wei Hai Wei, 5 September 1934

... A letter from you this morning dated 15 July, Piet's* eighth birthday. All your chat about him, Mum and Dad is always amusing and you give me a very good idea of that boy of ours. I liked your story of him knocking the other chap down. So long as he only hits one bigger than himself it shows he's not a bully, just pugnacious. I well remember the first black eye I took home to a most unsympathetic Mother who asked no questions and got no information. I too was eight. But Piet sounds a sympathetic lad when he's not fighting. I'm sorry to miss his first real schooling. I do understand how tremendous the difficulties of youth appear, and can look back at my own fences and how insurmountable they seemed (and still do sometimes) so I could have helped.

The fact is I've got about 800 'children' here to look after. But your vivid understanding letters help me greatly to know my boy.

Then today came your cable saying you were leaving 6 November arriving Singapore 16 November. Ten days from Cape Town to Singapore! Seems incredible. It's terribly exciting.

Wei Hai Wei, 22 September 1934

... I've sent a photo of the ship to Piet in a letter pointing out the catapult, aircraft, guns and things.

---

* Piet is the South African spelling of the English diminutive of 'Peter' or 'Pieter', and we fell into spelling it this way as did his contemporaries and relations.

The Commander-in-Chief has gone North in the *Falmouth** with Lady Dreyer so they can see Peking and the Great Wall of China before the Japs get there. While they're away my 'Fair Maid of Kent' is being given a new frock of light battleship grey.

A Chinese naval launch was wrecked here last week and was salved and beached by the *Cornwall*. Seventy bodies have been recovered – 40 of them on Gladys Hooper's beach.

The Chinese Admiral signalled to the Commander-in-Chief thanking us for our assistance. 'Without your timely and generous assistance a great calamity might have occurred.' Eighty-six drowned out of 200 seems to me to answer the description. The coxswain of the launch was executed yesterday for still being alive!

As a sideline on the Chinese mentality the repercussions will amuse you. Altho' it is entirely untrue the Chinese Admiral, to save his face, spread the story (including the press) that the launch capsized due to the wash made by the *Bruce*. In fact, the *Bruce* was 15 miles away at Shantung Promontory. He backs up his story by saying we are obviously responsible because we immediately offered to salve the wreck for him!!! That'll teach Freddie to offer anything for nothing to a Chinaman. They don't understand altruism. I expect by now Freddie has flames and smoke pouring out of his mouth, nose and ears. But luckily he's still in the *Falmouth*.

But I was very depressed when your last letter said that after the Imperial Airways articles you meant to give up writing. Then I bucked up, sure it was just a phase and I wasn't there to see you thro' it.

My sweet Joy-Joy, the thought and study you have to give to your subject to write a lively interesting article – which you do – is fine training for the mind. It means that you can talk with knowledge about that subject far better than if you'd only read about it. Read and cultivate the mind, travel

* The official yacht of the Commander-in-Chief China Fleet.

and cultivate the mind, observe what is going on around you. These things are splendid and help to increase your beauty, for the mind lights up the face – but *write as well* because that – for you – is the ultimate development of it all.

Good writing makes for style and precision which reflects itself in speech.

I feel strongly on this subject. Whether it is a book – a tremendous task – or articles, keep at it! Don't let go when you have a rattling good hold already.

Early in 1935 the *Kent* left Hong Kong to show the flag in Singapore and Penang, and then on to the Dutch Colony of Sumatra and French Indo-China (now part of independent Indonesia and Cambodia). Bertie couldn't take leave so I had to go without him to the jungle ruins of Angkor Wat, the Sacred Precincts of the vanished Khmers, where grey gibbers pranced and barked '*Thwark Maou!*' (Monkey!) on crumbling rosy parapets, while golden pheasants and gaudy peacocks strutted in one-time pleasances among tall trees inhabited by emerald parrots and blue-birds. Dark naked Cambodian children, with cigarette stubs behind their ears and bows and arrows in their hands, watched the birds and chattered at the gibbers '*Thwark Maou! Thwark Maou!*' I liked to sit alone there in the cool dawn or sunset and make believe that in times of trouble I would be able to send my disturbed spirit to this sanctuary of peace.

There is little peace in Cambodia now.

In the spring the Flagship was far north in Tokyo. I too was there beneath canopies of cherry blossom, both real and artificial. I stayed with the Naval Attaché, George Ross, and his wife who lived in a Japanese house, but it was bigger than most, with high ceilings, for it was the house of a wrestler and Japanese wrestlers were bred immensely tall and powerful and wore their lacquered hair in a topknot. The *Kent* officers were invited to the Emperor's Cherry Blossom Tea Party in the Palace gardens, where we walked in a long 'crocodile' of ladies in gorgeous kimonos and gentlemen in morning-coats and striped trousers. The shingle paths crossed streams and ponds where exotic fish flashed under gracefully dwarfed trees. We never saw the Emperor, for there was a hint of rain in the air and the Son of Heaven must not catch cold. Yet the only showers were flurries of petals from the double cherry blossom trees that made spring magic of the Imperial Park.

On my way south to Shanghai I joined friends in Peking and saw the once-upon-a-time splendours of the world's most cultured and arrogant dynasties hidden behind the high rose-coloured walls of the Forbidden City, which is the heart and core of China's long history.

May 1935 was the Jubilee of King George V which the Commander-in-Chief and his Flagship *Kent* celebrated officially in Shanghai with the British community. Far away in Cape Town my Mother and our son celebrated it too.

'Tees Lodge', 7 May 1935

My dearest Bertie and darling Joy,
I am sitting at my desk this morning to write you my Jubilee letter.

All the schools had a holiday and I was determined that our boy should see *everything* worth seeing.

At 8 a.m. Arend was at Rossal to fetch him. It was a glorious winter day.

The big Military Review was on Green Point Common. We waited in the car in comfort, but as huge crowds surged in front of us I sent Arend and Peter to get a place right by the ropes. At 11 promptly Lord Clarendon, the Governor General, appeared, God Save the King struck up, and the Show began. Arend said it was all he could do to stop Peter from patting the police horses and calling out to the troops!

After an early lunch we drove to the Cathedral to see the lying-in-state of the Governor General's son, killed in that tragic car crash. I wished Peter to realize what *Duty* means, and that Lord Clarendon was carrying on his job and representing the King in spite of his deep personal sorrow.

Then to banish sad thoughts we went to the *Plaza* to see Cicely Courtnedge in the film *Things are looking up*. It was a splendid funny show, full of children.

We got home at 6 for an early supper and then into the car once more. Daddy was not with us. It would have been too much for him.

'Now, Arend, to the Parade please. We want to see the illuminations of the City Hall.' The crowds were every-where, buzzing like a huge swarm of bees. On the dot of 7 the façade of the City Hall burst into a flood of light and the people cheered themselves hoarse as a picture of the King and Queen, the Crown, the Lion and the Unicorn, blazed in dazzling lights!

'And now,' I said to Peter, 'we are going to the Cableway to the *top* of Table Mountain.'

The night was perfect, not too cold and a bright moon. We stood on the summit and we could hear the breakers far below. We got a perfect view of the fireworks and the city and suburbs and the ships in Table Bay all picked out in lights.

Then suddenly a chilly little wind made us realize we wanted a cup of coffee and we hurried to the restaurant. The cable-car driver was there and we invited him to join us for coffee. After that we were asked to sign the Visitors' Book, Piet's tongue hanging out at the effort!

Now we had to hurry to get him back to Rossal before 9. We *just* managed it.

When I walked into 'Tees Lodge' instead of a white-faced anxious husband waiting for me I found a cheery rosy man sitting in the study writing to you both.

And there is the story of our Jubilee Day.

Your Mother

That summer in China we had our own home for a few months – 'Wooden Bungalow', no better than its flimsy name. But our wide veranda looked across the harbour to the blue mountains of the Shantung mainland and we had a little spare room where we could put up a friend or two. We were right on the path from the little jetty to the golf course so there was usually someone dropping in for a 'snifter' on the way back to the ship.

Goo, my amah, still came tapping in on her triangular

bound feet to washee-washee sew-sew and to press our clothes with her clumsy charcoal-heated iron and Ah Lin our 'Number One' was paid an overall wage and hired and fired as he thought fit. If we were not well served he would lose face. The pomegranates flaunted their polished splendour and the sunflowers in our tiny garden stood ten foot high. Bertie went early to the ship to go boat-pulling and so we were often up at sunrise to play nine holes before I strolled down with him to the little jetty where the *Kent* picket boat waited. At sunset the cicadas tuned up their high insect orchestra and the nights were cool.

The simple friendly things of life were all we had and all we wanted. There were concert parties got up by the ship's company, football matches, regattas, swimming, tennis, picnics, church on the Quarterdeck, the gulls mewing with the hymns, and out-of-date films on board on Sunday nights.

Autumn came with clouds of blue dragonflies known as 'typhoon flies'. They were warning signals that sent Tomato-Face, Tomollow-Fish and Yesterday-Fish to the safest cover on the mainland where they dragged their sampans far up the shore.

The typhoon season marked the end of our Wei Hai Wei summer.

We knew it was our last and we were sad to leave. We'd have felt sadder still had we known that in 1937 the Japanese would be in occupation. There, on the jetty, old Ugly and our sampan 'flends' would kneel with bowed heads and hands tied behind their backs while the executioner wielded his sword.

The New Year of 1936 began well for us.

Bertie was promoted to Captain and relieved. We sailed for Cape Town in a Japanese ship – for the first time in our lives, together! The boats from the *Kent* rowed and sailed alongside us and cheered us on our way. The Chinese members of the crew set off a *feu de joie* of firecrackers to wish our vessel fair weather, and overhead, as we sailed into Lyemun Pass with its junks and anti-piracy patrol warships, the little aircraft was catapulted from the *Kent*. She roared over us, dipped and roared away again, and I knew that my husband was heartsore at leaving his 'Fair Maid of Kent', such a happy ship.

When we went below we found telegrams and flowers in our cabin, and a letter addressed to me in a flowing unknown hand. When I'd read it I passed it to Bertie.

HMS *Kent, China Station, 13 January 1936*

Dear Mrs. Packer,
Please pardon me for taking the liberty of writing this letter to you, but I thought you could not leave Hong Kong without a word from the ship's company.

The men of the *Kent* wish to thank you for all you have done for them, you have helped to make their lives happy during your stay with us, you have been as it were a foster mother to us all. Your charming presence at all our football matches, concerts, dances, etc., has given us the extra will to win and now we lose two real friends, yourself and Captain Packer. We all hope that the next we hear of Captain Packer is that he will be appointed Flag Officer to a ship, which is bound to come. He is an officer whom all would follow and is loved by all his men.

In saying Goodbye to you, we wish you all you wish yourselves. In happiness there is no need for that because we know that Captain Packer will see to that. So God speed you and Captain Packer to your home and family and a very happy reunion.

E. L. Castle. Master at Arms.

Part Three: Diplomatic Interlude
1936 to 1939

13
'The duty of a diplomat is to ensure that his country will have the right allies.'

Naval Attaché	Balkans
1936 to 1937	Athens and Ankara

BERTIE'S foreign service leave, most of which we spent at 'Tees Lodge', was extended and, when we sailed for England, our son was with us.

Peter settled down quickly at the Dragon School in Oxford while Bertie worked at the Admiralty in Naval Intelligence to prepare for his next appointment as Naval Attaché to Turkey, Greece and Yugoslavia.

'When do we go?' I asked as Christmas approached.

'That's the tricky part,' he said. 'The appointment has to be approved by the King.'

The King! But *what* King? Rumours of Abdication were rife.

On 11 December I made my first note in the journal I had decided to keep while we were in the Balkans.

[11 December 1936 London] *It is all over. The shortest reign in history. We have just heard Edward VIII's Abdication Speech broadcast at 10 p.m. He spoke simply, in a voice tired but determined. 'You must believe me when I tell you that I have found it impossible to carry the heavy burden of responsibility and discharge my duties as King without the help and support of the woman I love.'*

So now he is on his way to some unknown destination on the Continent. She has already left the country.

[12 December] *Today at St. James's Palace at 3 p.m. Albert, Duke of York, to be known henceforth as George VI, was proclaimed King Emperor. The nation has accepted him with spontaneous goodwill, and the Commonwealth too. He is a family man and the British like a Royal Family. (Mrs. Simpson at 44 and, after two marriages, is childless.)*

While the new King tackled the pile of documents his brother had left unsigned we spent Christmas with Bertie's sister, Dorothy, and her husband, Professor Norman Capon, in their charming Regency home near Prince's Park in Liverpool. They had consented to be Peter's guardians in our absence. In *The Times* and *Morning Post* of 19 January 1937, my husband's appointment was formally announced.

Naval Attaché at Angora.

The King has approved the appointment of Captain H. A. Packer, RN, as Naval Attaché to His Majesty's Embassy at Angora, and to His Majesty's Legations at Belgrade and Athens with headquarters at Athens to date January 21.

In Part Four of *Pack and Follow* I have written fully and nostalgically of our two and a half years in the Balkans. I was enthralled with every aspect. For Bertie, in that troubled period on the brink of World War Two, it was an exacting post requiring him, among many other things, to project the fact that the Franco-British Entente was more powerful than the Rome–Berlin Axis, and that the Mediterranean was *not* an 'Italian Lake' but an important British naval sphere of interest.

Within a fortnight of our arrival we were established in an attractive modern villa on the coast at Glyphada, a few miles out of Athens and conveniently situated opposite the Golf Club, where we could also sail and swim. A married couple,

Jean and Ero, looked after our house. Jean, a willing and efficient young man, found us a good chef, Apostolis. Diki our chauffeur was a scholarly White Russian who lived in a flat attached to our garage with his wife and eight-year-old son, Basil.

An early spring that year covered the countryside with a froth of blossom and carpets of wild flowers, blood-red poppies and silvery asphodels while Athens, crowned by the Acropolis and the Parthenon, was a dazzling gem in a setting of mountains to match the blue of sea and sky.

Bertie was duly briefed by the British Minister, Sir Sydney Waterlow, an imposing figure, known to the Greeks and the Diplomats as 'Sir Waterloo'.

The British Legation and Chancery was housed in the mansion which had been occupied by the Cretan statesman and Dictator, Venizelos and it was there that the Naval Attaché to Turkey, Greece and Yugoslavia had his headquarters office and his Civil Service clerk, Mr. Richardson.

My husband had innumerable official calls to pay and was received in private audience by King George II of the Hellenes, who had recently been recalled to the Throne after the overthrow of Venizelos. The King and his brother, Prince Paul, the Crown Prince, had spent many years in London and, like the people of Greece, were democratic and well-disposed towards Britain who had played a major part in the Greek War of Independence against centuries of Turkish domination.

At the end of February, when these formalities had been completed in Athens, they had to be repeated in Turkey, and after that in Yugoslavia.

We were met in Istanbul by the Military Attaché, Colonel Alick Ross, and his dark Patrician-looking wife, Tania, the only member of her family who had escaped from Russia during the Revolution. Tania's English was accented and vivid and entirely disregarded the article 'the' or 'a'.

Before they left us at the Park Oteli, Tania said to me:

'You are dining with Ambassador tonight. Informal. If he stares at you and says nothing, keep quiet. I lose head and crash in with silly remark. Don't crash in. Remember!'

Sir Percy Loraine, the last of a long line of English baronets, and a career diplomat, had been Minister in Persia and Greece and High Commissioner in Egypt before being appointed Ambassador to Kemal Ataturk's new Turkey. He looked as distinguished as he was, tall and spare with iron grey hair, a close clipped moustache and the slate blue eyes of a young baby with much the same uncompromising gaze. This silent mesmeric stare upset nervous members of his staff and everybody had a different theory about it. Bertie's was simple. He reckoned the Ambassador disliked untidy ill-considered speech and was considering the most lucid words with which to express his opinions. And pretty strong they were at times.

We dined in the palatial Embassy at Istanbul in a small charming room with the Ambassador's exquisite Persian miniatures on the walls and his rare Oriental rugs on the polished floor. A cosy wood fire burned in the grate.

I had been prepared to find the Ambassador alarming but the moment we met and he smiled my misgivings vanished. At dinner we received a concise lesson in diplomacy which I recorded as soon as we got back to the hotel.

[28 February 1937. Midnight Park Oteli] ... *'What is war?' asked the Ambassador, clearly intending to answer his own question, for he had put down the two forks with which he eats his fish (fish knives are tabu at the Embassy). But Bertie took advantage of the characteristic pause to slip in an answer – somewhat to Sir Percy's surprise.*

'Surely, sir, war is the failure of diplomacy.'

H.E. wouldn't have that. He gave his new Naval Attaché the stare, and then said severely: 'Diplomacy breaks down when the man with the sword acts hastily on his own initiative creating a situation which nullifies the patient efforts of the diplomat. Take, for example, the case of General X.'

He made his point conclusively.

'I think, sir,' said Bertie, 'that the case of General X proves a sad lack of understanding between the Diplomatic and Fighting Services. If commanding officers knew more about the Foreign Office and if the Foreign Office had

*greater sympathy with the Commander-in-Chief expected to
keep order on the spot, there would be fewer inflammable
incidents.'*

*Sir Percy agreed. But added: 'There is one thing you
should know, N.A. The duty of a diplomat is not so much to
avert war at any price, as to ensure that, if war is inevitable,
his country will at least have the right allies. It takes years of
peacetime effort to do as much.'*

*He was thinking perhaps of his own formidable task in
Turkey, where German influence has been predominant
since long before 1914. Turkish troops were trained by
German officers and later fought against the Allies under
their leadership, including Kemal himself. If Turkey is now
to swing towards Britain – remain neutral – in the only too
likely event of another war it will be due to H.E.'s well-
known personal influence with Ataturk who admires him
for many things, not least his racing studs and his willing-
ness to dance or play poker till after midnight and then settle
down to a discussion of foreign policy till dawn, for it is
Ataturk's habit to turn night into day.*

The Ambassador liked to travel with a retinue, especially
his Service Attachés, so next evening the Ross's, Group
Captain Thomas Elmhirst, the Air Attaché, his wife and
ourselves went on board the Embassy yacht *Makook II*,
which had once been a river boat on the Nile, and crossed
the Bosphorus from Turkey-in-Europe to Turkey-in-Asia
and entrained with the Ambassador for the night journey to
Ataturk's new capital, Ankara. (The Foreign Office, well
behind the times, still referred to Ankara as Angora and was
also using Embassy notepaper headed Constantinople instead of Istanbul!)

Ankara, like all artificial capitals, was interesting but still
soulless. The Government officials and Diplomatic Corps
felt isolated in the vast emptiness of the brown Anatolian
Plain that had once long ago been the granary of Asia. Most
of them suffered from 'Ankaritis' – a combination of
claustrophobia and agoraphobia – from which they recuper-
ated during the summer in Istanbul or on leave.

We were bitten by bugs in our hotel, and Tania said, 'Don't worry. Bug is everywhere in Turkey. You will get used to bug, just like you will get used to protocol.'

There were two government-subsidized night haunts – the Russian Restaurant Karpitch, and the cabaret Pavillon – both much patronized by the 'Dancing Dictator' who was determined to exchange Turkish music for red hot jazz. The children in the fine new compulsory schools were taught phonetic spelling and Western lettering. Western fashions must be adopted, women unveiled and emancipated and any head seen wearing the traditional fez was struck off and impaled as a public example.

Most days we walked miles over the eroded plain with Sir Percy, who gave us some insight into the Dictator's flexible mentality.

'A magnificent soldier who, after 1918 turned the remnants of a defeated army into a fighting force that increased his country's territory and prestige. The nation worshipped him as 'the Ghazi' – the Conqueror. He is a very far-seeing reformer. If Turkey is to flourish she must about-face from East to West. He intends to re-educate his nation in one generation. Unlike other Dictators, he is determined to lead his people towards lasting peace and prosperity. They go together. So now he is known not only as the Ghazi but as Ataturk – Father of all the Turks. He'll guide his children ruthlessly, but for their own ultimate good.'

Sir Percy stopped in his tracks when two huge brown bears shambled down a ravine towards us.

'Don't worry. They are only the mascots of the Ghazi's bodyguard. Now the sheep-dogs really are dangerous. They are trained to fight the wolves who attack the flocks in winter – and they are not discriminating.'

Some young Turkish soldiers laughed and shooed the bears away. On the summit of Chan Kaya Hill above them was the rose-red mansion of the Dictator.

'Is Ataturk really as dissolute as he is said to be?' I asked.

The Ambassador's eyes twinkled.

'He *was*! Unfortunately his health now limits some of his wilder activities, so the scandals are less amusing.'

My journal, dated 8 March, notes: 'We went to a *thé dansant* at the Polish Embassy considered to be the finest in Ankara with pillared portico and tiled roof in the style of a traditional Polish country house. Ambassador Sokulnitska is a collector – a small pale man with sad brown eyes and a falsetto voice. When we admired the contents of his display cabinets he said tenderly, "Ah, yes, I love my treasures too much. Sometimes I could wish to be liberated from this passion".'

Wealth and glamour. That was the projection of Poland in Ankara in 1937. Later that year the impression was enhanced by a letter from Sir Percy Loraine. Bertie had recently given me a Leica, but it was the Ambassador who tried to teach me how to use it properly. He was a student of photography and his own pictures were gems of artistry. Mine were 'journalese' – human interest bang in the centre of the foreground, light and composition regardless.

Turf Club, Piccadilly, W1, 13 September 1937

So glad you liked the photographs and pleased to have your letter. Have been thoroughly on the move since leaving Istanbul 25 August. First we went to Count Potochi's shooting lodge at Julin, Polish Galicia, a delightful spot. Played golf on his private course, went for a long ride in lovely endless woodlands; and in the evening shot a roebuck. Then we went on to Prince and Princess (Charles) Radziwill, at Mankiewicze, in Polesia, quite near the Soviet border. Wild country, in its own way very attractive; it is right in the Pripet marshes. We shot a few duck and snipe. . . .

Then it was suddenly decided that Charles Radziwill was to take me out to try to get an elk (what, as a matter of fact, I call a moose, but there they call it an elk), the nearest living thing to the antediluvian fauna. This happens in virgin forest, where no one lives and the elk is King. It can only be done in the rutting season, which lasts three or four weeks; you may be out a week without getting a shot at one big enough to warrant killing. Our time limit was 36 hours, and the day after we left Mankiewicze for the elk forest, I got one at 5.30 a.m. probably about 55 stone! It was absolutely thrilling. We had to follow him up in the thick forest undergrowth. I could see the branches moving and hear the boughs cracking as he came toward me. I never *saw* him until he was at some 15 paces from me, and then more than half of him was blind to me. I had to fire then or never, handicapped at such range of course by a telescopic sight. After the shot he bounded away, madly, missing me by about six yards and my host by only three yards. And that, as we afterwards knew, with a bullet in his heart! He went 50 yards and was stone dead when we came up to him. You can imagine how pleased I was! Not a really big head but a nice one.

Then home, with a morning glimpse of Warsaw between two trains. Then Doncaster: bad meeting for me. Neither of my horses won, though both were good enough to win. The rub of the green was agin!

Tomorrow I'm off to Ireland to see the horses, especially the young ones. I hear the filly foal of my own breeding looks quite a likely racehorse. . . .

Date of my return as yet uncertain. I *may* have to go back third week in October, *en garçon*. If I do, will you both please come to stay in the Embassy 27 October when you arrive; in which case why not come up to Ankara in the train with me in good time for The Show?

Percy L.

'The Show' was Turkey's National Day, the Anniversary of the Republic on 29 October. One of our fellow passengers on the ship from Greece to Istanbul was the Turkish Minister to Athens, Unayden Pasha, a poet of renown with sad passionate eyes, a deep melodious voice, a powerful presence and a hennaed moustache.

'He's superb,' said Bertie. 'But he's a survivor at heart and by upbringing. He should have slaves and odalisques to fawn on him.'

He joined us for an aperitif before dinner.

'What can I offer you, Excellence?' asked Bertie.

'What are *you* taking, Captain Packer?'

'Gin and bitters. It is the aperitif of the British Navy.'

'Ah yes. "Pink gin" you call it? I should like to try it.'

He took very little water with it and savoured the taste thoughtfully. 'It's rather like vodka. Strong. I like all that is strong – including this pink gin.'

His wife, it seemed, would not be joining him in Ankara.

'She prefers our home on the Marmara. Ankara is a raw city – adolescent – and the wild Anatolian scene does not please her.'

Bertie led him to talk of his boyhood in Istanbul. While the poet spoke his tapering fingers passed a chaplet of amber beads to and fro across his palm.

'You want me to go back 30 years into a world already forgotten by our young generation of today? Very well, then. My father had a mansion with gardens, courtyards and fountains. The women of his household were veiled and lived in their own quarters. My mother was attended by young fair-skinned Circassians and, when she considered the time ripe, she selected the most accomplished of her maidens to initiate me into the delicate arts of love.'

Bertie's eyes were amused. 'Very civilized compared with the juvenile tumbles in the hay of my own uninitiated youth. Finesse in l'amour should not become a forgotten art in young Turkey.'

The poet raised his glass. 'I drink to those sentiments. Yet today the world needs warriors more than lovers.'

'The strategy of love and war are not incompatible – as history and Cleopatra have proved,' protested Bertie.

Unayden turned his expressive gaze on me.

'What do you say, Madame?'

'I agree with you both. On Saturday night at sea the Royal Navy has a toast you would like – "To sweethearts and wives – may they never meet!" '

He laughed and leaned forward to give me the chaplet still warm from his touch.

'We pass these beads through our hands – to stop us from smoking too much – or so we say. I have many – ivory, shagreen, sandalwood – this is amber from the Baltic.' The beads were extraordinarily light, warm and smooth as a woman's skin, rich in colour.

'Keep them, Madame – if your warrior permits – as a small souvenir of at least one old custom that is unlikely to die in our new Turkey.'

The day and night of 29 October were strange and memorable – the day an impressive display of modern Turkey's military might, the creation of Mustapha Kemal, 'the Ghazi'; the night an exposition of the diplomacy of Mustapha Kemal Ataturk, who had revolutionized his land and turned its newly enlightened face towards the West.

Ankara overflowed with visiting VIPs and representatives of the Balkan Entente. It was *en gala*, with the Old Citadel across the rift floodlit. We attended a reception given by Premier Çelal Bayar in honour of the Rumanian Premier Tatarescu, the Persian Minister of Foreign Affairs, and other official guests.

'But where is Ismet Ineunu?' I asked Bertie. I missed the deaf ex-Premier with his listening eyes and crest of white hair.

'He's being kept on ice to succeed Ataturk as President when the time comes. So he's suffering from a diplomatic indisposition.'

Early next morning we woke to an unfamiliar sound on those wide uplands so far from the sea. It was like the thunderous crash of surf rising and falling, a surge of mighty tides. Bertie came to the window and we looked down from Chan Kaya heights.

'Now it's near, now far – that roar! Now here, now there.'

'Ataturk must be driving round with his motorcycle outriders,' said Bertie. 'You're hearing the cheers of his people wherever he shows up.'

In the morning the Dictator received the Diplomatic Corps in all their glory of full dress. In the afternoon there was a military parade at the Race Course. For three hours Mustapha Kemal stood rigidly to attention taking the salute. We saw him then as 'the Ghazi' whose iron will commanded his failing flesh as it had once commanded his

112

troops. Overhead the bombers and fighters flew in perfect formation, led by Sabiya Gokçen, the young woman Squadron Leader liberated from the bonds of the harem to the status of an Air officer, already blooded in battle against Kurdish rebels. Parachutists – many of them girls – floated out of the sky to land on the grassy slopes round the Race Course. Balloons, painted with Kemal's face, and the words *'Varol Ataturk'* (long live Ataturk), hovered above us, yet every one knew that he would never celebrate another such anniversary – even the thousands of uniformed school-children goose-stepping past the Dictator who had brought them Western education and pride in their nation.

That night the Presidential Gala Reception was held at the Exhibition Hall and early next morning I wrote down my impressions before they could be blurred by much-needed sleep.

[30 October 1937. 8 a.m. Ankara] *Five thousand guests were at the President's Reception last night. A special room was set aside for the Diplomatic Corps. We arrived at 10.30 p.m. and half an hour later Ataturk entered with his Ministers. We missed the hawk-featured fiery Inenu. The new Premier, Çelal Bay, was on the President's right. He is dark, spectacled and unassuming. Marshal Fevzi, Chief of the General Staff, on Ataturk's left, is a grim granite-faced soldier with grizzled grey hair en brosse. Aras, the Foreign Minister, was nervous as a cat, limbs twitching, swollen eyes darting about from behind strong glasses.*

We formed a circle and the President shook hands with most of us.

He is medium height, well built, his tails and starched shirt immaculate. Evening dress is the only 'uniform' he wears these days (like Turkish or American diplomats) and he'll go straight from an all-night party to inspect a factory still wearing his formal evening clothes. His face is unforgettable – strong nose and chin, wide forehead, grey hair, thin mobile lips and eyebrows, with a Satanic upward twist at the outer corners. His eyes are extraordinary. Light grey,

113

penetrating and pitiless. His hands are small and fine-boned, limp in the handshake.

While he was in the room the atmosphere was electric. When he had left it a sigh and a flutter of talk broke the tension. Bertie touched my arm.

'Let's go into the public ballroom.'

The long hall was packed with a huge crowd pressed round a dais on which stood the Dictator and his party. The band was playing a slow waltz but nobody danced except a tiny figure on the platform in a long pink evening gown. Her face was round and wise, flowers clung in her black hair, her body was flat as a child's.

'She is a child!' I whispered.

'Yes. She's Ülkü, the Ghazi's mascot. Unayden told me about her. The Ghazi adopted her from the station master and his wife at a small village near his birthplace. He takes the little one everywhere and she adores him.'

At midnight Ataturk returned to the Diplomats' salon where a wide circle of comfortable chairs had been arranged facing a crescent of seats for the Dictator who summoned those he wanted near him. Tatarescu, the Rumanian Premier and guest of honour, was on his right, Sir Percy Loraine on his left. Then the Afghan Minister, the French Ambassador Ponsot, the Greek Military Commander-in-Chief, Papagos, and the Persian Foreign Minister.

Our friend Unayden Pasha took charge of Bertie and me. He sat between us and described the various official guests with realistic perception.

Having settled his audience, the Diplomatic Corps, Ataturk lectured everybody on all manner of subjects, educational, sentimental, theoretical and finally on matters concerning Turkey's foreign policy. He spoke in French and was never at a loss for a word. His glass of 'rakia' was frequently refilled, Sir Percy drank only his usual whisky and water, and the others took champagne.

At first Ataturk's listeners were attentive but, as hours passed and dawn seeped through the long uncurtained windows, an all-pervasive weariness produced yawns, slumber and a few snores. Tatarescu's puffy face with heavy-

lidded black eyes was sleepily inscrutable but when he answered questions addressed to him by the President it was clear that he was very wide awake. The Persian leaned forward intently, smiling a little, while Papagos sat stiffly to attention, his sharp features drawn with toothache. Marshal Fevzi, solid as a rock, never stirred; Aras dozed, mouth agape, fingers twitching; Ponsot, podgy and sulky, sat scowling. Every now and again Ataturk turned to H.E. and said, 'What are your views, my friend?' And Sir Percy responded with precise deliberation in his exquisite French, while Ataturk watched him with those magnetic grey eyes warm with approval.

Once Ponsot lost his temper when Ataturk goaded him about the thorny subject of Alexandretta. He began to argue angrily, his stubby finger thrust rudely at the Ghazi. He was rash enough to mention the possibility of a Turkish defeat in certain circumstances. Immediately the Ghazi drew himself up with a fierce shout that echoed through the room.

'Je ne sui jamais battu! Ou je gagne ou je meurs!' (*I am never beaten! Either I win or I die!*)

Everybody woke up. Even Aras, whose head had lolled on to his neighbour's shoulder, came to with a jerk, coughed loudly, got out his handkerchief, held it in front of his face and spat accurately into it.

It was 6.45 a.m. Sunlight slanted into the lofty salon. Ataturk called for his old Secretary who had been one of the great generals of the Greek–Turkish War in Asia Minor. The President, who always converses with Sir Percy in French, suddenly turned and addressed a little speech to him in Turkish. The Secretary, gentle and venerable, translated. When he had done, Ataturk patted H.E.'s arm and said 'Vous êtes mon ami.' Then he turned to his comrade-in-arms who leaned over his shoulder. '*And you too!*' He reached up his hand to stroke the furrowed cheek. Impulsively he drew the white head down and embraced the old Secretary, who kissed his master's hand.

Chairs were pushed back and the circle widened as Ataturk called for his Anatolian folk-dancers. Clarionets sounded and drums throbbed as the dancers – all male –

performed their athletic dances, dipping and springing with inhuman agility, uttering hoarse cries as they did so. They had waited all night for this moment. Unayden, beside me, was obviously affected. 'This is our own music – wild and stirring. See the athletic beauty of those dancers! They are true Anatolians.'

When at last we trailed after the President into the chill harsh light of the autumn morning, the great swelling roar burst again as thousands of voices bellowed 'Varol Ataturk!'

14
'The most beautiful of all was our Marina.'

Naval Attaché	Balkans
1938	Isles of Greece and Yugoslavia

1938 opened with a glitter of Grecian grandeur.

On Sunday, 9 January Prince Paul of the Hellenes, heir to the Throne, was married to Princess Frederika of Hanover.

Royalty flocked to Athens for the occasion and not only the Palace but the Foreign Legations were in a fine flurry over accommodating their various VIPs.

Bertie's log, with its brief entries, went overboard for the Duchess of Kent.

[Friday, 7 January 1938] *Everyone fussing about the Kents. Huge gathering to protocol them at the station at 6 p.m.*

Princess Marina very beautiful, dignified and gracious. Kind-looking. The Duke a bit worn since last I saw him. King of Greece arrived five minutes beforehand and gave everybody and everything a piercing look – like a tough commander of a battleship.

[Sunday, 9 January] *Wedding. Assembled at Legation 9 a.m. Cathedral 9.45 Everything excellently arranged. Princess Frederika very small, a merry childlike face, neat figure, looked like a little girl standing alongside Prince Paul who is over 6 foot. He wore naval uniform.*

Prince Dimitri was best man and three brothers of the bride were pages, also Prince Michael of Rumania, a good-looking young chap. Pages well-built lot. Bridesmaids plain. Splendid old Prince George of Greece, with his magnificent moustache, was in charge of the party.

My own journal adds a flamboyant touch of background.

'Sir Waterloo' was indescribably gorgeous in all his trappings of gold braid, sword (why a sword for a diplomat?), medals, orders, cocked hat with white ostrich plumes, his elegant nose more than ever in the air as his uniform collar was too tight. Diplomatic Corps in full regalia faced the Premier, Metaxa, and the Cabinet. No pews. Just standing room. The French Military Attaché was musical comedy in cardinal red trousers and sky blue tunic, the Rumanian Attaché sported a burnished coal scuttle on his head, but the Hungarian Minister took the palm in black velvet and astrakhan with a massive gold and turquoise chain, a scimitar, and a wonderful headgear with ospreys. As soon as the Royals had taken their places a platoon of Bishops entered in a blaze of brocaded gold, silver and purple. The Archimandrite alone must have been worth a fortune. Behind these potentates of the Greek Orthodox Church stood two sombre black figures, the Chief Rabbi and the Head of the Armenian Church in Greece.

On the following night there was a big reception at the British Legation which bristled with Royalties all related one way or another – a sort of twilight of the gods, for most of them were fated to end up as exiles or refugees. When the King laughed it dislodged his eyeglass and the severity left his face. Prince Paul, the Regent of Yugoslavia, presented us to his wife, Princess Olga, who was Princess Marina's sister. Bertie noted that 'the Duke of Kent talked for a long time to Admiral Sakallariou, Head of the Greek Navy, and did his stuff splendidly. ... I took old Prince George an enormous beaker of champagne. He said he never touched it, had been teetotal for years, and then poured it straight down his throat just like emptying a jug into a tin pail. I swear I heard it hit bottom! Then I danced a tango with MARINA. I was very proud. She is light as a feather and so charming. In fact the whale of an evening and everybody in crashing form. The most beautiful of all was our MARINA.'

A few days later, when the visitors had all departed, he

summed up the feeling of most of the Diplomatic Corps. 'A pleasant sense of relief after the tumult and the shouting.'

Early that spring we were in Belgrade, a city of lilacs and soldiers on the confluence of the Sava and the Danube, which is not blue but muddy grey.

We stayed with Sir Ronald Campbell,* the British Minister, and Lady Campbell, who were very easy and amusing.

The heart of Yugoslavia was Serbian Belgrade – tough, overbearing and of the Orthodox religion. In the mountainous province of Bosnia the people were Moslem and the women veiled and kept in *purdah*. It was there, in Sarajevo, that we saw the bridge where in 1914 the student, Prinçip assassinated the Hapsburg Archduke Francis Ferdinand and his consort with one bullet and precipitated World War One. In Dalmatia and Slovenia the religion was mostly Roman Catholic and the people fair and fresh-faced.

The most powerful man in Yugoslavia in the years preceding World War Two was the Serbian Prime Minister, Stoyadenovitch, a massive figure with darting black eyes and a quick tongue. In the Balkans, where assassination is an everyday hazard, he was a continual target. The most recent attempt on his life had been made in the Chamber of Deputies. Sir Ronald told us the story.

'It happened on Budget Day. The Diplomatic Corps turned out in full regalia for the occasion. When Stoyadenovitch was making his speech a good deal of heckling annoyed him and he said, "If you have any questions to put, come out here and ask them!" There was a scuffle and one of the deputies stepped forward right in front of the Speaker's rostrum and directly opposite the gallery reserved for the Diplomats. I was looking straight at the man who was clearly drunk. He swayed on his feet and then drew a revolver. In a flash the Diplomatic Corps was on its belly behind the barrier. I remained in my place to see what was

---

* Sir Ronald Campbell was British Ambassador in Paris in 1940 when France capitulated.

going to happen next. What I didn't realize, and couldn't have believed possible, was that any man – even drunk – could be such a fearful shot! As you know, Stoyadenovitch is an elephantine target and was at point blank range. He ducked, the bullet went wide and whistled past my ear. The would-be assassin was set upon and overcome, and, like a conjuring trick, a policeman popped up in the Speaker's rostrum and trained a machine gun on the deputies. When order was restored Stoyadenovitch calmly finished his speech. I give him full marks for nerve.'

Prince Paul, the Regent, and Princess Olga lived in a lovely house called 'Beli Dvor' (the White Lodge) in the woods outside the city as did the boy King Peter, still too young to ascend the Throne vacated by his father, King Alexander, who was assassinated in Marseilles in 1935.

We left Belgrade for the incomparable Dalmatian Coast where Bertie was to be shown over the Adriatic Bases of the Yugoslav Navy. Philip Rhodes met us at Split to return with us by sea to Athens.

While Bertie was swept off to the Seaplane Base by Commander Sandvich of the Yugoslav Navy, Mr. Perich the Honorary British Consul, took charge of Philip and me. He drove us to the top of a wooded hill. Behind us were snow-capped mountains; at our feet wild deer, hares, pheasants and partridges took flight, while far below the ancient walled city of Split rose from the shining sea. No traffic is allowed to cross the drawbridge into that Gothic gem of tall houses and narrow passages. Like its neighbour Dubrovnik (once Ragusa), the city state of prosperous maritime merchants, the influence of Venetian art and architecture was everywhere apparent.

Next day a naval launch took us to some of the lush green Adriatic islands. On one of them was a tiny Byzantine church. It still haunts me. Under the altar was a rough mat. The young naval officer who was our guide said, 'The people here believe that if a mad person can be forced to lie there for 24 hours Sveti Naum – the patron saint of this church – will exorcise the demon in possession.'

'Does it work?' asked Philip.

The officer shrugged and grinned.

'Who knows? Do punishment cells make a bad man good? Perhaps they help. And here there is Sveti Naum.'

Philip flew home for Easter and Peter joined us in Athens, taller, thinner, very full of life.

On Good Friday all the flags in Athens were lowered to half-mast. 'But why?' Piet asked our chauffeur, Diki.

The big Russian threw him a reproachful glance from behind his strong glasses.

'Jesus Christ died today.'

But on Saturday all the church bells pealed as midnight struck and the crowds poured out of the Midnight Mass and embraced each other saying 'Christ is risen' and answering 'He is risen indeed!' Torchlight processions of singing children were here, there and everywhere, while fireworks blew Pontius Pilate sky high.

Next day beaches, woods and gardens were misty with smoke and the appetizing aroma of meat turning on the spits, and noisy with families and friends celebrating Easter Day and the Resurrection.

It was a fresh clear night and when it was all over and our stretch of coast was quiet once more under the stars, the three of us stood spellbound on our balcony. Our arrogant white Ankara cat, Mustapha Atakat, brooded in the graceful branches of the pinetree in our garden. But he was deaf, as are most of his breed, and I doubt if he heard the song in the cypress grove. Behind us Hymettus, the Honey Mountain, was etched against the sky and out at sea we saw the lights of the fishing boats strung out behind the leading caique.

Bertie said: 'Listen, Piet! Our nightingale's getting up steam.'

We held our breath as the crystal scale mounted, a silvery madrigal thrown into the silence.

'He's stopped,' cried Piet. 'But he can't stop *now*!'

From the grove came the throaty crooning response of his mate.

Then once more the quivering trills of the rhapsody soared into the night.

Sometimes we went sailing to little-known islands in *Troll*, the beautiful yacht of our friends, Chris and Mary Carolou.* When we returned with the evening breeze filling the sails, Mary strummed her ukelele and Chris sang Greek folk songs in his fine baritone. We ate delicious snacks and drank the fragrant white wine grown in the vineyards of the King at Tatoi. And the tideless Aegean was indeed Homer's 'wine dark sea'.

I took Peter to the Acropolis in the late afternoon when the pure white marble of Pentelicon changes to amber, rose and lavender, he was deeply impressed by the Parthenon and its sacred precincts and with the tiny chapel hidden deep in the rocky hillside where, under the noses of the Moslem Turks, the people of Athens had kept the flame of their own faith alive for 400 years.

On the Hill of Mars I showed him the cave where Socrates was imprisoned.

'He was tried and condemned to commit suicide because he expressed the belief that there was only one God. He drank hemlock and went on lecturing his students and friends till he fell asleep and died. The idea of just one God was too awesome for the Pagan Greeks.'

Soon after Peter had flown back Bertie received a message that the *Repulse* would shortly be in Tribuki Bay off the Island of Skyros. The Captain of this fine battle-cruiser was John Godfrey, our friend of the China Station. A destroyer was to meet the Naval Attaché at Kimi, a little port in the Island of Eubea, and take him to the *Repulse*.

The drive to Port Kimi took about six hours through wine-growing country. All the villages smelt of fermenting grapes and the villagers stamped the fruit in home-made presses on the pavement. They waved to us as we passed, and carts trundled along stacked with goatskins filled with

---

* When King Paul came to the Greek Throne Mary Carolou was Lady-in-Waiting to Queen Frederika.

'must' (fermenting juice) which the carters held aloft, gulping great draughts and greeting us with tipsy gaiety. The spirit of Dionysus was alive in the dusty air.

We embarked in the destroyer *Ilex* which took us to Tribuki Bay in an hour and a half at 22 knots. The *Repulse*, long grey and watchful, and the destroyer *Icarus* lay in the sunset against the background of Skyros, a tiny lonely island of rocky mountains, where only a few shepherds and fisherfolk had their huts. Since there was nowhere I could stay ashore, John Godfrey, with a reluctant smile, offered me his cabin for the night.

'I didn't expect Joy,' he said to Bertie – reproachfully.

'I didn't expect her at Tsingtao – in that coolie-ship, as you may remember.'

'She destroys one's better judgement,' smiled John. 'What's more, I doubt if she came here to keep you company – or to see me.'

We were on the Bridge. He picked out a small spot on the Admiralty Chart of the Aegean Islands. '*Skyros. Rupert Brooke's Tomb. 23 April 1915.* Would that be the reason?'

We dined on deck. The night was windless and the air soft and pure. John and Bertie talked far into the night, for even here, in this place of solitude and starlit sea, the ghost of one world war and the threat of another were with us all. John already knew that he was likely to be appointed Director of Naval Intelligence and there was much to discuss with the Naval Attaché.

I woke at first light to hear the roar of floatplanes warming up and watched through the open scuttle as they took off, wing lights circling and vanishing into the grey dawn. I lay drowsily, observing the growing light discover hidden beauties in the Captain's tribute-silk coverlet which had come from the Forbidden City in Peking as had the blue and white rug in his after-cabin and the jade tree abloom with semi-precious flowers on his lacquer dinner-table. His pictures were Impressionist and there were sketches by Augustus John, a personal friend of his. In War all these things and his books – so important to him – would be whisked away and these quarters would be as bleak and austere as the sea-cabin he now occupied.

Sunday, Church on the Quarterdeck between sea and sky with the spirit free. Afterwards Bertie wanted to renew contacts with old shipmates and John arranged for the picket boat to take two of his officers ashore with me.

'Your pilgrimage,' he said.

A gorge cleaves one of the three mountains above the bay. In early spring it is a torrent swollen with melting snow. Now it was dry. We picked our way up the stony shepherd's track beside the gorge in the hot morning sun. In the heart of an olive grove we found the lonely grave protected by iron railings and four sturdy posts of Skyros marble. An olive tree leans protectively over this 'corner of a foreign field that is forever England'. All was peace and the spicy scent of silver-grey sage and thyme.

Rupert Brooke died at 27 years old of acute blood-poisoning in a French hospital ship – a Sub-Lieutenant in the Royal Naval Division bound for Gallipoli in the spring of 1915. Sailors with torches lined the rock ravine as the officers and men of his platoon carried the coffin up that tortuous track to the burial place his comrades had chosen for him to lie in 'shining peace, under the night'. Within six weeks most of those who had left there were killed or wounded in the Gallipoli campaign.

Before we returned to the ship we bathed in the gloriously clear water. I took a handful of pebbles from the beach, rainbow-coloured marble polished by the sea. The picket boat fetched us. We left the shadowed ravine in its solitude.

That afternoon the destroyer, *Icarus*, took us back to Kimi. Her Commander gave Bertie an *Icarus* crest set in good English heart of oak. The happy full-faced brass sun still smiles at me every day, for it is my doorstop.

15
'We would follow Ataturk anywhere and be glad to die.'

Naval Attaché	Marmara, Corfu, Albania, Ankara
1938 to 1939	Death of Ataturk

THE summer was idyllic.

Colonel Alick Ross and Tania were on leave in England and we rented their apartment in Istanbul complete with staff. It was in Pera – high above the city stewing in the heat – a Pasha's palace cleverly converted. Most of the diplomats were on holiday so for a few weeks that crazy merry-go-round had eased up. There was always a breeze on the golf course heights where a haze of mauve butterflies hovered over the mauve swaying heads of wild scabious. We often played a round in the cool of the evening, if we were not out with the Ambassador and Lady Loraine and various guests in *Makook*. Sir Percy always liked his bridge four on board and, as none of the staff played except the Air Attaché, Tommy Elmhirst, we were useful.

The Prince's Islands were green in their sparkling Marmara setting, and we usually anchored to swim in the lee of a ruined monastery.

In the mornings I did my rather haphazard housekeeping and wrote up my journal while Bertie worked at the Chancery.

[15 July] *Peter's birthday. Twelve today. Soon he will be with us here.*

Truly these Turks are an impetuous people! Here in Pera a man who was a bad sleeper was wakened very early each morning by a street vendor with a specially raucous cry. He protested in vain. At last, provoked beyond endurance, the insomniac sprang from his groundfloor window on to the back of the vendor and strangled him!

125

[25 July] *Yesterday a party of us went out in the Makook to Moda Yacht Club for the Regatta which was attended by Ataturk in his yacht Ertugrül. As she steamed into the gaily crowded harbour at 5.30 p.m. and took her place opposite the Makook right near us, sirens, whistles, hooters, bells and cheers welcomed the President.*

He stood bare-headed on the afterdeck, his white shirt open at the throat and he wore a blue blazer. On his right was Afet, the rather masculine-looking historian of New Turkey; on his left Sabiya Gokçen the girl Squadron Leader, then Makbule, Ataturk's sister. The other guests stood a little apart. The women were smart and pretty. Presently he sat down and his child mascot, Ülkü, climbed on to his knee. She looked wild and elfin with her black locks blowing across her little face.

Ataturk has no children of his own. He was married for three years to Latife Hanum, the lovely highly-educated young woman in whose house he had set up his headquarters when his army occupied Smyrna* and chased the unfortunate Greeks into the sea. They were divorced in 1925.

In 1926 Ataturk made polygamy illegal and really set the wheels of reform rolling, and a good many heads into the bargain.

In the late evening we picked up Fethi Okyar (Turkish Ambassador in London), Madame Fethi and General Ismet Ineunu, who will probably be President when Ataturk dies, which could be soon. We dropped anchor in a quiet bay backed by a sombre forest. As we dined on deck a full moon rose and lights spangled the islands.

Ismet, a gallant soldier and leader, is the Ghazi's most trusted supporter and friend. He is short and sallow with a strong beaked nose, a crest of snow-white hair and brilliant eyes that never leave the face of the person he is addressing. His voice is husky and uneven because of his deafness. He lip-reads French, Turkish and Greek and is learning Eng-

---

* *Now Izmir.*

lish! They say he is the hardest of all Kemal's hard gang and would, if necessary, sentence his best friend to death and attend the execution.

Ismet, the Ambassador, Madame Fethi and I made up one of the two tables at bridge. We played in French. In the last rubber Ismet drew me for a partner. He played like a gambler, with gusto, and cried out with enjoyment whenever I put down a good hand. Madame Fethi has a dreamy air but plays a brilliant game. It was long after midnight and the other table had broken up. Bertie and Fethi were standing behind Ismet. Madame Fethi opened the bidding with a spade, I called, 'One no trump' and Sir Percy passed. I glanced up at Fethi whose broad Tartar face was inscrutable. Ismet slapped his hand on the table face downwards and looked at me with triumphant glee.

'Grand slam in hearts!' he shouted.

A slow smile broke over Fethi's face.

When I set down my cards Ismet leaned across the table and clasped my hands.

'Très bien! We have it!'

'Just as well,' murmured Madame Fethi to Bertie afterwards. 'The General never stops till he has won. That's his character.'

The next day Peter arrived at Istanbul with a group of ten children by the Orient Express.

A few days later we were back in Athens and on our way to Corfu where Bertie was to meet his old sea-love, the *War-spite*, Flagship of the Mediterranean Fleet and of Admiral Sir Dudley Pound, who was to be First Sea Lord in the War years till his short illness and death in 1943. Bertie had served with Admiral Pound in the Mediterranean, a lean fearless forthright man with keen brown eyes.

We shipped our car with us. Unlike the barren Aegean Islands, Corfu was verdant, with great magnolias, cypresses, fruit orchards and orange groves. The country women were stately, and the horses wore flowered straw hats with holes for their ears and necklaces to ward off the evil eye. Early one morning we woke to the loud clanging of a bell and the street crier's resonant chant. '*Warspite* arriving! *Warspite* arriving!' Peter was dressed in a flash and on the breakwater. 'Just in time to see her anchor. Dad, what a ship!'

The King of Greece was on holiday in his villa high above the sea, secluded by olive groves and cypresses. Bertie wrote in his log:

[Friday, 12 August 1938] *Dined* à quatre *at His Majesty's villa, Joy and I and Mrs. Brittain-Jones. Very delightful and informal. Dinner on balcony.*

Took opportunity of telling His Majesty I'd get Their Lordships to agree to Greek officers serving in our Fleet. His Majesty all for it.

[Saturday, 13 August] *Drafted full telegram to Director of Naval Intelligence in bathroom at Hotel Bella Venezia. Nowhere else private! 9.30 a.m. picked up Vice-Consul Papadachi and called officially on Commander-in-Chief, Sir Dudley Pound, in Warspite. Fixed up Crown Prince's visit to Malta in Averoff and sent my long signal to DNI.*

[Tuesday, 16 August] *Signal from DNI to say would get full answer inside 48 hours.*

Went out with Piet exercising in Warspite. Also 15-inch Full Calibre. Jolly good show. Piet in fine form, not missing a thing. He had a chat with the King who was on board and he carried it off very well!

[Thursday, 18 August] *7 a.m. Orderly brought signal from DNI. Entirely favourable. We are leaving by car ferry at 9.30 for Albania, so wrote His Majesty private note. Didn't know how to start or finish – filthy old notepaper. All very quick work.*

Our journey from Albania to Athens across the wild mountains was extremely hazardous but Bertie was rightly sure that the new still-unfinished road financed by Italy was intended as a military approach to Greece. It was closed soon afterwards by landslides.

Meanwhile the situation in the Sudetenland had come to the boil and Bertie's log reports: [30 August. Athens] Pessimism here about Czechoslovakia. Things look bad with

Nazi Day on 5 September rapidly approaching. Due to leave today for Crown Prince Paul's Malta visit in Greek Flagship *Averoff*. Should I go?'

The answer was yes, so Bertie, with our invaluable butler-valet-barman, Jean, embarked – Jean armed with all the ingredients for producing any cocktail the Crown Prince might require. Jean was teetotal himself yet inventing cocktails was his idea of bliss. He and Ero were saving up for 'a little bar' of their own – and a family.

Greek Cruiser *Averoff*, *At sea off Cape Matapan, Wednesday, 31 August 1938*

... What a good boy am I to sit down and write to you and Piet when I'll probably get back before the letter. You'll be pleased to hear that almost the first thing the Crown Prince asked me was whether there was an Air Mail from Malta so that he could write to his wife! A good sign, I think.

Jean unpacked for me the moment we got on board and I changed into uniform and met Papavassiliou, Chief of the Naval Staff, who came on board to say Goodbye, and at 7 p.m. the Crown Prince and Prince Paul of Yugoslavia arrived and we sailed at 7.30. Jean at once made a little bar in my cabin! That's the first thing he'll do when he goes to heaven. And won't the angels like it!

So I asked Contoyannis (the Captain), Prince Paul (Regent) and *aide-de-camp* Vlachopoulos to try a dry martini, and we had a cheerful 'get together' with Jean hovering round, very smart in his white suit.

Then we had dinner *à quatre* with the Admiral (Economou), the Crown Prince and Prince Paul. Then Economou and the Crown Prince excused themselves and Prince Paul of Yugoslavia and I talked until 3 a.m.

Thursday last night had a real 'girl's gossip' with the Crown Prince. He's great fun, a first class naval officer and popular with the people, a very good mixer and extremely intelligent. What did we talk about? you'll ask. He told me he'd spent six months as a workman at Armstrong Siddeley's works in England absolutely incognito. Nobody knew who he was except old Siddeley himself. He talked about Charlie Chaplin and how interesting he was. And about Lord Lloyd and how rabidly anti-German he was and that last time Lloyd was in Athens he lunched at the Palace and, in front of the Crown Princess, aired his views freely on the subject. Not very good on the part of our head of propaganda abroad! The Crown Prince also said Sir Percy Loraine was very anti-German. I said I hadn't noticed it and I'd been with him when the Germans walked into Austria. The Crown Prince is very fair-minded but he is in love with his wife and would naturally resent her people being used as targets for custard-pies. We talked about boat sailing, athletics and the Greek Navy. He spent three years at the Naval College 15 years ago and finds it improved out of all recognition today and was certain this was due to the British Naval Missions. Good hearing!

I told him that the saying was common in Greece 'The King's Army, Metaxa's Police, the Nation's Navy and nobody's Air Force'. He agreed that there must be some roguery and incompetence at the top. The Greeks buy one machine in one country, one in another, and have as fine a collection of antiquated international samples as one could collect. The Crown Prince is out gunning after them for he is a fine airman. . . .

You remember the Meteorites with the little secret churches right on top where we had to be pulled up in a basket. Well, the Crown Prince told me that in 1921 or 1922 the late Queen Marie of Rumania went to the Meteorites at Kalambaka. At that time it was like Mount Athos and no women were allowed. However she insisted on being hoisted up in the basket. As she stepped out she was met by a priest who cursed her like fury. Since that day nothing went right for her. Family troubles all the time.

Later This morning there was an inspection by the Admiral and the Crown Prince, including all the officers who were criticized quite freely by the Admiral. He fairly bit chunks out of a Lieutenant-Commander who had a fountain pen sticking out of the top of his jacket pocket.

Malta was a hectic rush of official occasions for the Crown Prince and Prince Paul of Yugoslavia and for Bertie too, who was responsible for the *Averoff*'s welcome and all arrangements for the two Royal guests of the Royal Navy. He called at once on the Commander-in-Chief, Admiral Pound, and after ten years away from Malta found himself extremely homesick for the Navy at sea. His log on 2 September remarks: 'British Fleet looking fine. Saw friends in *Warspite*. Czechoslovakian situation dangerous. Mediterranean Fleet is always ready for war nowadays.' On Tuesday, 6 September he was on his way back to Greece with Crown Prince Paul in the Greek destroyer *Hydra*. 'Crown Prince really is a marvel. Always full of *bonhomie* and misses nothing.

7 *Wednesday* Arrived Phaleron 16.00 and landed with Crown Prince. Joy and Piet to meet me.'

A week later the September Crisis of 1938 was working up to its climax.

[Wednesday, 14 September] *Hitler's speech at Nuremberg on Monday about Czechoslovakia not too aggressive but pretty determined. This morning things look gloomier. His Majesty's Minister despondent for first time. So am I. Matters seem to be rolling on slowly and inevitably to a bloody war and I don't see how we can keep out of it. Sudeten-Germans' ultimatum for autonomy and Czechs turning it down.*

It's a fine cup of tea personally too. Here are Joy and Peter booked for England on Saturday by Lufthansa!! What to do about it? Joy's return fare already paid. And I am due to leave for Istanbul on Monday.

Live from day to day. That's all.

[Thursday, 15 September] *Neville Chamberlain visits Hitler. A very courageous move. For a man of 69, just recovering from an illness, to fly for the first time and then deal with a half crazy Führer shows guts. Meanwhile Czechs and Sudetens murdering each other.*

[Saturday, 17 September] *Saw Joy and Peter off by Lufthansa from Tatoi at 6.0 a.m.*

[Later] *Telegram from Joy they had missed the London connection in Vienna and been taken on to Berlin! Telegraphed Naval Attaché Berlin, Tom Troubridge. He is away.*

Imperial Airways bringing Philip Rhodes to stay with me failed to arrive.

[Sunday, 18 September] *Philip Rhodes arrived here. Joy and Piet safe in London staying with Charles and Maisie te Water. My Istanbul visit postponed.*

My journey to England was to see Peter's Headmaster and arrange that in the event of War our son should be flown to us without delay.

The War build-up was frightening. Sandbags against the buildings, men digging trenches in Hyde Park. My host, Charles te Water, the South African High Commissioner, was anxious. Mr. Chamberlain had flown to Godesburg for a second conference with Hitler and the talks were not going well.

Peter was worried when I saw him on Saturday, 24 September. Autumn leaves whirled about us in the garden of the Dragon School in the windy dusk.

'Take me back with you to Athens,' he said. 'We mustn't be separated if there's a War.'

'We won't be separated. That's what I'm here about.'

Back in London I found my cousin Maisie hunched over the fire.

'The Prime Minister got back from Godesburg this afternoon,' she said. 'Charles is with him now.'

When Charles came back, she sprang up.

'Is Chamberlain hopeful?'

Charles ran his long nervous fingers through his fair hair.

'He's exhausted, but not beaten. It's tragic – this inability of human beings to understand each other. Chamberlain said today "I found it very difficult to speak to Hitler. He was so hard and unapproachable". It didn't occur to him that he too can appear aloof and forbidding. When I urged him to go on trying for peace he put his hand on my shoulder, threw up his head and said. "I will!" '

132

Bertie's log reflected the mood in Athens.

[Tuesday, 27 September] *Things very tense. Philip Rhodes shot off back to London. Mediterranean Fleet mobilized. Committee here on air-raid precautions.*
[Wednesday, 28 September] *Very relieved to get telegram saying Joy returning by air this morning.*

What do I do for heaven's sake? Sit here and get fat! A young Captain of 43 is just the right age for command of a fine ship. Anyhow I'll not fuss yet. They've enough to fuss about at the Admiralty already. But I won't stay here long if War breaks out. *Perhaps Commander-in-Chief Mediterranean can give me a job afloat.*
[Thursday, 29 September] *Last night in House great sensation when in the middle of Chamberlain's speech, which, as it went on, made War look inevitable, a telegram from Hitler arrived and was read aloud, agreeing that Daladier, Mussolini and Chamberlain should meet him at Munich. German mobilization postponed for 24 hours. Queen Mary was led out in tears of relief.*

Should I – as a man of War – want War?

Does a doctor want a cholera epidemic?

All these days are very emotional.
[Friday, 30 September] *Three Imperial Airways came through distributing 60 Naval Control Service chaps in the Mediterranean. Triumphant return of Chamberlain to London broadcast at 8 p.m. Very moving. Aeroplanes now messengers of peace. This new form of diplomacy only possible due to aeroplanes. They carry people. Telegraph cables and wireless don't carry people. They carry misunderstandings.*

Three weeks later we received a cable from my mother. The message was long and distressing. My father was seriously ill and Mummy who had never asked anything of us – only given – said 'I am longing for Joy.'

On 21 October the entry in Bertie's log was brief.

[Friday, 21 October 1938. Trafalgar Day] *Joy left per* Circe

133

for Cape Town at 15.00 yesterday. People waiting here for birth of Crown Prince's kid. 101 guns for boy – 20 guns girl.

Ataturk very ill.
Leave for Ankara tomorrow by sea.

I flew to a home of sorrow.

Bertie sailed for Istanbul where a great Dictator and reformer lay gravely ill in Dolmabatche Palace.

In Greece there was keen disappointment when 20 guns announced the birth of a daughter, Sophia, who was to marry Juan Carlos, crowned King of Spain in 1975 at Franco's death. The boy Constantine was born later, and at the death of his father, King Paul, was crowned King of the Hellenes but was deposed.

Back in 'Tees Lodge' I was warned that my father might not know me. Yet, strangely, he did. He seemed asleep in bed in the sunny familiar room, but when I knelt beside him and took his cold hand in mine he opened his eyes, as if half waking from some distant distressing dream. For a moment the light of recognition lit them and he spoke my name. Then he lapsed into the deep coma that lasted for many weeks.

Bertie's letters during that period never failed me in understanding, or in news that would interest or cheer me.

Ankara Palas Oteli, Tuesday, 25 October 1938

... Owing to the Ghazi being ill, it's dull here. No parties, no Pavillon yet, no band at Karpitch's. The Ghazi has advanced cirrhosis of the liver and has been 'punctured' three times, makes short recoveries afterwards, but any time now is expected to die. Probably Ismet Ineunu will take his place.

It's lonely up here without you. Everyone misses you. I'm so anxious for news of you and yours. Don't forget I shall expect you to bring poor Mum back with you to stay as long as she likes. .... Have written Piet to continue writing to you in Athens. I'll read his letters and forward them straight on to you.

I see now that Hankow and Canton have fallen and Chiang Kai-shek has flown no one knows where. What happens now? The Japs have got China. What about Hong Kong? ...

Sunday, 30 October Now about yesterday's National Day. Well the Big Day was only a Little Day and soon over. All glamour missing without the Grand Chef. Illuminations and Parade very good, but little enthusiasm. ....

Ankara, Thursday, 10 November 1938

... At the end of a pathetic and exciting day I have just got back to my room at the Ankara Palace and it's late but I can't turn in without telling you all about it. You see, I know if you'd been here your journalistic sense would have found a hundred aspects that have probably missed me. But because you are not here and I miss you like hell, *I must tell you what Ankara was like the day the Ghazi died.*

Last night Tommy and Katherine Elmhirst and I went to Pavillon. It was its third night and we saw the 'turns' and dined. About midnight Tommy went out and looked at the news bulletin from Istanbul. One had just been issued from Dolmabatche to say the Ghazi's condition was *'très grave'*.

Everything seemed normal this morning and I went into the photographer's shop shortly before noon to meet Katherine and pick up the official photographs of H.E. and party on the National Day. Then quite suddenly the whole town seemed to go into a ferment. People started running from all directions to Ulus Square. I said 'Let's go and see what's up. Probably the Ghazi is dead and there could be a row'. I had in mind counter-revolutions because when I've seen that sort of trouble in Lisbon and places like that it's always happened in the same way. People rushing in masses, saying nothing, but having something in mind which one couldn't quite fathom. So off we went to the corner of the Square where the statues are and where there is a big plinth. On the plinth a lot of young people were addressing the crowd. The Square was a dense human mass increasing all the time while the orators on the plinth were talking and gesticulating like anything. There were a lot of men and women weeping into their hands fit to burst. I knew then that the Ghazi must be dead but didn't know whether the young men on the plinth were talking treason or what they were at.

Then suddenly the police arrived. They flooded the place on foot, in armoured cars and fire engines. A column of about 50 on horseback appeared and then some 500 soldiers formed a solid block on the far side of the Square and stood dead still.

The police were splendid. With no fuss or shouting they had control of the whole vast crowd in about ten minutes. The young men on the plinth had a herd of police around them but they just went on making their speeches. So I knew this was no counter-revolution or anything bad, for the police stood absolutely quiet.

Quite suddenly everybody took off their hats and sang. I suppose it was a *Hymn of the Revolution or Anthem of New Turkey*. But not a soul moved.

Then I knew that the passing of the Ghazi had gone as he would have wished and that the wonderful things he had done for his country without ranting and roaring had really sunk into the souls of the illiterate sullen people he had ruled with a rod of iron and an enlightenment that comes to few.

Saturday, 12 November ... Yesterday, at 11 o'clock on 11 November 1938 the same date and time as the coming into force of the Armistice in 1918 – exactly 20 years ago – Ismet Ineunu, the new President of the Republic, was elected unanimously here in Ankara.

Last night I asked my waiter – a *very* intelligent chap – if he was content with his new Prime Minister. He went off like a racehorse with a bee under its tail. Ataturk had done everything for the people – he was dead and every Turk felt his life was finished too. Who followed didn't matter. 'Look what Ataturk has done for me!' (I didn't think it much – an overworked little waiter in an Ankara hotel.) 'Under the Sultans I shouldn't be able to read or write. I speak French, Italian, Greek and a bit of German and can read and write them. He has lifted me and millions like me out of our ignorance. I have been a soldier, wounded twice. We would follow Ataturk anywhere and be glad to die.' Finally he burst into tears. I told him that Ataturk had given them education, inspiration and a future to live for and that there was no one better than Ismet to carry on the tradition.

Mopping up waiters' tears in an Ankara pub is a new occupation! He disappeared and came back with apologies and a postcard photograph of himself as a soldier. A loathly looking object. He's a damned good waiter. Perhaps he was a damned good soldier.

The body of Ataturk was to be conveyed by warship from Istanbul to Izmud and thence by train to Ankara. Foreign warships would join the ocean cortège on Saturday, 19 November; on Sunday Ataturk's body would lie in state in Ankara, and on Monday, 21 November the funeral would take place. The Government had commandeered the two big hotels in Ankara for the official representative of every Government in Europe and special trains had been laid on for VIPs. Great Britain would be represented by the Commander-in-Chief, Mediterranean Fleet, Admiral Sir Dudley Pound in the *Malaya,* and by the King's personal representative, Field Marshal Lord Birdwood, who had fought with the Anzacs against the Turks in Gallipoli. A Royal Naval contingent would take part in the funeral parade at Ankara. All the naval arrangements must, of course, be made by the Naval Attaché.

HMS *Malaya, Istanbul, Saturday, 19 November 1938*

... On Wednesday night I came down from Ankara and conferred with Turks like hell all Thursday. In the last rush I became the accepted authority on naval procedure, salutes, precedence and so on.

The one thing I was determined upon was that the Commander-in-Chief in the *Malaya* should lead the line of foreign warships. Protocol said all right, we'll put ships in alphabetical order of countries' names in French and will call you *Angleterre* and not *Grande Bretagne.* So that was decent and all right by me. Then at the last moment, when all orders were out, *Emden* said she was coming. That meant *Allemagne* led! *That I would not have.* Said so. Told Protocol they must put the ships with Admirals in the order of the seniority of the Admirals and the remainder could go in alphabetical order.

So today the *Malaya* had been leading the five foreign warships in the ocean cortége escorting the Ghazi's body in the *Yavuz* across to Izmud. The others were Russian, German, French, Greek and Rumanian.

We've just got back. It's 5.30 p.m. and at 7 p.m. our party lands to catch the special train to Ankara.

Ankara Palace Hotel, Tuesday, 22 November

... Well, up we all came, arriving Sunday afternoon for the funeral on Monday (yesterday). The Commander-in-Chief, Lady Loraine (Sir Percy was already here), any number of VIPs of all descriptions and our *Malaya* party, 12 officers, 150 sailors, six Marines and 56 bandsmen to take part in the funeral procession. Poor old Field Marshal Lord Birdwood, representing the King, had a badly swollen foot and had to be carried to the observation coach. He is a dear old chap – 74 – very bright and pleasant.

Protocol had booked me a front room here, and right opposite the Ankara Palace was a huge impressive catafalque with Ataturk's coffin lying in state on it and a bodyguard of officers standing on guard without a movement. Crowds filed past all night. It was icy cold and drizzling. Every now and then a burst of wailing would come from the crowd, last about three minutes and die away. I had never heard wailing before. A noise effect woeful and impossible to describe. Everyone crying their eyes out – men and women – and women having hysterics all over the place.

The Commander-in-Chief, H.E. and I went to the Ghazi Institute, where our men from *Malaya* were quartered, to see how they were, and then had tea with the Director of the Institute.

Yesterday (Monday) was the Funeral day. All 'Dips' and

VIPs were told to assemble at the Ankara Palace Hotel by 7 a.m. and wait until 9.30, for there was to be no circulation whatever in the streets after 7. So being here already, I could turn out at my leisure.

In due course the coffin was lifted down on to the gun carriage and the procession formed up – troops, etc., ahead. Our *Malaya* detachment looked fine and smart, the biggest foreign one by a good deal. I felt very proud of our men. 'Dips' in full dress, and Deputies followed the coffin. At the slow march we went downhill to the station, turned left and up to the People's Palace.

It was raining.

After one and a half hours we began to reach the end – the crowd was very thick and there were great bursts of wailing and everyone sobbing bitterly. The most extraordinary thing was the soldiers lining the route. They stood at attention with tears pouring out of their eyes, running down their cheeks and falling on to the road with the raindrops.

Then at the People's Palace we rounded the corner and there was our Field Marshal, Lord Birdwood, propped up behind a low wall. Very straight in his plumed hat, scarlet coat and Field Marshal's baton. He couldn't walk in the procession, so he'd been propped up with hidden soap-boxes, sandbags and things.

Everyone saluted him – as if he were taking a march past. He stole all the thunder.

Then the coffin was lifted off the gun carriage on to a trestle. We saluted and went into the People's Palace whilst the streets were cleared....

Bertie returned from Belgrade to Athens just before Christmas.

Athens, Friday, 23 December 1938

Cable to say that dear old Dad died – a very kind lovable person. All very sad for Mum and Joy.
Saturday, 31 December
Didn't feel like going out. Saw the New Year in alone with

Mussi, the cat. Piet is with Dorothy and Norman for his Christmas holidays.

Sunday, 1 January 1939. New Year's Day

Hope to God it will be a calmer year than 1938 which was jumpy as hell.

In Cape Town my mother, exhausted and heartbroken, felt unequal to accepting Bertie's invitation to come to Athens with me and stay as long as she liked. She craved the peace of her favourite brother's farm, 'Strehla', in the lonely expanse of the Transvaal highveld, and there she stayed till she felt strong enough to go back to 'Tees Lodge', the old home she could not bear to leave.

At last, in mid-January 1939, Bertie's log stated: 'Joy arrived, *thank goodness*, by *Caledonia* from Durban. Fine flight and a lovely day such as Greece tenders to a welcome guest.'

Part Four: Sailor at War
1939 to 1946

16
'Commence hostilities with Germany at once.'

Naval Attaché	Balkans
HMS *Calcutta*	North Sea
1939	Declaration of War

In January 1939, Captain John Godfrey, promoted Rear-Admiral and appointed Director of Naval Intelligence, rapidly assembled a growing team of brilliant and imaginative young men recruited from many powerful quarters. Lieutenant-Commander Ian Fleming, RNVR, later the famous creator of *James Bond, 007*,* was one of them.

Bertie felt his new 'Boss was the right man in the right place at the right time'.

In a letter to us from Sir Percy Loraine written from Istanbul that same January, change was again in the air.

... As for me, the appointment to Rome is now official. We are already packing up, the house is being gradually stripped and beginning to take on a bleak sort of air. If we had any dogs they would now be feeling and looking

---

* John Godfrey was the prototype of 'M', James Bond's boss, head of the Secret Service.

unhappy and desolate, and wondering whether there was going to be a rug left anywhere for them to lie on. . . .

It's a pleasing as well as difficult appointment, and I shall be annoyed if I can't enjoy it, but I shall have a sad parting from my Turkish friends. . . .

The Ambassador had told my husband that he was 'a damned good Naval Attaché' and wished to take him to Rome, but Bertie was convinced that war was imminent and while appreciating the compliment longed for active service. 'It can't be managed,' he wrote in his log. 'Am *determined* to go to sea. The Loraines have been very kind to us and of course Sir Percy Loraine has done a wonderful job here. He is not easy to work with till you know him well. The long silences are disconcerting.'

On 24 February, we were on Istanbul Station to bid the Loraines farewell according to protocol. Lady Loraine loved Rome and Sir Percy looked well and equal to his new 'pleasing' but highly responsible appointment. 'I shall be annoyed if I can't enjoy it.' Annoyed! It was a challenge doomed to bring the friend of Kemal Ataturk close to breaking point. Benito Mussolini, with his visions of conquest, *maré nostrum*, and a resuscitated Roman Empire, was 'the Man with the Sword' who created the situation 'which nullifies the patient efforts of the diplomat to keep his country in the way of peace'.

The 'patient efforts' were those of Sir Percy Loraine, 12th and last Baronet of Kirkharle, Northumberland, and Count Ciano, Italian Foreign Minister and son-in-law of *Il Duce*. Ciano was executed by the Germans for treason in 1944. Mussolini made no effort to save him.

Sir Hughe Knatchbull Hugessen followed Sir Percy Loraine in Ankara, a charming genial personality.

He was, towards the end of the War, to play the unwitting lead in an Ankara 'true spy story' written and filmed as *Operation Cicero*.

The Ides of March were heavy with premonitions and the entries in Bertie's log became less and less optimistic.

[Thursday, 16th March, 1939] Athens *This ruddy Hitler has gone wild in Czechoslovakia again and has flatly gone back on his agreement that territorial ambitions were finished. He is taking 7,000,000 Czechs into the Reich. . . . World opinion will certainly harden against him.* This time surely we will not give in? *It may mean war. If only UK, France, USSR and USA, will get together Hitler is for it. We are working up for another major crisis – blast it – but somehow we must stop this business. It will be Hungary and Rumania next and so on to the Ukraine.*

We lunched with Prince and Princess Ehrbach zu Schönberg (German Minister, she is Hungarian). An awkward party on such a day. But everybody quite unperturbed and pretending nothing had happened.

Saturday, 18 March *Jitters all over the place. Joy very upset. War looks quite possible. Dined with Henry and Alice Hopkinson.* The King had invited himself and paid us the compliment of saying he wanted us invited too. So party was King, Princesses Irene and Catherine, Mrs. Joyce Brittain-Jones, Joy, me, Aubrey Moody, Hon. Attaché to Legation, and our host and hostess.*

A very friendly pleasant party. Princess Irene† looking regal and beautiful but quite chatty. Said Hitler had gone mad and she thought revolution in Germany quite possible. Evening ended with the King on all fours playing with the dog and barking!

Bed at 3 a.m. after listening to the wireless.

Rumours about Rumania being threatened.

Wednesday 22 March *Local Defence meeting. What an able fellow Henry Hopkinson is!*

Thursday, 30 March *Germans looking dangerous* v. *Poles and Danzig. Piet arrived by plane. He has grown a lot.*

Sunday, 3 April *Piet riding with Joy. Yesterday he nearly killed himself by hanging on to a motor-bus on roller skates! One skate came off and he was dragged until the bus stopped. Silly ass! But lucky.*

---

* Henry Hopkinson now Lord Colyton.
† Later married Italian Count d'Aosta.

Things have really come to a head.

We will stand no more armed aggression in Europe and have departed from our old tradition. We have stated that if Poland's independence is at stake we will help her. France says so too.

Wednesday, 5 April *Albanian question looks bad again. Zog isn't 'taking it'.*

Thursday, 6 April *Dined with Hopkinsons, Michael and Atlanta Arlen.* A very amusing dinner.*

Good Friday, 7 April *Last night Italians bombarded Durazzo, Valona, Santa Quaranto and landed troops after having yesterday said in writing (Ciano) that Italy was not going to take military measures or threaten Albania's sovereignty!*

A nice Good Friday action. Poor Queen Geraldine, who had a baby boy two days ago, has left for Greece.

Easter Sunday *Wars and rumours of wars. Jitters all round.*

I hear King Zog beat the rest to the frontier! Presumably frightened of his own folk?

The hymn in Church was 'The fight is o'er, the battle won—'. Like hell it is!

On 14 April, Princess Catherine came to see us. She told Bertie that the weekend at the Palace had been 'nerve-wracking' and that her brother, the King, was 'haggard and drawn'. Bertie noted: 'She told me what she thought of Mussolini and Hitler in no measured terms. I said it was up to someone like herself to sit on a sofa beside Mussolini and spellbind him as she was doing to me. She answered that the trouble was they spellbound everyone else. We decided to be optimists and not believe in War. But at heart we know there will be War.'

On the following day Neville Chamberlain made his speech in the House of Commons giving guarantees to Rumania and Greece. Bertie's comment: 'It seems the only

---

* Michael Arlen was Armenian, the witty brittle writer of *The Green Hat* which was 'shocking' in the 'thirties. His Greek wife was the daughter of Count Mercati.

thing left to do is to get together an opposition gang which, *if backed by USA*, would be very powerful.' But USA was to prove in World War Two, as in World War One, a fence-sitter where Europe was concerned. On 28 April, Hitler's *Reichstag* Speech denounced the British Naval Treaty and Polish Treaty, and 'the Mediterranean Fleet has moved into the Eastern Mediterranean based on Alexandria. Some units visiting Greek waters. Western Mediterranean is now in hands of French with some British stiffening.'

On 1 May, Bertie and I were in historic Navarino (where, in 1827, a combined British, French and Russian Fleet, under the command of Admiral Codrington, finally defeated the Ottoman Fleet). My husband was to meet the battleships *Barham* and *Malaya*.

[Monday, May Day, Navarino] *Lovely weather, hard journey by road. Public holiday in Greece. Peasants in national costumes, dancing, singing and wine drinking. Changed, and on board* Barham *to dinner with Geoffrey Layton. Long interesting talk with him and my old Captain of HMS* Kent. (*China Station*) *Ion Tower, now Captain of* Malaya – *a fine chap.*

[HMS *Warspite*, Thursday, 4 May, Alexandria] *Arrived by air 2.30 p.m. Long session with Rear-Admiral Andrew B. Cunningham. He talks a lot and is very quick.*

Then here to Warspite *at 6.30 p.m. Dined with Commander-in-Chief (Admiral Sir Dudley Pound) and his Chief of Staff, Algy Willis.*

10.00 p.m. ashore with Commander-in-Chief to 'beat up' in Coldstream Mess, Mustapha Barracks. Back on board 04.00, fearsome drive with Commander-in-Chief as chauffeur.

Slept like a log. A ship is a lovely place.
Friday, 5 May *To sea in* Warspite. *Important talks with Commander-in-Chief and Chief of Staff.*
Saturday, 6 May *Took off 04.15, back in Athens 09.15. Very successful journey. Learned a lot, and hope they learned something from me too.*

Monday, 8 May *Dined Hopkinsons. King, Prince Andrew and Princess Catherine to dinner. Told HM of my visit to Fleet and how we had taken over the Eastern Mediterranean until things settled. Most opportune.*
Tuesday, 9 May *Telegram to hold myself in readiness for Staff talks in Turkey. Letter from O'Donnell to say he is to relieve me mid-July.*

From then on the pace quickened. Bertie was sent to Belgrade, Ankara, Sophia, and to London for talks with the Director of Naval Intelligence, and conferences with the combined Services and Foreign Services' representatives – French, Turkish, Greek, Yugoslavian, Egyptian and various others. After spinning round like a top, he returned to Athens on 6 July to welcome five visiting British warships.
'*Monday, 10 July* Dined in the *Glorious*. Have never seen such crowds. The Greeks checking up on their guarantee! Packing like mad.'

That was the last entry in his log.

We were due to fly back to England two days later and our pretty villa was in a turmoil of packing. Mustapha Atakat, in his usual independent way, made his own arrangements. He simply moved in with the Diki family where he was warmly welcomed by that kindly Russian *ménage*.

Here, in this pagan sunlit land of flowers and nightingales and shooting stars on summer nights, our little family had shared glamour, excitement and, above all, a home.

Bertie had two and a half months' foreign service leave due to him and we had planned to spend the latter half of Peter's holidays in the Scottish Highlands. In the meantime we had rented a small furnished flat in Chelsea by the week. We had also, while Bertie was still enjoying diplomatic privilege, bought a duty free SS Jaguar to be delivered to us on arrival in London. Our great friend, Hillie Longstaff, who had stayed with us in Athens after the sudden death of her husband, gave us a mascot most precious to us – a little chromium sailor who had been at the helm of the Daimler limousine 'Cuddie' Longstaff had lent us on our wedding day to take us from Portsmouth to London. That sailor is with me still on my XJ6.

Piet sent a postcard from the Dragon School to his father on 17 July, addressed to the United Services Club, the only mail address he had. 'Could you and Mom come for the Sports on Saturday? Then I can can come home with you next day. ...' *Home?* The bare impersonal little flat. Everything we possessed, including all Bertie's uniforms and most of our clothes, were at sea somewhere between Greece and England.

We went to Oxford in the new Jaguar and, among other things, arranged with Mr. Lynam, the Headmaster, that Peter should write his entrance exam for Dartmouth towards the end of the year. He had worked hard and the Dragon School had a high scholastic record. The Head was confident that he would pass.

It was a strange unfamiliar London to which we took our son.

Silver barrage balloons floated overhead, air-raid shelters burrowed into the earth and skeletal bunks lined the main tube and underground stations. These preparations for War excited Piet and made me shiver in the sun of a late lovely summer. But we spread out our AA maps and the three of us pored over them, planning our mythical Highland tour.

Early on the morning of 24 August there was a knock on the door.

'Name of Packer?' asked the telegraph messenger.

I signed for the pink flimsy and opened it.

11.30 OHMS ADMIRALTY LONDON OF LAST NIGHT CAPT H A PACKER FLAT 901 NELL GWYNN HOUSE SLOANE AVENUE SW1 = YOU ARE APPOINTED CALCUTTA IN COMMAND AUGUST 23 JOIN AT HULL FORTHWITH = FROM ADMIRALTY +

Bertie said, 'Hell, and I haven't got a uniform! I'm going to Gieves at once to get a reach-me-down. Piet, you and Mom get Jaggy filled up. Then you and I will drive to Hull. Mom will pack up here and catch the first train she can. We'll meet her – or you will – at the Station Hotel in Hull.'

The midday post came just as I was leaving to catch the train. There was only a small buff envelope addressed to me OHMS. I opened it in the taxi. It contained a card and duplicate and an addressed envelope for return of one of the two cards. An anchor was imprinted on the left-hand corner. I filled it in at Euston Station and posted one of the cards as requested.

ADMIRALTY CASUALTY CARD

If I am killed or seriously injured during an air raid please notify my *Husband*

(insert relationship)

RANK (in full)	CAPTAIN RN
CHRISTIAN NAME(S) (in full)	HERBERT ANNESLEY
SURNAME	PACKER

PLEASE WRITE IN BLOCK LETTERS THROUGHOUT

Fill in your own name and address here NAME (Mr *Mrs* or Miss) JOY PACKER
ADDRESS C/O STANDARD BANK,
9 NORTHUMBERLAND AVENUE

WC2

Peter met the train at Hull.

'Dad said you'd be on this one! He doesn't know when he'll get ashore and he'll be sleeping on board. He's booked us a room at the Station Hotel.'

'But where is the *Calcutta* right now?'

'In the Albert Dock here. I've seen her.'

His eyes were brimful of excitement. He had more news for me.

'There's a Bomber Station near here – Leconfield – and Group Captain Elmhirst is in charge. We're to stay with him and Mrs. Elmhirst for the next few days – till we know what's happening.'

Tommy and Katherine Elmhirst? But already Ankara with its Air and Naval Attachés and late-night parties seemed a century away.

'The *Calcutta* – what's she like?'

'A little anti-aircraft cruiser – 20 years old. She was in the

Reserve Fleet. Dad has to bring her forward for active service. She'll sail any day.'

'Where for?'

'He's not allowed to say.'

In fact, HMS *Calcutta*'s immediate destination was Scapa Flow and she was to sail two days later at 4 p.m., 28 August.

Piet and I were on the quayside to see her go. Katherine Elmhirst and the two little Elmhirst children, Jane and Roger, were with us. As the gap between us widened Piet saluted smartly and the Captain on his Bridge returned the compliment. A bearded officer with a white cockatoo on his shoulder stood beside him. From the day of commissioning to the very end 'Cocky' was *Calcutta*'s mascot.

For the next week we stayed on the Bomber Station. Katherine was putting up black-out curtains, and we criss-crossed sticky paper strips over windows, packing away anything of value. Tommy's bombers were ready in the camouflaged hangars and before dawn we heard them roaring off on unknown reconnaissance missions.

The children were to go to their grandmother in Fife. Piet got the Jaguar's headlights hooded to comply with black-out regulations and then he and I drove Jane and Roger as far as York, where their aunt took charge of them for the train journey to Scotland.

We went into York Minster. I tried to pray. But the huge historic cathedral was so empty that even the Holy Spirit seemed absent and one could almost hear the death-watch beetles reducing ancient sacred timber to common dust.

On 2 September the news vendors in Hull cried '*Speshul! Speshul!* Poland invaded. Poland and Germany at War!' Piet and I were on our way to the Station Hotel to see if there was any mail for us. The station was thronged with children carrying gas-masks, iron rations and labels round their necks. The great evacuation from danger areas had begun. Meanwhile in Poland the Nazi armies were across the border. Far north in Scapa Flow, the Home Fleet waited for the inevitable announcement.

... The censorship regulations allow me to put the name of the ship on the paper but not where she is or what other ships are here. You know my address, c/o GPO London, and already you and Piet may have left Hull – where for? – so I can only write to you c/o Standard Bank, London.

Well, War has been declared, so now we know. I still think Hitler is mad.

Shall I tell you how the day passed here?

The day broke cold, wet, misty and a gale blowing up from the southeast. So I decided to spend Sunday forenoon inspecting the ship's company and the ship. This I did very thoroughly, took two hours over it and had a good 'shake up' all round.

Then came running the RNVR Midshipman to tell me the PM was about to speak. Of course the Wardroom's wireless didn't work so I shot over to the Warrant Officers' Mess and at 11.15 heard Mr. Neville Chamberlain's statement about the ultimatum, and a state of War now existing. I thought the statement clear, impressive, logical and unhysterical.

Curiously, naturally perhaps, there was throughout the ship a feeling 'Well, thank goodness for that!' Apart from the rights and wrongs and the deeper issues, the tension has been so high now for so long that the natural reaction has been one of relief to know where one stands. The Navy is not introspective, thank goodness, it faces what's in front of it and deals with it to the best of its ability.

I at once had the hands piped to muster on the Quarterdeck and told the ship's company we were now at War with Germany, that, as they knew, we had tried every way of keeping the peace.

Told them we should again win and, as in the last War, it would be the old qualities of our race – determination, persistence, a cheerful acceptance of hardship, a laugh when things were worst – that would give us the victory.

Told them that, like seamen through the centuries, we should have to face, maybe, the discomforts of cold, tropical heat, rough weather and dangers of all sorts. It might be for one year or three or five (I said the last bit slowly and when I reached 'five' there was a good hearty laugh, I'm glad to say.)

Told them that when a day should come when they felt they had had more than enough they were to remember what I had said and to remember also that the enemy was sure to be worse off than they were, and see it through.

Told them many had just left their homes at short notice, and whether they were Active Service, RFR, RNVR, RNR, or pensioners, they were now all one – the ship's company of the *Calcutta* – and that their womenfolk at home would say with pride that their husband or brother or son was on Active Service in the British Fleet. Ended 'Good Luck to you all!'

There was a hearty chorus of 'Thank you, sir!' Like a cheerful growl. I was surprised because on these occasions the sailors, when a bit *emotionné*, usually keep a stolid silence and look self-conscious like when 'God Save the King' is played, or two minutes silence on Armistice Day, or you commiserate with them because their mother has died.

So off they went and I got a signal *'Commence hostilities with Germany at once.'* And I felt very helpless because there weren't any Germans nearby to get at. So I popped over and saw Bradley, late Naval Attaché Washington, and drank to 'Bloody War' and 'Damnation to Hitler' and shot back again.

So, you see, we are all merry and bright and determined and don't give a damn for an odd war or so.

But if many of them feel like I do, that the hardship lies with those left behind, I'm sorry for them.

You, my sweet, and young Piet will have the bother and uncertainty and fuss and difficulty of life in wartime. And you particularly when Piet goes back to school and I'm not there to calm your fears and fix things up.

We have no home, you see.

At the time of writing the air menace is still an unknown quantity – no news yet of any raid. Go to a quiet place till things clear a bit and we know where we are.

151

I can give you no news of my movements. In any case I do not know them. One lives, of course, from moment to moment, never knowing where one may be sent.

We are getting on well. I am very proud to be afloat in command of a cruiser the day War was declared. I'd be miserable tucked away in Athens.

17
'Hold the fatalistic war idea. It's always the other chap who gets it.'

HMS *Calcutta*   Scapa, The Humber, North Sea
1939

HMS *Calcutta, Tuesday, 5 September 1939*

... Eight days since we waved farewell from the ship to the quay and today I had your letter of Friday, 1 September and was I mighty glad to get it! You hadn't had my first one yet. Well, my dear, you still had to wait 48 hours before your uncertainty was put at rest – in a disappointing way. *But there was no other solution.* If Hitler had got away with this it was the end of all things. Hungary, Denmark, Alsace-Lorraine, Rumania and the Colonies. Occupy the place, then say, 'now then, who disputes it?' Rig a plebiscite, vote the right way or get a crack on the head, and so on.

So far, 48 hours after War was declared, it's interesting to see that there's been no mad bombing and slaughtering as was predicted, but I am not deceived. Things may well work up to the worst we have imagined.

That sounds pessimistic, but it is not meant so. I do know how a rat will fight when really cornered. And it will be 'all in' before the War is over unless some sensational upheaval begins in Germany. This I doubt for a long time to come.

Meanwhile we are developing daily and visibly into a grand little ship with a 'full out' ship's company. None of us has been ashore since we left. Our 'butchers, bakers and candlestick-makers' are learning fast and become more sea-manlike and efficient by the day. (My best able seaman is a curator from the British Museum!) *But* they have not yet experienced a rough sea. We'll feel it when they do. We have our immediate problems and deal with them straight-forwardly. If a chap makes an ass of himself you tell him so quite pleasantly and no bones broken, if he's done well you say so equally simply and no swelled heads. What a change from the last three years of dealing with foreigners and lying like a flatfish, or else telling the plain truth and not being believed and being considered very subtle.

Thursday, 7 September I listen to the radio news in English, French and German and it's all very shrouded. South Africa declared War today; good for Smuts!

Please ask Piet if he could tell the difference at 15 miles between a *Skua* and a *Heinkel III*. I couldn't and wished I had his book of cigarette cards. If he *has* got it with him, would he send it to me? It might get spoilt by weather but he would have to excuse me.

As Piet would say 'all well and happy this end' but I'll be glad when I know you two are in Robin Hood's Bay ...

Peter and I had decided to spend the rest of his holidays at Robin Hood's Bay, a pretty little seaside spot on the Yorkshire Coast below the moors in a safety zone. We spent the first night of the War in a shelter on Leconfield Bomber Station, looking like pigs in our gas-masks and fully expecting to be gassed and buried alive. In fact, Tommy Elmhirst's bombers were zooming overhead on their way to Germany and Piet was extremely disgusted next day to hear from the cook that they had dropped pamphlets and not bombs.

Petrol was rationed to ten gallons a month, but, forseeing this, we had laid in a store and next day we set off. Piet had a pair of binoculars Bertie had given him and we'd sit on the cliffs and watch for the coastal convoys, wondering if the little anti-aircraft cruiser sailing with them from dawn to dusk was HMS *Calcutta*. A Fox Terrier puppy called Dinah attached herself to Piet and when we took our long walks across the moors, or scrambled down to the seashore, she came with us.

Luckily Piet had his cigarette cards album with him, so he was able to post it to his father, who used it on the Bridge throughout his time in command of the *Calcutta*!

. . . Now you are in a quiet peaceful place please take things easy and enjoy the countryside as much as possible. We must get used to the idea of War. It will take a big slice out of our lives and it's bloody. But it's on us and that's all there is to it. One day I'll come roaring back from the sea with a face like a bcetroot and tasting all salty and what a whale of a time we'll have!

I hope you'll send me Mum's letters from South Africa.

We are getting on fine here. What a funny mixed lot we are, but we all fit into our places quite amazingly. Some of us are stupid, some clumsy, but we all pull hard on the rope together. So it gives one a great thrill to be in command, to guide them from one's experience, teach them from one's knowledge, shake them up and keep them active. They are becoming just like our *Kent*'s ship's company. Confront them with anything at a moment's notice and they are quite unshakeable and go to it. And always a sense of humour. As a matter of fact, we are a Chatham ship's company like the *Kent* and all our RNVRs are London Division and so 'Cockneys' too. They are unbeatable.

My newly acquired wireless is a Godsend to me, but most of all I wait for your letters, because outside this ship that is where my life lies, as you know.

Just write, as you do so beautifully, of the ordinary things – what the moor looked like, the place and people.

Today I went ashore for the first time in a fortnight. I went with Stephens, a passed over Lieutenant-Commander who'd been First Lieutenant of the *Bee* up the Yangtze. An RNVR crew pulled us ashore – rather self-consciously. There was no habitation in sight. Suddenly a pack of grouse got up out of the heather. A shot rang out and one was down.

We found an elderly Scot with a Labrador pup. I said 'Good-day to you. We are from the cruiser. We'll walk with you so as not to spoil your shooting.'

After long reflection the elderly Scot said, 'I think I'll be turning back.' Not very matey. 'Maybe tho' you would like these.' And he gave me five snipe. 'I'd give you the grouse too,' he added, 'but I canna for they must go to the owner.' So we thanked him and took the snipe. As we were leaving, the elderly Scot called back, 'Tell them on board ye caught them in a mouse-trap. They'll no believe ye. But ye can do so. I've done it.'

So you see we are easily amused. We walked four miles saw no one else, and five rabbits, but enjoyed ourselves thoroughly. May you and your companionable Piet do the same in your corner of the Yorkshire moors.

15 September 1939

... Three very tough days in a snorting gale. My brave lads were sick as dogs all day, but not so quietly. But they stuck it, and there wasn't a single case of one not turning up for his watch altho' they were turning up everything else!

By now I had received a warm-hearted letter from Hillie Longstaff asking me to share her home in Southsea for as long as I wished. Peter would always be welcome and of course Bertie too if leave was given. A naval port was a military target but for the present, with France our ally and the Low Countries neutral, it seemed safe enough. Bertie approved.

After the holidays I left Peter at Oxford and went to Southsea where Hillie and I heard on the wireless that the Aircraft Carrier *Courageous* with a ship's company of 1,200 had been sunk. By 21 September Poland was being partitioned by Germany and Russia. Where now were Ambassador Sokulnitska's beloved treasures, and where the noble Elk, 'King of his virgin forest'?

21 September 1939

... The *Courageous* is sunk – well we are sorry and we wonder who got away with it and how it happened – and all the time we have our own immediate problems to cope with.

Don't worry, darling. Hold the fatalistic war idea. It's always the other chap who gets it. . . .

The War at sea is merely in its infancy. By this time last War lots of warships had been sunk and Lord alone knows how many merchant-ships captured or sunk by *Emden* and Co. Now it's all different somehow. The idea of a big battle is impossible at present as we have no enemy fleet to fight – as yet. It seems a contest of one trying to destroy merchant shipping and the other trying to protect it.

An interesting struggle to watch and partake in, but long, I fear. . . .

I have a feeling that Russia has done the dirty on Poland for two reasons – one to stop the Germans getting into the Ukraine and other to get on the Rumanian frontier and stop the Germans moving towards the Black Sea and the Dardanelles. Now Sarajoglu (the Turkish Foreign Minister) is going to Moscow. What for? I fancy it's to get together with Russia on both their aims, and that Russia will be content for the Turks to control the Dardanelles so long as she, Russia, gets special favoured treatment. This she has at present by the Montreux Convention, in which Germany would never join.

Of course Russia can supply Germany. So can Italy, the Balkans and Scandinavian countries, and the Low Countries. Except for Russia, so they could last War too!

But how is Germany going to pay for supplies? She will be too hard-pressed to pay in exports and will they give her credit if they can find a safer market elsewhere? Before the last War Germany's credit was high. Before this War started 23 Marks officially was worth about 11 or 12 in the world.

In any case, that aspect will not take effect for a long time. Our capacity for economic warfare is tremendous. HMS *Calcutta* is doing her bit. The pressure is relentless and if I were Hitler I'd be very worried. But like Napoleon, he just doesn't understand the sea.

Off at 5 a.m. Must sleep. Be of good heart, my lovely. We're just bridging a gap and will be back together again.

On 2 October, I cut out the *Daily Telegraph* report of

Winston Churchill's broadcast on the partition of Poland by Germany and Russia.

Poland has again been overrun by two of the great Powers which held her in bondage for 150 years, but ... the heroic defence of Warsaw shows that the soul of Poland is indestructible and that she will rise again. ...

Russia has pursued a cold policy of self interest. ... But that the Russian armies should stand on this line was clearly necessary for the safety of Russia against the Nazi menace. ... An Eastern Front has been created which Nazi Germany does not dare assail. When Herr von Ribbentrop was summoned to Moscow last week it was to learn and accept the fact that the Nazi designs on the Baltic States and on the Ukraine must come to a dead stop. ... It cannot be in the interests of Russia that Nazi Germany should plant herself upon the shores of the Black Sea, or that it should overrun the Balkan States and subjugate the Slavonic peoples of southeastern Europe. ... Here these interests fall into the same channel as the interests of Britain and France. None of these three Powers can afford to see Rumania, Yugoslavia, Bulgaria and, above all, Turkey put under the German heel.

Through the fog of confusion and uncertainty we may discern quite plainly the community of interests which exist between England, France and Russia to prevent the Germans carrying the flames of War into the Balkans and Turkey.

I had no sooner clipped this cutting to Bertie's letter than I received an almost incoherent note telling me to go to Grimsby.

Grimsby, at the mouth of the Humber, is a North Sea fishing port as grim and grey as its name. Its heart is the Fish Market, the dock where the trawlers lie. Its people are tough, slow-speaking, capable of ferocious fury and equally of understated sympathy, expressed in action rather than words.

I had never been there but Hillie looked it up on a map

and we saw that it was not far from Hull, where I had left a cache of petrol at Leconfield Bomber Station. I packed a suitcase and awaited confirmation. It was posted ashore on 30 September.

... My God, I'm so excited! Booked a single room for you at Darley's Hotel, Cleethorpes for next Thursday, 5 October. Cleethorpes is to Grimsby what Southsea is to Portsmouth – but, oh, so different! Every other day I reckon to be with you from midday till 8 p.m. I am out *every* night. There's a golf course, so that'll be our recreation – and I'll need a bit of sleep in your single bed in the afternoons!

Darling, I feel I could take on the whole German Navy and Air Force single-handed.

I don't know how long this will last, or if you can stay very long as this is a five-star danger area for bombers.

I won't be able to meet you, so just get yourself installed. *If anything goes wrong and I don't turn up* do not hesitate to tackle the 'local Emperor' – Lord Monsell, the Naval Officer in Charge. He's a wartime Commander tho' he was First Lord of the Admiralty some years ago. He is helpful and not a bit stuck up. I'll tell him you are coming. He lives at Darley's Hotel.

It's no use bringing Jaggy because of no petrol....

I disregarded that last line and with Dinah, golf clubs and a suitcase, I set off at once for Grimsby, stopping briefly at Oxford to tell Piet the news and give him a scamper with Dinah, then spent the night at Leconfield. Next day, with a full tank, I headed for the Humber.

There is no beauty so poignant as beauty threatened. Oxford, mellow and cloistered; Lincoln Cathedral with virginia creeper covering ancient walls in autumn ruby, peaceful meadows, great trees holding on to the last golden leaves before the storm should scatter them – all these seemed to symbolize a mood not yet blunted by the years of destruction to come.

My small cold room at Darley's looked out upon a narrow street of semi-detached brick houses with grimy chimney pots. Rosie, the plump blonde manageress, introduced Dinah to her own shaggy dog, Tangles, and to Doozoo, her rheumatic Persian cat.

'Tangles is a Terrier,' she explained, 'even if he is rather well developed and his ears do stick straight oop. He was frightened when he was a pooppy, and oop went his ears! They never came down.' Rosie usually carried lame Doozoo about in a basket not unlike Dinah's. Dinah flirted with Tangles, but didn't take to Doozoo, who was too old to care one way or the other. Rosie was also queen of the Long Bar where the trawlermen and 'commercials' gathered of an evening. Dinner was at 6.30 p.m. I had a table for two but no companion. I noticed a tall thin grey man with an ascetic face and a detached air sitting by himself. He wore naval uniform and the three gold rings of a commander on his sleeve.

He stopped at my table on his way out of the diningroom. 'Mrs. Packer?'

'Yes. And you must be Lord Monsell.'

He nodded and smiled in the anxious remote way of a man who dreads being asked questions or giving answers.

'Your husband *should* be here tomorrow about noon,' he said, and drifted away without elaborating on the forecast.

Next morning I took Dinah for a walk along the seashore which smelt strongly of ozone and seaweed and vaguely of sewers. The day was wintry. There were no children, for they had been evacuated. The tide was out and the only person I saw was a dilapidated old beachcomber collecting shellfish. She wore a long shabby coat, no shoes or stockings, a red muffler and a man's peaked cap, and was followed by an aged moth-eaten dog. She was the widow and the mother of a fisherman and we came to know each other well enough during the next fortnight.

When the ancient dog showed a nostalgic interest in Dinah, I said: 'Will they fight?'

She cackled. 'My Laddie fight a poopy? Bless you, no. 'E wouldn't be disgoostin' with her either. 'E's a daicent dog – always 'as been, even in 'is youth. So don't ye worry.'

I laughed, and she gave me a toothless grin.

'You look 'appy. What's to be 'appy about? Fish oopset, kids gone, black-out, mines in 'Oomber, wreckage too and them sirens wailin'—'

'All the same I *am* happy. Be seeing you—'

Soon after midday my little room without a view came alive with pale sunlight, a salty sailor, and a relief and joy more profound than anything we had ever known. Dinah, who usually snapped nervously at strangers, didn't snap now.

'Your uniform fits!'

He chuckled. 'Gieves recovered my gear from Athens and sent it to me. So I returned their awful straight-jacket.'

He looked well and vital.

'But your eyes?' I touched the swollen lids gently.

'Just a bit of strain – and lack of sleep.'

'Can't you wear goggles on the Bridge?'

'The weather mists goggles. Steaming in and out of the Humber in the dark is quite a performance.'

'When did you dock?'

'After midnight. We're lying out in Grimsby Roads. There'll be a motor-boat to take me off from the Fish Market at half-past eight tonight. It's grand you could bring Jaggy!'

So the pattern of the next fortnight established itself. Bertie was now Senior Officer of three anti-aircraft cruisers based on the Humber.

'We pick up our convoy at dawn,' he explained. 'That may mean several hours of night steaming to reach the rendezvous. We protect the convoy against air attack all day. At sunset we creep carefully back up the Humber. What time we anchor depends on where we leave the convoy. When we are safely anchored I can snatch a few hours' sleep. The morning is routine ship's work and arranging recreation and transport ashore for my sailors. And off again the same night.'

'Never a full night's sleep or a whole day off?'

'Not at present. It may get worse, it may get better. Take what comes.'

He didn't mention the treacherous mudbanks in the

161

blacked-out Humber, the fierce seven-knot current at the ebb, the mines, the uncharted wrecks that marked collisions overnight, or the fact that U-boats were reported at the river mouth. I heard these things from Rosie who had them from trawlermen in the Long Bar. Many fishing trawlers had been converted into mine-sweepers.

Jaggy was a blessing. I was at the Fish Market at noon 'every other day' with a packed lunch and our golf clubs if the weather was fine. We'd play a round on the deserted course, eat and go back to Darley's. Then he'd sleep for a few hours – 'go down to 100 fathoms' – while I curled up in the easy-chair and read a book and Dinah dozed twitchily in her basket. At 6 o'clock we'd go down to the Ladies' Bar and after dinner we'd drive down to the Fish Market in the icy black-out and find the *Calcutta*'s motor-boat waiting alongside with the Captain's Coxswain.

Coxswain Frank Corney was a young Leading Seaman from the Isle of Wight who was to share my husband's service career from then until the end. He was powerfully built with a fresh complexion and a wonderful smile; and he was eagerly waiting for leave so that he could marry the girl he'd left behind.

I'd been ten days at Darley's when the mysterious new peril first made itself felt.

The moon was at the full, everything sharply defined in its cold radiance although no lights shone ashore or afloat. I stood by the Fish Market dock and watched the gleaming wake of the motor-boat cleave a silver path to Grimsby Roads where the *Calcutta*'s silhouette swayed tall and stately in comparison with the squat high-masted trawlers turned mine-sweepers. It should be easier navigating to-night, I thought.

I was in bed when the sirens wailed and the enemy mine-laying aircraft pulsed over the Humber. We had no night-fighters then and few searchlights. Dinah whimpered. I patted her and fell asleep when she had settled again in her basket at my bedside.

At lunch next day Lord Monsell paused at my table as he went out of the dining-room.

'Your husband didn't sail last night. He may be along late this afternoon.'

'That's great news! I didn't expect him till tomorrow.'

He nodded and passed on, unsmiling.

Rosie came over to me and glanced round the empty room to be sure we were alone.

'Did Lord Monsell tell you what happened last night?' she asked.

'Yes, my husband's ship is still in Grimsby Roads. He may be here this evening. Isn't that nice news for me?'

'No, loov, it's not. D'you know what the Jerries dropped in 'Oomber last night?'

'Mines, as usual, I suppose.'

'Mines – yes. *But not as usual.* I've been listening to the lads in the Long Bar. Those mines is *Hitler's Secret Weapon* – and ships blowing up all over the place.'

I took Dinah to the seashore for a walk in the bitter wind. The old beachcomber was there with her dog, Laddie, and her tin pail for shellfish.

'The Jerries is oop to their tricks,' she muttered. 'Remember 'ow they bombed the Lightship last week? Noothin' left of those poor lads but blood and bones and scraps of 'air. Well, joost afterwards my boy's trawler picked oop two Jerries in the ditch and brought 'em in. The women was waitin' at the Fish Market with boat-'ooks to shove the buggers back again. Fair mad they was! If there 'adn't been no naval guard those Jerries wouldn't be alive today.'

'My husband's in the Navy.'

'Then I 'ope 'e's safe ashore this day.'

'Why specially today?'

' 'Cos o' them mines they dropped last night.'

'They'll be swept and the ship'll go down the swept channel to the sea.'

She straightened up and set down her shellfish pail the better to shake her fist at Jerries in general.

'There's *no way* to sweep them mines. They're waitin' on the coast and 'ere in 'Oomber. Them new mines *find* the ships an' blow 'em to hell. It's the Secret Weapon.' She turned to her decrepit dog. 'Coom 'ere, Laddie! Noon o' that nah, an' she pooppy!'

When Bertie came to Darley's that evening I told him the rumours about the Secret Weapon. He made light of it and I learnt nothing from him.

For two days and nights after that there was no sign of the *Calcutta*. No cruiser entered Grimsby Roads.

Rosie found excuses to join me in the lounge after dinner with Tangles and Doozoo. 'We'll share your fire, loov. It's good for Doozoo's rheumatics.' The three animals dozed while she took my mind off my gnawing anxieties with tales of her own life and varying fortunes.

Lord Monsell was seldom to be seen. If it's the worst, I thought, surely he'd have told me by now. The next of kin are always informed!

At last, on the third afternoon, he came to my table and dropped one of his passing remarks.

'You've got your car here, Mrs. Packer. Why not take a drive over to Immingham later this afternoon?'

The sun was low when we reached the marshes of Immingham. A few destroyers and mine-sweepers and a couple of depot ships were anchored in the Humber, and at the end of a long wooded jetty lay the *Calcutta*. The mud flats, pink in the sunset, were scarred with the imprints of innumerable birds' feet; gulls circled and mewed overhead and more orderly formations of birds flew in from their feeding grounds to the reeds.

Here was sanctuary for birds. Maybe for ships.

I left the car and approached the jetty with Dinah frisking beside me. A tall figure was there to meet me. Coxswain Corney flashed his splendid teeth.

'We saw the Jagger and the Captain sent me to fetch you. We knew you'd find us.'

'Just a minute, Corney. I want to look at her – your ship. I haven't seen her since you sailed from Hull. ... Out in Grimsby Roads she was just a shape.'

Her flanks were bloody with the red-lead scars of grazes

and near-misses. Her indefatigable armoury was canvas-covered.

'She looks very brave – but she has scars everywhere.'

'She could do with a coat of paint. But we don't get much time.'

The bearded officer with the white cockatoo on his shoulder was pacing the deck.

'That's Lieutenant-Commander Arkwright with "Cocky" our mascot.'

'Cocky's done your proud – brought you here safely through those awful new mines.'

Corney's smile widened.

'By the skin of our teeth. But you know what they call us? The "Lucky *Calcutta*".'

'It's a good name.'

'It's the Captain. He knows the way to make a happy ship, and what with him and "Cocky" we're lucky too.'

'Am I really allowed on board?'

'It's illegal, Madam. But the Captain can stretch a point – just once in a lifetime.'

My husband was at his desk when Corney showed me into his day-cabin. He sprang to his feet and Corney disappeared. There were new lines and shadows of fatigue on his face.

'I know about the mines,' I said as we drew apart. 'It was on the news. They're magnetic mines. They *are* the Secret Weapon.'

'One of many, no doubt. But there's always an answer. The boffins'll find it any moment. Darling, you must go back to Hillie tomorrow. We're not going to be around these parts for a bit. When we are, I'll get you a message.'

'Shall I leave Jaggy? I'd never get the petrol to bring her back here.'

He knew what I'd read into his answer. The hesitation was slight, his voice firm.

'Yes, leave her. Corney and I'll find a safe place for her till we get back.'

There was a sharp double knock on the door. A young man stepped briskly in with a batch of signals. The Captain went through them quickly, scribbled a few replies and handed them to the young man with a brief order in the bitten-off tone he sometimes used to Peter and very seldom to me.

'Aye, aye, Sir.' The young man saluted and was gone.

Bertie smiled. 'My yeoman of signals is a postman in private life. He always gives a postman's double knock. Now I've got some paperwork to finish, Joy-Joy. You and Dinah relax for half an hour and we'll go ashore for a bite of supper.'

'Let's have a bite here.'

'*NO*. It's irregular enough to have you here at all.' He pushed a slip of paper across his desk. 'I wrote to our friend, the Bishop of Dover, and asked him to look out some new rousing prayers, good fighting stuff to put heart into my jolly lads and never mind turning the other cheek. I like this one – though it's hardly *new*.'

I read it while he returned to his papers.

The Prayer of Sir Francis Drake
(On entering Cadiz, 1587)

'Oh Lord, when Thou givest to Thy servants to endeavour in any great matter, grant us also to know that *it is not the beginning but the continuing of the same until it be thoroughly finished which yieldeth the true glory –* through Him who for the finishing of Thy work laid down His life – our Redeemer, Jesus Christ. Amen.'

The italics were the Captain's.

An hour later I gave him Jaggy's keys and he saw Dinah and me into the trolley-bus for Grimsby.

'*Auf Wiedersehen,* my dear.'

'So long, Unkie.'

It was too dark to see his face, only a faint blue light illumined the bus. The wind was sleety but the little terrier was warm in my lap. It would be icy on the Bridge tonight.

18

'Sea warfare is slow, relentless and seldom spectacular. It demands endurance and toughness.'

HMS *Calcutta*	North Sea Convoys
1939 to 1940	*Altmark* Boarding

HMS *Calcutta, Thursday, 19 October 1939*

. . . What a gap there is now you have gone . . .

As you saw, one leads a hard, responsible, preoccupied existence, usually short of sleep and living from hour to hour.

The big news today is the Turkish-Anglo-French Pact *at last*. I've seen it start and taken part in it. As you know, I never doubted Turkey's good faith.

It is an excellent pact – more important than anything which has happened diplomatically this last tense year or two. It will influence the whole Arab world enormously. And the Balkans, of course. Italy too. It is real statesmanship. All honour to Percy Loraine who never wavered in his opinion against all sorts of heavy guns. And of course the French too who were wise enough to give in on the Alexandretta question. Do you remember Ataturk pitching into old Ponsot at 6 o'clock in the morning at Ankara in October 1937? And Ponsot bringing his 15 stone of square flesh into activity and not doing badly. It was about Alexandretta, and Ataturk knew damn well what he was at, and that time was pressing in the affairs of the world and in his own span too.

Well, it is settled now and all the patience we showed in Turkey last June and July has been repaid.

Later Your letter with enclosures has just arrived. Thank you darling for your sweet note. It was a thrill to have you on board 'illegally' and, knowing you, I think you had your thrill too. If you disliked parting once more, I felt it as much and maybe more. . . .

I see that two German aviators got ashore at Whitby yesterday. What an adventure for them – and then to be arrested by a Special Constable! I might have done it so much better myself but for the darkness. . . .

Of course I instantly looked up Whitby. So he was still in the mine-infested Humber. His letter written on the night of 21 October, Trafalgar Day, gave me further clues, for of course Hillie and I never missed news broadcasts and that evening we had heard about a heavy bombing attack on a large convoy, magnificently repelled by anti-aircraft cruisers and RAF coastal fighters with big losses for the enemy. 'A grand day's sport and my men were cool and collected as old hands – on their toes and jumped like cats.'

Next day, at Grimsby Fish Market he was able to assess some of the results of that 'grand day's sport' and find out from Lord Monsell where his other two anti-aircraft cruisers might be.

Sunday, 22 October 1939

. . . Got ashore this morning to try and find the whereabouts of my other two 'children' and there was the Lord, quite immaculate as usual, walking up and down inspecting salvage of all sorts collected from various aircraft shot down. It was all ranged on the jetty, being 'inventoried'. Brought things home to one somehow – drawers, vests, uniforms, apart from all the other stuff. But of course it was all from rescued chaps – so one said to oneself, well even if they are prisoners they'll be well looked after, which they will be.

26 October 1939

. . . Just by accident an opportunity for a quick line. Have had no chance of writing for some days and unlikely to for some days to come.

All goes well but hellish strenuous. Will expect you 1 November, as arranged on 'phone, but cannot guarantee to meet you. Same old racket only more so. Jaggy is in a shed at Immingham.

Am on tenterhooks to telephone you tonight at Philip Rhodes' to hear how our brave Piet got on with his interview. Have been thinking of him all the time. . . .

He couldn't telephone London that night and if he had done there was no good news to give him.

Piet, who had passed his entrance exam for Dartmouth with flying colours, went to the Admiralty for his interview and medical on 26 October, and we stayed the night before with Philip Rhodes in South Audley Street. I was to stay on till I could go to Grimsby. Philip was determined to get some sort of job in the Navy and was in touch with John Godfrey who wanted him for Naval Intelligence.

'Your chances of getting into the Navy are rather better than mine,' he said to Piet as he dropped us at the Admiralty on his way to the Stock Exchange. 'Good luck!'

I settled down in a waiting-room. Piet came back cheerfully from the interview. But later, after the medical, which seemed to me to take forever, it was a different story. He was taut and pale.

'Everything was okay and then they did the eye-test – lanterns and a Japanese book where you have to pick a figure out of a lot of dots. I got it all wrong.'

I knew there was nothing to be done. My brother Norman had difficulty with distinguishing certain colours. The fault is transmitted through the mother though she does not have it herself.

I took him to Paddington. The winter evening was foggy, the train ghostly, lit only by small blue bulbs.

'Tell Dad they've done me in,' he said as I left him. 'Tell him it wasn't my fault.'

I told Bertie in the bare little room at Darley's when we met again. We took it hard, all three of us.

I stayed in Grimsby for over a fortnight. It was bitterly cold, the worst winter in 40 years they said, with sleet and storms and short hours of daylight. The *Calcutta* at Immingham was often weather-bound and Bertie could seldom come ashore. When I left he told me to take the Jaguar back to Southsea as the ship was going to 'God knows where' and might not come back to the Humber. She went to the Thames Estuary where Amy Mollison, on air ferry service, lost her life.

Tuesday, 28 November 1939

... We got here all right and how long we stay is a mystery. It's bleak as hell, miles from anywhere but gives us time to lick our wounds.

It was fine seeing you on Sunday – even if only for a couple of hours – and we had as lovely a five days as one can these times.

As you know, at the very first opportunity I shall cry out to have you with me.

I had a letter from Piet which I enclose. I've written to him. So now it must be Wellington and he'll have three or four years to make up his mind what he wants to do. He's a grand boy and there are countless heights left for him to conquer. So that's that. But in spite of my nice philosophical words, I'm sick at heart for him and wish you were here with me.

Saturday, 9 December 1939

... About Xmas, I'm afraid I'm helpless. As I wrote, if there's a chance of getting you two and Dinah around, I'll be on it like a knife. So it must rest like that. As a matter of fact I'm 'fussed' too about my 400 'children' in this ship who'd hoped for Xmas leave. Well, I must just do my best for them wherever we are – probably at sea.

I received a lovely wool helmet from you, which I think you did not knit. Perhaps you put a couple of pounds of wool into Jaggy's fan and it came out as a helmet. Anyway it's just the thing.

I try to keep in touch with the European situation. I have

infinite faith in Percy Loraine in Rome and am sure that if we become more anti-Russian, Italy will become more pro-British. *But* Turkey and Greece are so anti-Italian. What a cup of tea! Meanwhile I am confident that at sea the situation is fine. But sea warfare is slow, relentless and seldom spectacular. It demands endurance and toughness – always has done. In spite of enemy aircraft, submarines and magnetic mines, I see no real alteration in the general scheme of things at sea. As well expect rain to be dry or the earth to become transparent. . . .

By mid-December he was based on Scapa again.

Back here in the greyness. As you've heard said many times 'war consists of periods of intense fear punctuated by periods of intense boredom'.

Water it right down, right here, and you get the answer. We've had our moment when there's been the sort of feeling that one's going to have an operation with the reaction 'to hell with it anyway'. For the present we are in a quiet period. Not bored – but damn nearly!

It's light at 8.30 a.m. and dark at 3.30 p.m.

We have none of the facilities of a big ship. No cinema, recreation spaces, or 'Schooly' to teach us a bit. We read or talk in our time off and 'fug' in our messes between decks because it's so icy and wet on deck.

And our talk is that Hitler really *is* mad, and the Russians bloody, and if the ship is not given an active job in the face of the enemy the Germans may well win because we are a terrible menace to them – even if there's no German ship we can catch and sink and no German ship which can't catch and sink us – this, of course, is true. But we don't worry because there is some peculiar thing about an old under-gunned, out-of-date, rather slow British Cruiser which makes her more than a match for any German modern warship in the North Sea! We are convinced that the moment they see us they will flee. The thing really is how to catch and sink them before they can escape.

So that is fine.

Happy days with Piet during the holidays. I feel so sore at not being able to be with you two.

Sunday, 17 December I have just finished conducting a Church service with Charlie Noble* at the harmonium, and I even produced a prayer of thanks for our victory over the raider *Graf Spee* in the River Plate. I also read the most bloodthirsty Psalm of David I could find, in which David asks the Lord to tear his enemies to bits and stop their lying propaganda. I felt it was hardly the moment to read about how they wrapped the Babe in his swaddling clothes and all that!

I went for a walk with Joe Oram† yesterday and for the first time he spoke of the *Thetis*. It is a terrible story and his description of the effect of CO_2 poisoning was vivid. It makes concentration on any one point impossible. It took him two hours to plan the escape – normally a matter of a few minutes – and twenty minutes to get his gear on and get into the escape chamber. Then his description of Professor Haldane subsequently deliberately poisoning himself with CO_2 till he was nearly dead and then putting on an escape apparatus to see if he would be sick was wonderful. He *was* sick, terribly sick, which of course prevented the use of the apparatus and proved his theory of why the second party failed to get out and were all drowned.

On Christmas Day he wrote from the snowy desolation of Scapa.

. . . We celebrated our Christmas Day yesterday because it seemed unlikely we'd be able to do so today.

First of all I went in the boat on Saturday with ten officers and we filled it up with greenery and decorated

---

* The son of Admiral Sir Percy Noble. 'Charlie' Noble, after the War, was Conservative MP for Chelsea.
† Senior Submarine Officer & Technical Adviser on board the new submarine *Thetis* when she sank in Liverpool Bay on her final trials shortly before the War.

things up a bit. In some mysterious way the two RNVR doctors got a young fir tree for a Xmas tree. (They don't grow here!) I think they stole it because they brought it on board after dark and won't say how or where they got it!

On Xmas morning I made a speech to the sailors – sweating cold sweat – but it seemed to go all right.

Then I gave all the officers a glass of champagne and conducted Service.

The sailors sang their Xmas hymns like mad – fairly raised the deck. Then I inspected the men's dinners – didn't go round the mess decks. They couldn't put up much of a show, poor chaps, so I thought I wouldn't 'uncover their nakedness'.

We had that stolen (?) Xmas tree in the Wardroom – very well got up, with silly presents for all which made much fun. I was given a box of very tough dog-biscuits with on it 'To Bulldog (Sir) with best Xmas wishes'. (It's not a bad nickname if I must have one.)

But the joke of the tree was that it was adorned with lots of lovely balloons of all colours with faces and things painted on them. Darling, in my innocence, I didn't tumble till right at the end that the medical faculty had come up to scratch again. They were Government *FLs* and the inventive and logical brains of the faculty had agreed that as there was not a chance of their being used (alas!) for the purpose intended they could well be expended and expanded to adorn the Xmas tree!!

The incongruity of using them to decorate a tree celebrating the Nativity is still tickling my odd sense of humour.

The day went with a swing, marred for a short time by a sailor falling overboard from a ship nearby. We picked him up but he was already drowned so we had a corpse on board for the rest of the day.

We had a trawler alongside with a midshipman in her and as the man was picked up in the searchlight beam, for it was pitch dark, this eager youngster, who reminded me damnably of Piet, dived after him without a moment's hesitation followed by a Signalman and our RNR Engineer Lieutenant-Commander.

As a matter of fact I had my coat and shoes off and was just going in off the Quarterdeck when these three went. So I was able to direct the rescue of all four! It was ice-cold and the midshipman was suffering from shock when we got them aboard the boat that picked them up. He was all right again this morning and is doing his Seamanship Exam for Sub-Lieutenant!!

Darling, I thought so often of you and Piet and Hillie during yesterday and what bricks you all are and had some difficulty at the Morning Church Service in reading the Prayer the Bishop of Dover sent me 'For Home and Friends'.

About this time between Christmas and New Year, we heard over the wireless one of the 'bad news' messages broadcast by Lord Haw-Haw, the British traitor who was Germany's best propaganda weapon for causing despondency at home. Too often he told the truth. The *Nelson* had been mined and was lying useless in a Scottish lake with two anti-aircraft cruisers to guard her. 'It was Loch Ewe.'

'That's probably Dad – *must* be!' said Peter.

He was right. The *Calcutta* had been called to stand by the crippled *Nelson*. The little anti-aircraft cruiser had set off at full speed and at dawn she was waiting to enter the heavily-mined Loch. Bertie received explicit instructions. *'When entering port today approach in a line as near the western shore as possible. ... The fore part of the ship should be cleared and as few men as possible below deck. ... Speed should be as slow as possible.'* The *Calcutta* had not yet been degaussed against magnetic mines, but she was lucky, and on New Year's Day Bertie wrote to me from the Loch.

1 January 1940

... You would love this beautiful place. Only a few houses, snow-capped mountains, peaty-brown moors and clear water after the muddy Humber. There is something wonder-

174

fully freshening about the wildness and loneliness. One can see its effect on the sailors – and perhaps on oneself.

We ate the excellent turkey you sent us in the Wardroom last night and everyone gave you a vote of thanks ... On deck it was frosty with a clear sky and no wind, the mountains pale in the starlight and we could smell the damp heather-scent of the earth. As the youngest member of the Mess struck 16 bells at midnight the moon came up over the mountains as if someone had pressed a button. We sang 'Auld Lang Syne' on deck and then back to the Wardroom before we got frozen. . . .

At 6 p.m. all the New Year promotions had come out. Rather pathetic in a way. You know what an excitement it always makes in a ship. Of course in my ocean greyhound there is *no one* interested. They are all passed over, retired or reserves. . . .

But at last there was belated Christmas leave when the *Calcutta* was given a 'Job Number' in Chatham Dockyard to be degaussed. Bertie was able to snatch a week with Hillie, Peter and me at Southsea and Coxswain Corney married his sweetheart in the Isle of Wight.

During that week together we discussed many things.

'Hillie's been wonderful to me – and Piet – and it's been a comfort to us both, not being alone in wartime, but I can't go on like this. When Piet's gone to Wellington I want to take a flat in London and do some sort of War job.'

'This'll be no short War, Joy-Joy. It's hardly begun. I know how you feel. But *London* – if Hitler cut loose with his *Luftwaffe*—'

'That's why flats are cheap there now. We have friends at the Admiralty – I'll feel more in touch. I'll get a voluntary job I can leave whenever we can be together.'

So it was decided. Our old friend, Jack Borrett, was a Duty Captain at the Admiralty and his wife, Joy, had a flat in Onslow Gardens. Their children were in Hereford – a safe area – with Joy's parents. I rang her up and she told me that there was a furnished ground-floor flat in a block right opposite theirs. 'You could put up Bertie and Peter easily and the flat opens on to a little garden, just right for Dinah.' The rent was minimal. London was hollow with empty flats.

Tommy Elmhirst had been promoted to Air Commodore and was at the Air Ministry and he and Katherine had taken a house in Walton Place and the children were with them.

'Tommy'll know when things are likely to hot up,' said Bertie. 'He won't let the children stay.'

Hillie too realized that Portsmouth might at any time become untenable and was prepared, when necessary, to share their home in Hampshire with old friends of hers.

We arranged that I should take Peter to Wellington and go straight on to London, thus saving petrol. It distressed Bertie that he would not be able to introduce his son to his new school himself. But by then he was in the Arctic Circle. 'It has been just as bad as it can be at sea,' he wrote. 'Wind, frost, snow and damnably cold. We were iced all over by the spray as it froze on us, and, where we are now, pack-ice forming fast. It looks so silly to see the seagulls skating past or standing on the water, so to speak. At times today I couldn't see the forecastle head for the snow blizzard. Thank goodness for our woollen gear. Without it our chaps couldn't exist.'

HMS *Calcutta, 18 February 1940*

... I have not written for five days. The reason I will leave to your imagination.

My news must only be personal but – rather like you on your wireless – I have had a stirring day or two following the *Altmark* to the final dénouement. It was a fine piece of work, believe me. Tracking down the ship in darkness and snowstorms, putting a destroyer alongside with that ship trying to ram you and great navigational hazards, is no mean feat, to say nothing of the boarding and the rescue of 300 naval prisoners. I don't think anyone but a sailor can really appreciate that part of it.

The diplomatic arguments about taking the chase into neutral waters will go on and eventually fizzle out. The feature which is so splendid is the virility of the Admiralty and the Government. Usually the wretched Senior Naval Officer is left to hold the baby and is apt to find himself the scapegoat. Here the Senior Naval Officer was told unreservedly to do his stuff and was backed up publicly and immediately by the Admiralty and Government.

That is heartening beyond belief to the fighting man. We must give Winston, the First Lord, the credit for this attitude which will make itself felt consciously and unconsciously by every senior officer afloat.

The *Calcutta* had been on the spot, standing by throughout the capture of the *Altmark* which became famous. Philip Vian, Commander of the destroyer *Cossack* which pursued the *Graf Spee*'s one-time supply ship into Norwegian waters, was decorated for his piratical boarding in which officers and sailors swarmed over the side, released their 300 comrades and took the ship. Soon afterwards I happened to be dining with Tommy and Katherine Elmhirst. To my surprise and delight they had a guest with narrow vital blue eyes and a mellow Canadian voice who looked at me with humorous recognition.

'So it's Joy Packer back in my life.'

'Bax! I can't believe it. How long is it since you gave me a job on the *Express*? Eight years?'

Beverley Baxter was now the Member of Parliament for Wood Green. The turbulent 'Max–Bax' partnership had temporarily broken up (though in a friendly way) and the inspirations of this brilliant controversial journalist were harnessed to the Kemsley Press to boost morale on the home front. The *Sunday Graphic* gave him the whole front page, he was doing the *Atticus* column in the *Sunday Times,* and his syndicated articles from Westminster received maximum publicity in Canada, the land of his birth. His attractive Canadian wife, Edie, and their two children, Clive and Meribah, were in British Columbia.

'They're safer there for the present,' he said. 'And where's that sailor of yours?'

'Out in the grey. At sea.'

We talked about the *Altmark* rescue. I had brought

Bertie's letter with me to show Tommy, but Bax too was interested in Bertie's reaction to the exploit. The point of view of the Navy afloat was new to him. From that evening on, it caught his receptive imagination and, with responsible regard for security and anonymity, he quoted views from Bertie's letters that he reckoned would 'hearten' millions of readers at home and at sea.

But the letter that made me happiest had no news of ships and sailors and enemies. It was written on 20 February 1940, the 15th anniversary of our wedding.

. . . This is a lovely date on which to write you a little love-letter. I am thinking of you and all the loveliness and happiness that goes with you wherever you go. It is not my way you go as often as I could wish but, whenever there is a chance, you come my way with a wholeheartedness which is a beautiful thing for me. . . .

So, darling, I'm telling you what I've told you in so many lands – in the clear moonshine of South Africa or Greece, or on the shores of the China Sea, or on a mountainside in Monte Carlo, or in the squalor of Grimsby – that I love you before anyone or anything in the world. And if there's no news in this little letter but old news, it is news that's stood the test of time, and I'm not giving a thought tonight of wars, pestilence and horrors. I'm just thinking of you so that if Hitler walked into my cabin this moment I'd merely look up from my desk and tell him to sit down in a chair, keep quiet and not interrupt.

19
'I am where you would want me to be – actively doing my job.'

HMS *Manchester*	Norwegian Campaign
1940	Landing and Evacuation of Troops

I WAS settled in my little flat in Onslow Gardens and doing a voluntary clerical job in the Royal Navy Depot for Knitted Comforts. The Depot was in charge of Lady Louis Mountbatten who was the organizer of many different War efforts.

It was in Eaton Square and we had a key to the long rectangular gardens. So, in my tea-break, I always took Dinah for a scamper under the trees. Admiral Pound was now First Sea Lord and Lady Pound came to the Depot almost daily. Sometimes Mrs. Churchill came in too and impressed us with her elegance. The beautiful Georgian rooms were crammed ceiling-high with heavy mine-sweeper jerseys, seaboot-stockings, helmets and gloves and pervaded by the sickly smell of oiled wool intended to defy blizzards and drenching seas.

Just before Easter Bertie was relieved from the 'Lucky *Calcutta*' and appointed Captain of the modern cruiser *Manchester* and Chief of Staff to Admiral Geoffrey Layton. The *Manchester* was the Flagship of Admiral Layton's Cruiser Squadron which had been recalled from the East Indies Station to patrol the Scandinavian coast and Northern approaches to the Atlantic.

His leave came at just the right time – the Easter holidays – and we fetched Peter from Wellington. As we walked across the playing fields – Dinah frisking ahead of us – we met an athletic young man in shorts with a shock of red hair. He stopped to greet us.

'The Master,' whispered Peter in a tone of awe. Evidently the Sports Master, we thought.

179

Bertie was in uniform and the young man said: 'I have a brother in the Navy, lucky devil!'

'What's his name?' asked Bertie. 'I'm afraid I didn't catch yours.'

I heard Peter gasp and saw his look of horror.

'Longdon,' grinned the young man.

'Hell's delight! You can't be the Head?'

'I'm afraid so.' Longdon laughed, and Peter relaxed. 'I envy my brother. This is no time to be in a safe billet.'

'Sorry,' said Bertie to his son afterwards. 'I'm not up in the jargon. So Wellington's Headmaster is simply "the Master"? Quite Biblical.'

On 8 April the papers blazoned 'NORWAY AND DENMARK INVADED'. Bertie said in the clipped way he did when he was excited or angry, 'So now the War has *really* begun!'

He could hardly wait for the order that would cut his leave short. Peter and I saw him and Coxswain Corney off by the Flying Scotsman on a stormy night, both of them eager to join their new ship *Manchester* at Scapa Flow and be 'in the thick of things' again.

My first communication from HMS *Manchester* was a blue pencil scrawl on a signal pad written on the Bridge and dispatched by some mysterious means.

Naval message, 16 April 1940

... A really hurried note in the middle of great goings-on. I have found a way of getting it to you – I hope. I cannot say where I am but I am where you would want me to be – actively doing my job. Very fit and full of pep after our shore leave.

I must tell you of my journey. To my horror I found the train – non-stop – had no sleeping car, so had no dinner or anything at all – caught a 'plane at Inverness (by ten minutes) to Kirkwall. Got a car and another 'plane and was on the water alongside my ship by 2.40 p.m. We sailed 3.15!! Hot work.

I have nothing but the suitcase we packed – left Corney and gear at Inverness.

Bousfield (my predecessor) went over the side as I came up it – no time to turn-over – and off I went in the same clothes I left the cocktail party in on the evening before – 20 hours after leaving London.

Was I lucky or not? Half an hour later and I would have missed the ship and been out of it all.

Terribly busy every moment – right in the thick of it.

Geoffrey Layton in great form.

I've never had a happier leave, bless you. All the best to our Piet.

The *Manchester* was engaged in taking troops, including the French Chasseurs Alpins, into Norway, already overrun by German army and *Luftwaffe*. It was a short disastrous campaign for the Allies. The *Glasgow* had already evacuated King Haakon, his family and coffers of Norwegian State gold from Molde. Later Bertie showed me a copy of the Captain's report written on 9 April 1940. '... I am unable to refrain from remarking on the tremendous impression made on us all by His Majesty and the Crown Prince. His Majesty had undergone the severest ordeal and was broken-hearted at the fate of his country; he had remained in his field uniform for days on end, and had been subjected to continuous bombing whilst without sleep. His embarkation and departure had taken place under the most trying conditions with night bombing ... his composure and dignity, his kindliness and thoughtfulness for others, his confident and cheerful bearing when in public, were an inspiration to all of us and unforgettable.'

HMS *Manchester, 19 April 1940*

... A week today since I made my pierhead jump on board this ship.

It is difficult to write, as I cannot tell you of the strenuous and interesting things we are doing. I can only tell you I am fit and well, that I like my officers very much from what little

I have seen of them, and the ship's company seem cheerful and steady. I have so far had no chance to get among them and 'get hold' of them.

I have neither Corney nor my gear yet and don't look like getting either!

Geoffrey Layton is too busy at present to be jolly and hearty like he can be. But he's in fine condition – no non-sense, the hell of a thruster and most capable. We shall get on well. A certain readjustment of outlook is necessary when one has been very much cock of one's own roost in an independent command. . . .

29 April 1940

Geoffrey Layton is grand – a superheated ball of fire and never loses his head. And now, like a shot out of the blue, I hear he is off as Commander-in-Chief East Indies! He ought to be Commander-in-Chief Home Fleet. Anyhow, I stay here and the Lord knows what horror of an Admiral I shall get. I've asked Geoffrey Layton to advise his successor to hoist his flag in another ship of this class as *Manchester* is due for a refit and others of this squadron have had theirs. That would mean I could have *Manchester* all to myself.
3 May . . . By the time you get this you will have heard the PM's broadcast and know what we have been up to.

What they had been 'up to' had been worse than the in-itial stage of the operation. The evacuation of the defeated army in the teeth of the victorious enemy was a much more scarifying ordeal than landing them. The Prime Minister's speech, announcing the successful evacuation of the troops by the Navy, was precipitate, and those ships, like my hus-band's, that were last out of the fjords received concentrated attention from the *Luftwaffe* on the strength of it. Bertie wrote:

. . . It has been terribly strenuous, but the Navy hasn't failed – we have done our stuff in the most impossible con-ditions, not realized, I think, except by those on the spot.

182

There have been, by comparatively obscure or inexperienced naval officers in command – some only young Lieutenants – really epic stories of guts, courage and determination which leave even my tough heart gasping. I daresay most of them will never be heard about. My old *Calcutta* has distinguished herself greatly. Tonight I was able to get Number One, Chiefy, and the Pay over for a drink and a yarn. That ship has made the grade from 'asshole to breakfastime'. I was so delighted to see them again!

And what does our Air Force do? It should help the Navy to move the Army, and help the Army to defeat the enemy on land and to occupy and maintain its occupation of enemy territory. . . . The personnel of the Air Force is splendid, the aircraft are excellent, but the conception of their role as visualized at the top is deficient.

As I see it, the Coastal Command quite rightly has gone flat out for naval co-operation, I have great experience of them and they are splendid.

The Fighter Command is full of the finest material but doesn't know where the hell it should go full out.

The Bomber Command seems to act in a rigid independent kind of way and bombs marvellously – when quite possibly it would have done much better in this last business to fill bombers with machine guns to act as battleships of the air that no one dared approach, and so it would safeguard the Navy and the Army in the same way that battleships definitely ward off attacks on convoys.

The whole of this very small business has been a big unnecessary struggle by the Navy and Army against desperate odds – those odds are due to the direction of the Air Force – the Head of the Air Force primarily – ultimately the War Cabinet which should give the Head of the Air Force his directions.

What I have written is the opinion of my Admiral and of General Paget, late Commandant of the Military Staff College, with whom I had a long talk this morning. . . .

By the time I received Bertie's letter the operation had been completed and Jack Borrett was able to fill in many gaps for me. As Duty Captain at the Admiralty all vital signals came to him.

'The *Manchester* and her destroyer screen, and Bertie's beloved "Lucky *Calcutta*", were the last out,' he said. 'I hated to think what I might have to tell you.'

The ships had steamed up the long fjord in the few northern hours of darkness, lit by the red glow of Aandalsnes, all its timber houses in flames. ' 'Ands an' knees' the sailors called the blazing port.

General Paget and his waiting troops had been through hell, bombed and machine-gunned without any let-up for a fortnight. Destroyers ferried them on board where they collapsed in bunches, only stirring to gulp the hot soup offered them.

Next day, when the *Manchester* was clear of the land, Bertie and General Paget walked round together talking to the troops. Bertie wrote in his log:

... A lot were still 'out 'and the real youngsters 'cooked', but ... I was much impressed by the good condition of the older men and regular soldiers ... who were shaving and sprucing themselves up. They all said they would take on as many 'bluidy Bosches' as they could find but they couldn't cope with the aeroplanes which gave them no chance. We have 840 on board and the total taken off by our party last night was 2,200. My old Calcutta *took 740 – a big effort after 12 hours of being attacked with over 150 bombs.*

In the sickbay we have an enormous number of bad feet, swollen blue, black, blistered and bleeding. This party from the rearguard had entrained the night before. The train crashed in a bomb crater. The troops, already pretty well worn out, had to march 17 miles to a tunnel to take cover during the day. There they rested and got another train to about four miles from Aandalsnes, then marched the rest. I was delighted to see that most of them still had their rifles and equipment, and also they brought off a lot of ammunition and anti-tank guns.

Our Admiral's drive and decision is largely responsible for the successful accomplishment of that most difficult

operation of embarking a rearguard in the face of the enemy.
The Germans were in Aandalsnes today!

At present we are steaming W at 27 knots – and for the
first time *we have some air protection – a Sunderland flying-
boat and three Blenheims!*

To me he wrote on 8 May, from Scapa Flow in Orkney.

... As you can guess we are having a 'sit back' until the
next spot of bother. We are cleaning and sprucing up a bit
after a very busy time ...

I am sending you a parcel of Orkney tweed – sort of
bluey-grey, good stuff, I saw it being made.

... Last night Geoffrey Layton and I had a long moderate
sensible discussion about all this Air business. He was getting all worked up and trying not to, and finally he jumped
up and stood with his legs apart and his jaw jutting out. 'By
God, here we've been operating on the enemy's coast in the
teeth of their Air Force – over 150 bombs in one day and by
the grace of God and our own anti-aircraft guns not a
bloody hit on us. And we hear that our Air Force has done
this and done that, while for three bloody weeks I've looked
up into the air to see what our Air Force is doing for *us* –
and what do I see? Not even a f——g butterfly in the sky!'
And out he stumped.

I laughed myself sick and wished to heaven he could have
said his bit to the War Cabinet. He would certainly have
startled them. . . .

On 10 May 1940, Germany invaded neutral Belgium and
Holland. On the same date, at Westminster, a bitter debate
on the Norwegian fiasco forced Neville Chamberlain to
resign and a Coalition Government was formed with Winston Churchill as Prime Minister and Clement Attlee as
'alternate'.

So the Navy lost a vigorous First Lord but the Commonwealth of Nations gained the most dominating War
leader of all time to oppose Hitler's legend of invincibility.

By mid-May Germany's Mechanized Divisions were

striking deep into France and the British Expeditionary Force had been driven back to the Channel ports.

Katherine Elmhirst telephoned me early one morning, her voice scarcely recognizable.

'I'm in bed with tonsillitis. Tommy says the children must go to my sister in Tring at once. Can you take them if he fills Jaggy's tank for you?'

So I knew that Tommy – at the Air Ministry – must be expecting the bombing to begin in earnest very soon.

In Eaton Square there were changes. Quite near our Naval Depot the Women's Voluntary Service, for which I also worked, had set up a Clothing Depot for refugees from Europe, and almost next door to us the flag of the Netherlands flew from the mansion which housed the Dutch Royal Family, evacuated by a British destroyer. When I took Dinah into the garden I often met Princess Juliana watching her two chubby little girls at play.

On 13 May Bertie wrote: 'Anyway for the time being we now have a Coalition Government which represents every form of political opinion and which has one united idea – to win the ruddy War. God bless Hitler for doing that much for us. One other great point is that Hitler loathes Winston, which probably means that Hitler is at heart frightened of him.'

Two days later, after the evening News on the BBC – always disastrous now – my telephone rang. The exchange was Scottish. Bertie's voice was urgent and excited.

'Can you make the night train for Edinburgh? You've only got an hour—'

I rang my immediate boss at the Depot. She understood. Sudden leave was never denied us, nor was our destination asked. I also rang Marion. Short and sharp. She was thrilled for her brother and me. She and I and her Dachshund Fritz and Dinah spent most of our Sundays together – either at my flat or at her bungalow in Ruislip. She was in charge of Glaxo's personnel and, though various important manufacturing branches had been dispersed to safer areas, the main factory was still on the Great West Road. It was near Ruislip and also unpleasantly near Northolt Air

Station where many Polish airmen had established a reputation for dauntless bravery. Marion's boss had insisted upon giving her an air raid shelter in her garden. 'Do nicely for Piet when he wants a friend to stay,' she said.

Corney was on the platform at Edinburgh next morning, weathered and beaming. As he drove me off in a small naval car, he said: 'The Captain's taken a room for you at South Queensferry, Madam, just across the Forth Bridge. Nothing grand. But Mistress Maconochie doesn't mind Dinah. She runs the place – it's a boarding-house like.'

'Sounds fine. You look as if you'd been on a pleasure cruise—'

'Wait till you see the Captain. He thrives on excitement! Now General Paget – we took him and his troops off – he was terribly seasick and his feet were in an awful state. We lent him a pair of the Captain's socks that your Nannie knitted.'

He told me about the ship's mascot, Leslie, the black cat, who'd joined the *Manchester* at Tyneside where she'd been building. 'Not much to look at, mind you, but she finds a Tom in every port and always has her kittens in the boiler-room. A proper sea-going cat – had her Tyneside kittens in the Red Sea, an' after them some Indian kittens out East. She brings 'em up a treat – wash behind the ears and all. But we nearly lost her at 'Ands an' knees. The place was blazing and Leslie caught the last destroyer off by the skin of her teeth. They sent us a signal after they'd ferried the final lot of troops to us.'

I saw that signal later from the destroyer *Delight* (suitably named from Leslie's point of view) to *Manchester*.

'I have a black cat in exchange for 400 soldiers discharged to you. Does she belong to you please? 03.22.'

Manchester made instant reply.

'Please return our black cat. You can have the 400 soldiers back, 03.26. 2/5/40.'

'I wonder what happened to "Cocky"?' I said to Corney. He laughed.

'The *Calcutta* was with us in them fjords, Madam. And

there was "Cocky" going up the rigging claw-over-claw, proper seaman-like.'

At the Forth Bridge he stopped the car and pointed down the gleaming Firth between green banks studded with bleak stone villages.

'That's where we're lying.'

Warships lay in the silver camber of that long arm and above them, over Rosyth Dockyard, the balloon barrage floated lazily.

The next few days were long and sunny and, in the midst of increasingly desperate news from across the 'English moat', we enjoyed our personal peace to the full, though we didn't try to shut out reality. We must have covered many miles over the grassy hills and vales round the Firth of Forth as we told each other all the silly little things that made up our lives apart – some funny, some sad, and others funny-sad like my husband's story of the Chasseurs Alpins the *Manchester* had taken into Norway. A few years ago, in the Alpes-Maritimes, we had been guests in the Officers' Mess of these dashing mountain troops. 'And then I find them in Scotland,' said Bertie, 'waiting for us to embark them *with their mules*! We couldn't take their mules. It was impossible. They were completely heartbroken. They wrung their hands and cried out that it was *incroyable* that they – French mountain troops – should be expected to campaign in Norway without their animals. Their mules were their fellow-campaigners, their porters, their sisters and brothers, and without them they would be betrayed – the War would be lost – everything! Well, a lot was lost in Norway, but the mules of the Chasseurs Alpins remained safe from the enemy. And *don't* ask me what became of them. Joy-Joy!'

On 23 May I was back in London.

Thursday, 23 May 1940

... The news last night was lousy. Italy apparently still hanging back. To hell with Italy anyway. I heard Attlee's speech, it was stimulating and the Government has assumed powers I never thought possible. Good luck go with them. We *are* awake at last.

I woke at 4 a.m. yesterday thinking I ought never to have let you go south, but you promise me *really* to get ready to go if things boil up. Don't leave it too long. You can always go back to London if you've made a false judgement. Don't worry about Piet. That boy will be all right at Wellington with his fellow toughs – *men* I mean!

Bless you, darling. I'd take on any German ship in this old *Manchester*, for we are getting to know each other.

28 May 1940

... The news this morning that Leopold has surrendered his entire army to Germany is tough. I've been expecting the Belgians to collapse but not so quickly. Nor did I think Leopold would ever chuck his hand in like that!

I am lost in admiration for our RAF. I never doubted that they and their aircraft were tigers when it came to fighting. It was only that their scope was so limited by the conception of their 'high ups' that worried me.

As far as the armies in Flanders are concerned let's hope for a miracle. They'll need it, poor chaps.

The 'miracle' was already underway as the 'little ships' gathered to evacuate the British Expeditionary Force from the blood-stained beaches of Dunkirk, the only Channel port not yet in enemy hands. The sea was smooth and a heaven-sent canopy of fog shrouded the astounding performance of a shuttle service conducted by destroyers, transports, fishing smacks, tugs, yachts, steamers, launches, anything with an engine or a sail, and a man, a woman or a boy at the helm. Even the paddle-steamer, *Gracie Fields*, played her part, and, like her famous Lancashire namesake, was good for a laugh when the *Manchester*'s Yoeman of Signals solemnly handed the Captain an intercepted SOS. 'Gracie Fields making water fast.' Alas, she was lost to the Cowes Paddle Fleet, but two-thirds of the BEF, 333,000 men in all, including French, Dutch and Belgians, were

189

brought home – weary and wounded – their equipment gone, but their lives saved to fight again.

Now Britain prepared to repel invasion and Bertie wrote to me of 'the miracle of Dunkirk' as it was called at the time – and always will be. 'It seems that our tremendous evacuation is going so well that very soon we shall claim it is a victory! It is a marvellous achievement – as a man of war I say that. At the moment I am champing at the bit. We are watching and waiting instead of being in the forefront of a battle.'

It was now that Winston Churchill showed his tremendous powers as an orator and a leader. Not just in Parliament or on a platform, but to the people in their homes. We tuned in our radios, alone or with a friend, and we were strengthened at times when hope seemed lost. *We were all in the front line now*, he told us. We would fight for our Island – on the beaches, in the fields, in the cities and hamlets, street by street, house by house. We would never give in. Already bombs were falling on coastal military targets and we must prepare for parachutists. Home Defence must be vigilant and stand firm – the old, the young, men, women and children. It was all very dramatic, stirring and occasionally ridiculous. The old were armed with broomsticks, the Home Guard with wooden guns, housewives had pepperpots ready to throw in the faces of parachutists, children charged their water-pistols and everybody said: 'Let 'em come!'

But in Eaton Square I no longer saw Princess Juliana and her little girls playing in the gardens. They had gone to Canada to preserve a dynasty. Old Queen Wilhelmina stayed on alone. Dreadful tales were coming in daily with refugees from the occupied countries. 'Extermination' was a word to chill the heart. Boys on the verge of manhood, it seemed, would 'not be allowed by the enemy to develop as potential fighters'. So the seavacuees – the children – were being sent across the Atlantic to grow up in safety and prepare to return and take up the struggle when their time should come.

Dear Lady Pound, with the shadow of a fatal illness

already upon her face, stopped at my desk at the Depot.

'You know Mrs. Waterson of course?' she said.

'Yes, I do. Of course.'

Sydney Waterson had followed Charles te Water as South African High Commissioner in London at the outbreak of War.

'She's taking a big party of children to South Africa this week. Her own son is one of them. He's Peter's age. Have you considered that it might be wise to send Peter to your home?'

I looked at the wife of the First Sea Lord. Was it as bad as that?

'It's too late,' I said. 'Betty Waterson sails tomorrow. I know that.'

'It's not too late. You'd find her at South Africa House now. She deals with a great many emergencies – and fast.'

She bent down and patted Dinah's head. The little dog started and then licked her hand.

I borrowed the rusty key to the garden and took Dinah there. If only Bertie were here. And Peter. In my bag was a letter from my mother. 'The doors of "Tees Lodge" are wide open for you and your boy whenever you want to come.'

By some merciful chance Bertie telephoned me that night. From the accent of the exchange, I assumed it was from Immingham. There was little time to say anything because an air-raid warning cut our conversation short.

29 May 1940

... I am writing this evening after talking to you on the telephone. I can only repeat that you are right to take this chance which has suddenly presented itself. It was a big decision and, having made it, I know how hard and quickly you must have worked to get things fixed up – even the cadet's safety waistcoat from Gieves! I am little help to you, but it is now that we rely fully on our women-folk. ...

As I write you will have Piet with you and tomorrow I shall think of you two on Waterloo platform at 11.15. ... I'm afraid it will be terribly harrowing for both of you, Piet will feel he is leaving you in danger and hate and resent it because he has a high spirit. *But it is a right decision. Whatever happens never regret it.* . . .

Perhaps it was a 'right decision'. I have made countless wrong ones and regretted them less.

There had been no time to inform my in-laws. It had been a matter of 24 hours from the suggestion in the Depot to the parting on Waterloo Station.

I forwarded Bertie their characteristic reactions to the news. There were no reproaches. That was not their way. My mother-in-law, who was living in a residential hotel in Heswall not far from the five-star danger area of Liverpool where her daughter Dorothy and son-in-law continued to live and work, wrote briefly that she was 'naturally shocked to hear of my grandson's departure but of course your mother will be very happy to have him with her in South Africa'.

Dorothy replied with sympathy and understanding. She added: 'At first, when Norman and I read your letter, we found it hard to believe. It was as if the King and Queen had suddenly decided to leave England.'

Winifred expressed herself more academically as befitted the Headmistress of a fashionable girls' school. The education of the young would not be allowed to suffer, she said. Schools would be evacuated if necessary. It was a pity South Africa was so far away.

Marion, who never put pen to paper, sat with me on Sunday in Kensington Gardens while Fritz and Dinah chased each other in the sun of that warm clear summer.

'Unkie backed you up, Joy-Joy, and of course it was the right decision in all the circumstances – for any boy except Piet.'

A week later two of the first bombs to fall on a home county landed on Wellington College. The young man with red hair and the charming smile, who had envied his brother, Longdon, in the Navy, was killed instantly.

'You'll be very sorry,' I wrote to Peter by airmail. 'I know you admired the Master.'

He received it the day he arrived at Cape Town – the day Paris fell.

20
'We shall continue to control the sea routes of the world.'

HMS *Manchester*   Home Waters
1940

THE day Paris was evacuated, on 10 June, Italy declared War on Britain and France. The *Manchester* was on constant North Sea patrol.

11 June 1940

. . . When I telephoned you on Sunday night I had just heard that *Glorious* and two destroyers were sunk. Of course I could say nothing. It was depressing. But Mussolini and the battle in France attract all attention. It is a right perspective. In carrying out our duties of controlling the world's sea routes we must have naval losses. It will be give and take. We sink their pocket battleship *Graf Spee* and they sink our carrier *Glorious*. But we shall continue to control the sea routes of the world.

If you refuse to be beaten you can't be beaten. Remember the Ghazi letting fly at Ponsot that night in Ankara? *'Je ne suis jamais battu. Ou je gagne ou je meurs!'*
15 June It was wonderful to hear you on the telephone last night and to know that Piet had arrived safely. How happy Mum will be!
18 June These fateful days drag on. France is packing up. What will happen to her Navy? If only she will go on *fighting anywhere* – Algeria, Morocco or Cochin China and her Navy and Air Force will join themselves with us we shall be home. If they surrender we've got a very long and arduous fight ahead. Even then we shall make it, but it will be a business of years.

Surely if Holland and Belgium can go on fighting in their Empires France can do so too.

But on 21 June, Marshal Pétain accepted Hitler's Armistice terms and the surrender was signed in the same railway-coach at Compiègne where the Armistice of 11 November 1918 was signed, when it was Germany who was forced to her knees. On 24 June the Franco–Italian Armistice was signed near Rome. The battle for Western Europe was over.

That night I was dining at Beverley Baxter's beautiful home in St. John's Wood. The garden had exchanged herbaceous borders for vegetables, as the parks of London now grazed sheep under the tall plane and chestnut trees where children used to play. Bill Mabane,* MP for Huddersfield and Under Secretary for Home Security, was for the time being sharing Bax's house. Clever, brittle Stella Duggan, who was later to be his wife, and her equally attractive sister, Sylvia, were already there when I arrived. Our sixth was Canadian General Critchley in charge of Air Training.

Bax was playing the piano and singing softly in his mellow tenor. The lyric and music were his own – nostalgic echoes of peace.

Bill and 'Critch' stood with their backs to the empty grate; Sylvia hummed an accompaniment to our host's composition, while Stella exercised her ability to appear relaxed when she was not. The long windows of the lofty room were still open to the lingering midsummer twilight.

Bax rose from the piano stool.

'A *Dubonnet*?' he said. 'To drink to the resurrection of a moribund Ally. To France resurgent!'

It was Bill, tall and gaunt, who said, with grim satisfaction, what was in all our minds.'

'At least now we know where we stand.'

Bax looked at him, for once without amusement or challenge.

'In Europe we stand alone,' he said. 'But there is the Empire.'

---

* Later Lord Mabane.

'What about the French Fleet?' cut in Critchley.

'Surely it will fight on with us – from North Africa?' Bax was always optimistic.

Bill said, 'If not, we'll have to sink it. We can't risk it being handed over to Germany or Italy.'

'Critch' made an impatient gesture. 'We should, but we'd never have the guts.'

Suddenly some control within me snapped.

'Of course we would – if it was necessary! I'll bet you a fiver.'

'I'll give you a fiver to half-a-crown,' 'Critch' smiled. 'And I hope to lose.'

General Critchley was a very brave loser. He lost his sight some years afterwards, and learned to live actively and usefully without it.

He said: 'Now we can use our aircraft and our pilots for our own defence and stop pouring them into France to bolster up a lost cause.'

Somewhere near the lands of the Midnight Sun, Bertie was thinking along the same lines.

HMS *Manchester, Monday, 24 June 1940*

... As I write tonight I expect you are going a Small Slam – and getting it – with Bax's gang.

I had your letter last night and cannot discuss the news James S. gave you, but I know a lot about it. ...

'James S' was Admiral Somerville, a compelling personality noted for his lightning wit. In the summer of 1940 he was at the Admiralty straining at the leash to get to sea. His wish was granted under tragic circumstances. Their Lordships gave him command of his famous Force H and assigned him the task of persuading Admiral Gensoul, in command of the French Fleet at Oran in North Africa, to join the British Navy and continue the fight, or to take his ships to a safe French or British colonial port, or to scuttle them. If he refused all of these three alternatives Admiral Somerville, flying his flag in the *Hood*, and backed by the carrier *Ark Royal* and the *Valiant* and *Resolution*, had orders to sink the French Fleet. The *Hood* opened fire at Mers el Kébir on 4 July – 1,500 Frenchmen were killed.

Six days later, at Vichy, France became a totalitarian state with 84 year old Marshal Pétain as *Chef d'Etat*. That day I received a letter from Bertie. 'I am delighted the Cabinet's decision about the French Fleet at Oran was unanimous. It shows we are in deadly earnest. The only thing that succeeds now is force. The French Fleet was given every opportunity to join us, but their Admiral would not even see our envoy – 'Hooky' Holland, who'd been Naval Attaché in Paris before the War – so there was nothing for it but to sink the ships and so make sure that they would not fall into German or Italian hands. This James did with two casualties to us and God knows what to the French. It was a terrible thing to have to do, but there was no alternative. The French ships at Portsmouth, Plymouth and Alex. all gave in – very wisely, for France will get them back eventually. . . .'

Meanwhile Britain prepared to repel invasion. With good reason, for after the French collapse Hitler ordered the planning of Operation Sea Lion (*Seelöwe*). An extract from a directive issued by Hitler to his Combined Services' Staff on 16 July 1940 was quoted later by Winston Churchill. 'Since Britain, in spite of her militarily hopeless situation, shows no signs of coming to terms, I have decided to prepare a landing operation against England . . . the preparations must be completed by Mid-August.'

Every beach from Scotland to the Channel was one mass of barbed wire entanglements and concrete defences. The church-bells of the embattled Island were silenced, only to chime if a parachute air invasion was seen by any Home Defence Commander or if the Code Word CROMWELL went out to Home Guard headquarters, signifying 'Invasion Imminent'. Hillie Longstaff had left Southsea to go to her friends near Liphook in Hampshire, and Bertie wrote to me: 'On the wireless tonight I was greeted by the news that all children from Gosport and Portsmouth were being evacuated. Not comforting for my long-suffering sailors who are mostly Portsmouth men. All the same, it shocks me to find certain men on board who put personal consideration before their duty. It makes me vomit. This applies only to a few, I am glad to say. I've had to be very ruthless. It is the only way. Fortunately it is the common trait with us that if one is fair but ruthless the majority back one up.'

The Battle of Britain was in full swing, the raids on the ports were heavy. The Humber was getting full measure, and Bertie observed with pleasure 'our fighters going after the night raiders. Very thrilling to see them rush out of the blackness and pour bullets into the bombers and then watch the bombers crumple up and hit the ground or the sea. ... We've had enough of defence and evacuations. It's about time we found a way of giving Hitler a pill or two. The RAF are keeping at him. There is scope for us too. I wonder how many soldiers and police Hitler needs to look after his occupied countries!!'

In London the air-raids were not yet really alarming though, when they were noisy enough, Dinah and I slept in the dressing-room. The window was small, so less likely to shatter.

For some time I had been worried about Dinah's eyes. I confided in Marion as we sat in the park.

'She doesn't even chase the sheep now, Marion.'

'I've noticed, Joy-Joy. There must be a good vet—'

'I could ask Lady Louis at the Depot. She has two lovely Sealyhams she always brings with her.'

Lady Mountbatten's dark blue eyes were sympathetic.

'Yes, of course – in Elizabeth Street, just round the corner. He's a first class vet and very kind with animals.'

The vet was kind with humans too. When he had examined Dinah's eyes, he said: 'Have you a settled home – in the country perhaps – somewhere she knows her way?'

'We have no home. Just a rented flat in Onslow Gardens. She goes with me whenever I go away.'

'There's a shelter in your street – but you do realize that it's prohibited to take an animal into a public shelter?'

'I know.'

He turned away and looked out of the window on to

Elizabeth Street. Not much traffic that summer. Mostly vapour trails in the sky. I sat in a comfortable chair with Dinah on my lap. She was shivering a little. He came back to us.

'I'm sorry, Mrs. Packer. This is a very rare thing – especially in a young animal. Like an eclipse. She will soon be blind.'

'Both eyes?'

'Both.' Then he said: 'Go home and think it over. If you want to bring her back I can give her an injection to make her sleepy. After that you can hold her on your lap, as you're doing now. She'll fall asleep and not wake up.'

I'd known all along. There was no need to think it over.

There was a note for me when I opened the door of the little flat.

7 July 1940

... Keep in touch with Jacko. Very soon now I hope to get you a message tho' I'm not building on anything till it happens.

I'm so sorry about Dinah's eyes. It really distresses me to think of that live intelligent little creature confused and quenched by something you can't explain to her.

I think you're wise to sleep in the dressing-room and put cotton wool in your ears. One gets used to air-raids. If one takes reasonable precautions there is little more to be done.

I have written to Piet for his birthday and sent him the ship photographs he wants.

The very next evening Jack and Joy Borrett came in for a sundowner. Jack had splendid white teeth and an infectious grin which he flashed as he handed me a message written on a signal pad.

Go to the Eversfield Hotel at Southsea tomorrow. Apply for supplementary petrol to join your husband. It may be for a week or a month. You will need an Admiralty Pass to enter the perimeter.

'I have the petrol coupons and the permit here for you,' said Jacko. 'Don't lose them!'

The well-known Portsmouth Road had never seemed more hauntingly beautiful, the woods heavy with summer leaf, the sky woven with battle trails.

The sentries on Cosham Bridge stamped my Admiralty permit, smiled at me and my sailor mascot and waved us on.

Crossing the bridge that connects the great Naval Base and arsenal of Portsmouth with the rest of Hampshire was a shivery experience touched with awe and a sense of history, past, present and to come. On Portsdown Hill the old forts stood sturdily as they had done in the Napoleonic Wars – first line of defence against invasion by sea. But now it was common knowledge that the *Luftwaffe* intended to wipe out the RAF and cut all communication between London and the west of England as a preliminary to crossing the Channel with the barges and troops assembled at Rotterdam, Antwerp and Le Havre.

Goering was confident that his *Luftwaffe* was invincible and could protect the landing after first pulverizing the RAF. The German Naval High Command, however, had misgivings. 'According to Dönitz, subsequently Commander-in-Chief of the German Navy, it was generally accepted by the German leaders that their Navy would be no match for the Royal Navy, which they expected to be sacrificed to the last vessel and the last man to counter a landing.'*

The friendly busy face of Portsmouth was disfigured by blockades at strategic points; the Canoe Lake and grassy playgrounds of Southsea were deserted – the children gone. So sandcastles on the beach had given way to wire and concrete man-traps.

The Eversfield on Clarence Parade was run by Miss Heawood, grey-haired, practical and dauntless. She exemplified

---

* Extract from Winston Churchill's written Parliamentary Statement on Operation Sea Lion issued at Westminster.

the spirit Goebbels grudgingly noted in his diary two years later: '*20 February 1942*. Although England is fighting against tremendous obstacles, it cannot be said that morale is low. The English are used to hard blows and, to a certain extent the way they take them compels admiration. In times of crisis the British Government profits by the pig-headedness of the national character. . . .'

Miss Heawood and I had played tennis together at the United Services Club when first I was married. She had been a dogged opponent and a reliable partner. She showed me into a comfortable sitting-room with a view of the sea.

'The bedroom is rather small,' she said.

'It's a single—'

'It's what Captain Packer reserved.' She smiled. 'These are queer times.'

'Of course. The flowers in the sitting-room are so pretty—'

'A welcome. There's another welcome, not quite so nice.'

She gave me a leaflet. 'Your Invasion Instructions. This is the latest issue from Home Security. In the first, civilians were told to *stay put*. Winnie had it changed to *stand firm*.'

We agreed that Winnie was incomparable. As we did so the 'wailing banshee' sounded the air-raid warning.

'Even *that*,' she said. 'It was called the *Alarm* till Winnie instructed that it be known as the *Alert*. I'll get some tea. Your husband will be late coming in.'

Soon after the music of the 'All clear' announced the raiders' departure Bertie came ashore.

'At nightfall I must go back to the ship. With any luck, we'll have part of most afternoons together so long as we keep inside the port perimeter, in case of emergencies.'

Shipping in the Channel was being harassed by submarines, E-boats and bombers and the *Manchester*, much in need of a refit, was on invasion guard, her guns re-inforcing the anti-aircraft shore batteries and Coastal Command aircraft.

We played some tennis or went for walks and Bertie pointed out the forlorn French ships in port, their guns manned by British sailors, and a new Dutch cruiser which

Commander van Holthe* had managed to get to England before the Occupying Forces could lay hands on her. I made the acquaintance of a Free Frenchman who had escaped from Dunkirk in a destroyer and abandoned her in favour of the *Manchester*. Coxswain Corney persuaded the Captain to allow me on board for half an hour, especially to meet this new member of the ship's company.

'He's very excitable-like, Madam – being French. But if you'll speak to him in French he might calm down a bit.'

'I haven't talked French for ages—'

'He won't criticize your accent,' Bertie assured me. 'His own is a bit shaky.'

Corney disappeared and returned with the Free Frenchman who rushed into the cabin like a tornado and dashed out again. However, encouraged by all of us, he returned less emotionally and kissed my hand with unnecessary fervour. A very cold wet kiss it was. He was obviously in excellent health.

'Ordinary-Dog Shrapnel, Madam. He used to pull a milk-cart in Dunkirk. See the marks of the harness on his shoulders.'

I stroked his glossy coat. 'Strong shoulders and a hound's whippy tail. How does he get on with Leslie?'

'Like a brother. Kind to her kittens too. While she catches rats he frightens the gulls – fair blasts them when they bombard the Quarterdeck.'

'He's more sensible than he seems,' said Bertie. 'Shows a proper respect for the Quarterdeck.'

On one occasion Winston Churchill came on board, accompanied by a pugnacious little figure.

'Winston talked to the sailors and they hung on his words,' said Bertie. 'Then into the hangar he marched, smoking his cigar against all rules, fired off a volley of questions and turned round and said, "Make a note of that, Max!" The Beaver snapped, "I've already done so." ' Lord Beaverbrook was then the Minister of Aircraft Production.

Bertie made sure that batches of his ship's company with

* Later Chief of the Netherlands Navy.

homes in the perimeter should have opportunities of getting ashore, and Corney was able to go to the Isle of Wight and his young wife. But during 'the critical period of moon and tide' every man was at his post, and we who waited knew that the *Manchester* and her men might influence the course of history, and that what happened to us was immaterial.

I would turn off the dim electric light in my bedroom, open the black-out curtains and the sash window and watch the long geometric dance of the searchlights across sky and sea. I knew that my man out there *wanted* the invasion – 'something to bite on and defeat'. Phantom *carillons* echoed in my ears. Were the parachutes opening like evil moon flowers above the Hampshire meadows? But the church bells were illusory.

The 'crucial period' came and went and at last, towards the end of August, the *Manchester* was in dry dock for repairs and Bertie was able to snatch a week's leave with me in London before sailing north to Scapa.

HMS *Manchester, Monday, 26 August 1940*

. . . It is a week since I pecked you goodbye outside Gieves. These wartime goodbyes aren't funny, are they?

I had William Davies to dinner. He was at Oran. You can bet he was interesting and we had a grand gossip. He admired James S. very much indeed.

I was up all last night what with one thing and another and this afternoon took the Navigator ashore for a round of golf. The course is the one we made last War. It has been brought to life again out of the heather and the bog. So it's more fresh air and exercise than golf.

On Saturday night I dined *à deux* with Tom Troubridge – late Naval Attaché Berlin. He left a week before the War. His centre-piece was a silver plate, a gift from the German Commander-in-Chief Admiral Raeder!

He says that Hitler has consistently acted against the advice of his Generals and Admirals and, because he has got away with it each time, he puts less and less trust in his military and naval advisers.

But, says Tom, his Service advisers were right for they foresaw the ever-increasing impasse in which quick victories would put Hitler – unless he can conquer *us* – and eventually he would find himself with both feet in the soup. I give you this for what it is worth. In any case, after three years in Germany, Tom is much more likely to be right than I am.

Meanwhile I hear the air-raid news on the wireless. Portsmouth seems to have 'bought it', including a cinema and a hotel on the front. Could it be ours? The London area too. I hope like mad it was far from you. . . .

It *was* Eversfield Hotel in Southsea; and it was *not* 'far from' me. The nearest shelter to Onslow Gardens received a direct hit and everyone in it was killed. All the windows of our little flat were blown in despite the sticky tape crisscrossing them. I found another furnished flat in Swan Court, nearer the river and Battersea Power Station. Stupid. It was a bright and cheerful penthouse. Stupider still, but of course very cheap – as London flats were then, especially top floor. I wrote and told Bertie I had moved. My letter crossed with one from him. His Admiral, the successor to Geoffrey Layton, had once more hoisted his flag in the *Manchester*.

Friday, 30 August 1940

. . . The Old Man of the Sea came back yesterday. . . .

I *don't* like you being all alone in the flat with these air-raids going on. It tears the guts out of me to think of it. . . .

As Tommy Elmhirst told you, we had some 'attention' on the way here. Good for the 100 newcomers we collected at Portsmouth.

Some of my men have had their homes at Portsmouth blown to pieces and I am glad to say have asked to see me about it. Have told them all that their duty is here and their wives and families must keep things going in the danger zone at home. They show me their wives' letters. They are mostly very brave. It isn't funny for poor people to lose all their possessions with no real recompense – let alone their houses into which years of savings may have gone.

They are good about it. I do my best to fortify their courage. To one, after I had read his wife's letter, I said, 'Your wife is a fine brave woman. You are a lucky man that it was your house and not your wife you lost.' 'Thank you, sir,' he said. 'I am lucky.' It is difficult to put it properly. I do wish the Commander-in-Chief would do a 'Little Father' act to his 10,000 men up here and let them feel he had their troubles at heart. Not a sign. That isn't leadership. However, you know my views about lifting up the sailors' hearts. It isn't that they are 'down'. Not a bit of it. But now is the time to insure against the future and get their complete confidence against the times which must come in the end when both sides feel they have had enough and the 'sticker' wins.

Two grand letters from you today, one of 21 August and one of the 25th. Your description of golf at Croydon in an air-raid was superb. I'm sticking it in my log. I laughed my head off. Of course Bax and Charles Graves and Clarence, 'Critch' and company are right up your street. They are people of both ideas and action – and so are you.

I read Bax's paragraph from the *Sketch* with very great interest. It is so goddam true, wartime leaders in the field and afloat should *not* be old. The source of this information was so obvious!

So necessary to get across. I note too your discretion when crusading!

Bertie's next two letters were still from Scapa.

1 September 1940

... We have 15 Newfoundlanders just joined – absolutely raw Ordinary Seamen. I fell them in, welcomed them on board under my command, hoped they would be happy, they had come a long way and I valued their services. Said I knew their country and had once tried and failed to blow up a small iceberg blocking St. John's harbour. They must dig out, learn their work, and I hoped one day we would find ourselves together in action against an enemy worthy of us.

They stood to attention, and registered nothing till the last sentence when every one of them produced a grand, hopeful grin. Good for them!

Tuesday, 3 September Today two letters from you. One enclosed Miss Heawood's after the destruction of the Eversfield. It's a fine sturdy letter and I have given it to my Admiral to read.

Today you will have moved. I'm glad Sylvia Duggan has a flat at Swan Court too. As a matter of fact, I believe 'little flat' lost its appeal for you with no Piet and no Dinah. Am I right?

Friday, 6 September I was all of a twit getting through to you early this morning and hearing about your new flat and that you manage to ignore the air-raids to some extent.

My new Commander takes a lot off my shoulders and is firm but good with the ship's company. I'm getting to know a lot of them now and am glad to hear them whistling and singing. Lord Louis (Mountbatten) was on board to lunch today and we had a talk in my cabin afterwards. The King of Greece's photo was a help!! Lord Louis is full of go, damned efficient, a real live wire and leader. He and I saw eye to eye very quickly about getting on with the War – and how.

Here is a true story which he told me. As you may have seen, a destroyer was damaged the other day. She had her bow blown off up to the Bridge. The Captain was killed and probably some 30 of the ship's company. She was lying helpless in enemy waters and being bombed. The First Lieutenant was left in command. The Sub Lieutenant quite badly wounded with his head in bandages was in charge on deck.

Lord Louis arrived in another destroyer to tow her back stern first. He got into a boat and went on board. As he arrived over the side there was the Sub in his bandages standing at the salute and the boatswain's mate piping him over the side – as one does to a Captain of a ship coming aboard in peace time.

Perhaps it sounds a stupid piece of nonsense but it is a real example of morale.

I've also had talks with a couple of other first-class Captains lately. The spirit among all these Captains and younger officers is magnificent. There is only one place they want to be and that is within range of the enemies' guns. And they are all determined to get there somehow. Well, it's grand it should be so.

I am glad you have taken our naval pictures to your new flat. There is something reassuring about *Nelson* and *St. Vincent* and the battles of the past – especially if one has read one's history and knows that once we were the sole opponent to the might of Spain (Elizabeth) and once to Napoleon (Pitt – not George III). And here we are again facing the whole of the world.

Tonight the BBC told me 50 USA destroyers are on their way. Cash and carry, but all the same a bigger triumph than Italy coming in on the side of Germany, believe me. It will take some laughing off on Goebbels' part.

I love you. You are being splendid.

21
'Everyone was in the highest of spirits when action was to be joined.'

HMS *Manchester*	Northern Patrol
1940 to 1941	Mediterranean.
	Battle of Spartivento

HMS *Manchester, Tuesday, 10 September 1940*

... My darling, was I in a state! Jacko's message came in the middle of dinner – and of course I had to say it was nothing. You were safe but the block of flats had been hit. You see all the stewards were listening and I had to say 'One must expect that sort of thing' and sit out the dinner.

10 p.m. Wednesday, 11 September Your telegram of yester-day midday has just arrived – 36 hours on the way! I got Jacko at once. Direct to Admiralty. He's on duty tonight. He says you and his Joy left for Hereford in Jaggy this afternoon to go to her folk. That takes a big load off my mind. He said the Fire Brigade dug Jaggy out and put the hoses over her, but it'll be a week or more before anyone will know if the building is safe, much less habitable, because naturally no light, gas or water.

I'm dying to hear from you but if a telegram takes 36 hours what about a letter?

Thursday, 12 September So the King has had one in Buckingham Palace too! Well, it's good that everybody should know that *no one* is exempt from these wild bombings. ...

Goering, who had justifiable faith in his *Luftwaffe* and had not yet learned the extraordinary 'pig-headedness' of the British character in general and the tough jaunty Cockneys in particular, was convinced that London could be isolated from the rest of the country, by intensive bombing. Certain vital War, scientific and industrial departments were wisely shifted to places of greater safety but the Government remained in Westminster, the War Office, Air Ministry and Admiralty in Whitehall and Nelson on his column in Trafalgar Square with lions at his feet and pigeons round his head. And when the King and Queen were not visiting devastated ports or cities they were at their post in Buckingham Palace.

If I had been born and bred in Britain I might have taken the stubborn tenacity of the average man and woman for granted. As it was, I found in the civilians under dire stress the spirit Bertie appreciated most in his sailors, the ability to mock at a bad moment. Swan Court was struck at 4 p.m. by a tip-and-run raider jettisoning his load after an abortive dart at the Power Station. I was reading my South African mail when everything happened at once. The Alert, the roar of a low-flying bomber and a noise like an express train in a tunnel as high explosive gutted the lift-shaft alongside my penthouse. The wall swelled, cracked and settled back but *Nelson* and *St. Vincent* were not dislodged. I was, however, and as a fire-engine clanged down the King's Road I dashed on to the landing slap into the arms of a middle-aged lady in a dressing-gown and curlers. Smoke and the dust of disintegrated masonry poured up the lift-shaft.

'The fire escape's over there,' gasped the lady in curlers. 'Let's dash for it! The bastards caught me in my bath. I knew they would sooner or later – but at tea-time! That's *too* much!'

Bertie was on Northern Patrol and anti-invasion from the Norwegian coast. The *Manchester* was based on the Humber at Immingham.

HMS *Manchester, Sunday, 15 September*

... Here we are watching and waiting and 'ready aye ready'. We all hope that Hitler will really have a go at us. I heard on the 9 o'clock News tonight that 165 enemy bombers had been shot down and once more the RAF had given the coast ports a hell of a doing. I have no fear of the outcome of this air battle.

After ten days of blissfully unreal peace in Herefordshire

bordering on Shropshire and the Welsh Hills, I went to Marion's Ruislip bungalow and resumed part-time WVS work in London with Alice Hopkinson whose husband Henry was now at the Foreign Office. She was driving a mobile canteen to the East End Docklands where Herman Goering had done some devastating 'slum clearance'. We served hot dinner to the dockies on the wharf in the Albert Dock. Most of them were homeless, tenements gutted, their eating-houses blitzed, yet they didn't grumble at unloading the battered ships that had evaded the U-boats to bring vital cargoes to beleaguered Britain. They called me 'Gracie Fields', but though I could laugh with them I failed them when it came to singing. For their part, they increased my respect for London.

My Swan Court flat was a liability with no amenities likely to be restored, so I gave it up. *Nelson, St. Vincent* and the 'battles long ago' found themselves protecting Marion, who welcomed them on her bare bungalow walls.

'They'll be hard-worked. We're rather near Northolt.'

I spread our Turkish rugs on her polished floor.

'What about Glaxo's?'

'We got a landmine two days ago – in the only place it could do no harm.' She chuckled. 'Straight through the Women's Loo – and not a girl caught with her pants down!'

We went about our respective business by day and slept in the garden shelter with Fritz when the Warning sounded. Sometimes we lingered outside it in the autumn chill to watch the impressive magnificence of the 'fireworks' – star-shells, flares, searchlights, the flash of ack-ack and tracer.

'There's a new instrument in the orchestra,' I said. 'That barking gun.'

'Our anti-aircraft defences have been strengthened.'

Early in October Joy Borrett got through to me at Marion's during a lull.

'Listen, Joy, I'm at Bedford now, with Uncle Noel Symonds and Aunt Mabel. I've brought Daphne with me as it's time that child went to a good school. Jack stays at the

210

Admiralty but commutes here for 24 hours each week – no, don't interrupt, we may be cut off by a Warning any minute. The point is our WVS Citizens' Advice Bureau needs help. We're flooded with London, Midland and Dover evacuees – all with problems, lost relatives, lost homes, wage-earners killed, God knows what not all. Can you come here for a bit and help out? You can p.g. with Aunt Mabel. When? As soon as possible. Jack mentioned the idea to Bertie on a direct line. Yes, Bertie reckons it's your duty. Try to make it, *please*! Why not tomorrow?'

'It's a plot,' I said to Marion in the shelter afterwards. 'A well-presented case to get me out of London.'

'It's an SOS, Joy-Joy – on several levels. You'll be back. In the meantime Unk has plenty besides your safety to worry about. Give him a breather.'

HMS *Manchester Wednesday, 9 October 1940*

... Before I settle in to a couple of busy hours with my papers I must write you a word – on my birthday.

It's very much a wartime birthday. There's a gale blowing like hell – you know how it can blow here! – but we are at anchor with steam up.

A year ago, in the *Calcutta,* my birthday was the worst night of the War for me. A gale, blinding rain and the whole night in the middle of a convoy of 27 ships, all with no lights. I couldn't get out of them without a collision and had to go with them as best I could right past the Humber at midnight, until daylight at last let me get clear and make for the Humber again. But last night was grand. I had a telegram from you followed by your letter of 4 October after doing your salvage and seeing Mr. West at Gieves in Bond Street. So all my naval gear stored there went when Gieves caught it! Well, I hope to get compensation on *that,* at all events. Then I had a long combined letter from Dorothy and Norman who are taking the Liverpool Blitz in their stride, and a very admirable one from my old mother in Heswall.

One must be a fatalist these days, but not a stupid one.

There's no need to feel it necessary to *test* the extent of fear and courage. Courage and fear are funny things and I am unable, and somewhat unwilling, to think about them, much less analyse them. I am a great believer in 'playing the rules' and then, if there's something coming with one's number on it, that's that.

We were bombed objectively and not haphazardly for some three weeks in the Norwegian show, and before that in the *Calcutta*. Sometimes we could shoot back, sometimes not. We got tired and sleepless and rather bored. A few got windy. Not many. Moving about in command of a ship with no lights in pitch darkness and storm is, to my mind, much more alarming.

Our gear stored at Portsmouth! Well there it is – or rather was. When things break loose like this we must be satisfied if we get out with a victory and a whole skin. If we lose all our belongings we are companions with millions of others and can probably afford it better. In any case, my sweetie, I'd rather be penniless with you than lolling in the lap of luxury and safety with anyone else in the world.

Yesterday at 8.0 a.m. I heard on the BBC that Jack Tovey* was taking over Commander-in-Chief Home Fleet. It's a real breath of fresh air, approved by everyone who knows him. He'll stand up to anyone – including Winston! It's given us all a great kick.

By the way did you rescue my King's Medal – the gold one? (That sounds like Piet writing.) You used to keep it with your jewels. It's one of the few possessions I treasure.

I enjoy your letters so much. They keep me in touch with ideas other than ships and things and you write so graphically. Your description of your night at Bax's is wonderful, even if it made me shudder as much as laugh. It's going into my diary. Bax putting out incendiaries with a wet bridge cloth, the *Götterdämmerung* record at full strength to drown the other noises, and all of you rushing round with

---

* Later Admiral of the Fleet, Lord Tovey.

buckets of sand and a hose pipe till the Fire Brigade showed up. . . .

By the end of October, Greece had defied Italy's ultimatum and was at War with the Axis Powers. Bertie wrote on 30 October. 'My dear – our *only* Ally in the world! I can't keep my mind off our Greek friends and only hope poor beautiful Greece will not be overrun. There are only six million of them, they have damned few guns, tanks or aircraft, yet they are prepared to back us winning in the long run and fight for their liberty and for democracy and the old ideals of being able to say what you think. No country will fight unless she believes there is a chance of winning and the Greeks are shrewd and cosmopolitan. It's a magnificent gesture on Greece's part. If only we can really help her! We shall be hard put to do so. I wonder if the Italians will take that savage mountain road via Koriza from Jannina? Remember when Piet, you and I took it from Albania to Patras? What a journey!'

Within hours of opening his letter I heard his voice on the telephone and two days later I was with him. The mud-flats, railway lines and chimney pots were no more beautiful than they had been, the snatched hours together fewer, if anything, but for a week we were able to see each other. There was no question of my going on board, but sometimes Able Dog Shrapnel joined us for a walk, as French and exuberant as ever, the terror of the seabirds. Leading Cat Leslie was expecting again, 'probably a red-haired Scot', said Bertie. 'One thing's sure, the kittens will be brought up real seaman-like, to quote Corney.'

The kittens were born in the Mediterranean, for when the *Manchester* left the Humber she headed for Gibraltar to join Admiral Somerville's Force H.

23 November 1940

. . . It is most unlikely that you'll hear from me for some weeks after this. Nor I from you.

We live on our toes here. I find my fellow Captains in

great heart and a tremendous spirit in all the ships. Everybody swears by A.B.C.*

Saw James Somerville again and he sent you his love. He's in crashing form.

My new Admiral, Lancelot E. Holland, is most invigorating. Such fun and so cultivated, has a mind sharp as a razor and deep. Not fussy. The fussy ones are those who doubt their capacity. L. E. Holland is arrogant and intelligent. A beautiful combination. I know so many who use arrogance to hide a lack of intelligence.

We are busy day and night. It is right that we should be. . . .

No wonder they were all 'on their toes' for the 18th Cruiser Squadron in company with Force H was preparing to escort a large and vital convoy of soldiers, airmen and supplies through the Mediterranean to Alexandria in readiness for General Wavell's first great Desert Offensive. My war-horse clearly 'scented the battle from afar', and when Jack Borrett telephoned Joy from the Admiralty one evening at the end of November he gave her a cryptic message for me.

'Congratulate Bertie's Joy on a jolly good show! The enemy turned tail and fled and couldn't be seen for smoke!'

The following day the BBC elaborated, but of course no ships were named. A numerically superior force of Italian cruisers, destroyers and battleships had been engaged by the Royal Navy off Cape Spartivento and had been put to flight with two of their cruisers on fire and many ships damaged. The British Force had sustained no casualities. Thirty-four years later, in 1974, I came upon a faded roneoed report of the NAVAL ACTION OFF CAPE SPARTIVENTO, SARDINIA, 27 NOVEMBER 1940. It was held together by a rusted pin and was signed by H. A. Packer, Flag Captain and Chief of Staff to Vice-Admiral L. E. Holland. Even without the signature

---

* Admiral Sir Andrew B. Cunningham, Commander-in-Chief Mediterranean Fleet.

I would have recognized characteristic remarks as Bertie's. Each paragraph was numbered. Many were purely technical, so I have recorded only part of a document that is now a fragment of naval history.

SECRET No. 0191/588, HMS *Manchester*, 4 December 1940

Sir,
I have the honour to report that HMS *Manchester*, flying the flag of Vice-Admiral Commanding, 18th Cruiser Squadron, was in action with Italian naval forces to the south of Sardinia on 27 November 1940.

2. Since the conduct of the battle is being covered by the Vice-Admiral's report, the remarks below are mainly confined to points of interest relating to HMS *Manchester*.

3. The Squadron consisted of MANCHESTER, NEWCASTLE, SOUTHAMPTON and SHEFFIELD, formed on a line of bearing of 075°, with BERWICK some way back on the eastern flank, NEWCASTLE had not taken up her station when the action started. ... MANCHESTER had no difficulty in maintaining 30 knots with paravanes streamed, and could have increased speed by 15 revolutions. ...

4. Smoke was sighted to the northward by the masthead-man at 12.01 and shortly afterwards masts were sighted and reported at 12.03. Visibility was very good and, with the sun behind, the light was in our favour.

5. The composition of the enemy forces was difficult to determine, but it was evident that forces of cruisers and destroyers were approaching on westerly and south-westerly courses.

6. ... At 12.21 MANCHESTER opened fire on Target No. 1. This was the right hand cruiser of the left hand group. ...

7. At 12.36 Target No. 3 was obviously under fire from other ships of the Squadron and fire was shifted to Target No. 2. This was the left hand cruiser of the right hand group. This ship was altering away under smoke and then altering back, and was a poor target.

8. At 12.41 Target No. 3 was engaged. This was a destroyer . . . laying a smoke screen.

Many straddles were obtained and at one time the range was down to 1,500 yards. When it was seen that the destroyer was being engaged by other ships of the Squadron, fire was shifted once more to the right hand group of cruisers who had been firing with accuracy at MANCHESTER while being engaged by BERWICK only. Two of those cruisers were almost continually enveloped in smoke and were only firing from their after guns and this very slowly.

9. At 12.46 Target No. 4 was engaged. This was a cruiser belonging to the right hand group . . . MANCHESTER'S fire was heavy and accurate and at about 12.54 she was seen to be heavily on fire aft. She altered course and was eventually hidden in smoke.

11. At 13.01 enemy heavy ships were sighted approaching end on. . . . From their size and top hamper it was evident that these were heavier ships than any yet sighted and I had no hesitation in reporting them as battleships. This was confirmed when they opened fire. . . . The splashes were clearly made by heavy shell and were very much bigger than anything yet seen.

12. ENEMY FIRE. The enemy fire was accurate at the beginning of the action and MANCHESTER was straddled for range repeatedly. . . . Salvoes appeared to be mostly short, but occasionally they would creep up to hitting range.

13. AVOIDING ACTION. Full advantage was taken by MANCHESTER of the well-known difficulty of keeping correct line on an end on target when zig-zagging. . . . I have little doubt that MANCHESTER would have been hit several times if the ship had not zig-zagged when end on.

16. TROOPS TAKING PASSAGE. The 35 officers and 623 other ranks of the Army and RAF taking passage were dispersed between decks throughout the ship. All bathrooms were filled with troops. Their behaviour throughout was excellent and they were most enthusiastic about their unique experience, which they

thoroughly enjoyed. Two RAF Ratings formed part of 'A' magazine crew throughout the action. A number of officers and men were formed into willing parties to transfer ammunition from 'X' and 'Y' Turrets to 'A' and 'B' after the action.

It was not pleasant to contemplate what the result would have been had the ship been hit. I am glad to say the situation was accepted philosophically by all concerned as merely another risk of War.

18. Everyone on board was in the highest of spirits when it was apparent that action was to be joined. During the action I was delighted to note the calm and unruffled manner in which all on the Bridge carried out their duties in spite of enemy salvoes falling round the ship and the noise of shell passing over, and it is reported to me that this admirable bearing of the ship's company prevailed throughout the ship.

There was a hearty cheer ... when, as the first 6-inch salvo was fired, the silk Ensign presented by the City of Manchester was hoisted at the masthead.

20. AMMUNITION STOWAGE. I wish to bring to your notice that the foremost turrets fired many more rounds than the after turrets.

This is an experience common to many, if not all, of HM ships in action, both in this War and the last, and I am prepared to prophesy that it is a situation which is likely to continue. I suggest therefore that it is logical and necessary for the allowance and stowage of ammunition for the forward turrets of British warships to be increased, possibly at the expense of the after turrets.

I have the honour to be, Sir, Your obedient servant H. A. Packer

CAPTAIN

In Bertie's personal log he noted that: 'Just before the action started Able Dog Shrapnel carried out a quick tour of inspection of the ship, starting with me on the Bridge. He didn't mind the guns firing. 'Nothing after Dunkirk!' he said. Leslie, with British *sang-froid*, gave birth to yet another family in the boiler-room.'

The convoy got through to Alexandria two minutes late.

In Bedford I opened a cable from Alexandria dated 3 December 1940.

WE ARE ALL WELL AND HAPPY GOOD SHOW HOPE YOU ARE BEST LOVE UNKIE PACKER, NO. 101 CENSOR

On 10 December there was a follow-up. SANS ORIGIN

ALL BEST LOVE VERY MUCH ALIVE AND KICKING, PACKER, NO. 120 CENSOR

Jack Borrett laughed when I showed him the cable.

'You might have him back for Christmas. Just a chance. He's due for a month's leave sometime soon.'

That same evening I received a very unexpected telephone call from London.

'Joy, old girl, what about meeting me in London tomorrow? I've just arrived from Cape Town.'

My surgeon brother, Norman, now a Major in the South African Medical Corps, had been sent to England to study the methods of the famous plastic surgeons, Gillies and McIndoe, who were making new faces and hands for burned young airmen and other victims of battle and blitz. I found that Norman would be working out of London during the week and would be homeless on weekends.

That settled it. I went to see our indomitable old friend Gladys Hooper from Shanghai and Wei Hai Wei, who was living in a spacious flat in Bayswater which she had taken after the Japanese occupation of Shanghai. Her two daughters were also in England with their husbands. Sheila,* the younger, was driving her own car in the transport pool assigned to Fighting French Officers under General de Gaulle. Her husband, Lieutenant-Commander John Boteler, RN, was at the Admiralty.

'My dear Joy,' said Gladys. 'Of course you want to come back to London. I'm terrified whenever the sirens wail, but I wouldn't miss a moment of it.'

---

* Now Madame Pierre Fourcaud.

She whisked me into a taxi. Blitz or no blitz, London's taxis were still on the job.

'Number Eleven King Street, St. James's,' she told the driver, and turned to me as she sank somewhat heavily into her seat. 'It's just the place. It's where we China people always stayed when we came back to London. Handy for everywhere, full service in your flat – and it has atmosphere. Edwardian.'

A man opened the massive door. His saturnine face broke into a smile and his squint increased slightly with pleased surprise.

'Mrs. Hooper!'

'Frederick! Still going strong?'

'Me and Cyril too. And Ella and Kate and the cook.'

'I can't believe it's true.' She introduced me and surged into the marble hall. 'Now what about a flat for my friend, Mrs. Packer? By the week, of course.'

Frederick showed us into a second-floor suite furnished with antiques – not too many. There was a sitting-room with a divan which could be used as a bed and a double room with bath. It looked across King Street to the bombed Prince of Wales Theatre and Boodles Club disembowelled by high explosive. There were Pruniers in St. James's Street, and St. James's Palace and Park all within a stone's throw. Next door, and sharing a wall with Number Eleven, were Christie's Auction Rooms.

'And of all things an open fireplace – a real one!'

'Of course,' said Frederick with a smug glance at the full coal-scuttle.

So it was settled.

Joy's Aunt Mabel found someone to take my place in the Bedford Citizens' Advice Bureau and Uncle Noel, a distinguished House Master of Bedford College, long since retired but still a wise disciplinarian, said sternly, 'What will your husband say to this? London again.'

'He'll understand, now my brother's going to be based on London for a bit.'

'Well I hope you're right. But if you change your mind or need a refuge, don't forget us, We'll find a corner for you.'

It was good to be back where things were happening – too much at times – but London still remained the strong heart of the Commonwealth of Nations and the base of the occupied countries who were prepared to continue the fight. I rejoined Alice Hopkinson's mobile canteen.

Philip Rhodes had given up his house in South Audley Street, and he now wore the three gold stripes of a Commander RN. He was frequently away on mysterious missions and when he returned he often took a bachelor flat in Number Eleven. So did my mother's step-brother, Colin Bayne-Marais, a tall handsome fair man who had been South African Minister to France at the time of her collapse and was now Minister to Fighting France and the Governments in Exile of the Low Countries established in London.

Sheila and John Boteler occupied the suite next to me and Norman was my regular weekend lodger.

John Godfrey was living quite near St. James's in the luxurious apartment in Curzon Street which had been occupied in World War One by his famous predecessor, Admiral 'Blinker' Hall, Director of Naval Intelligence. It was full of strange devices and recorders and when I dined there it was like going into a spy-story.

One evening when a few of us were in my flat Philip Rhodes introduced us to a thin elegant young woman who had been driving military transport in France and Dunkirk and who was now working in his Department of Naval Intelligence. Her name was Elspeth and in 1944 she and Philip were married.

The *Manchester* returned to Scapa Flow and the bitter cold Northern Patrol. No Christmas leave was given and Norman and I celebrated 25 December 1940 alone at Number Eleven.

It was a strange night. *Quiet*. No raid! No church bells either. For 24 hours there was peace.

In the New Year Bertie was summoned to the Admiralty to discuss various matters. His business took a week which ended with a grand farewell party at the Café de Paris for Norman, who was standing by to join a convoy to South Africa, and for Jack Borrett who had been appointed in command of a cruiser bound for Madagascar. 'Snake Hips' Johnson and his Negro Jazz Band excelled themselves for the last time, so did the cabaret girls. It was a happy and hilarious evening. Next night a basket of 'Molotov cocktails' was received by the Café de Paris at midnight.

Bertie had ascertained that the *Manchester* would go into dry dock in Newcastle for a much needed refit. 'About two and a half months,' he told me. 'After that we'll most likely go out into the oceans. Somehow we must get you home to South Africa. Colin may be able to help.'

So that was our New Year resolution.

'Hood *is avenged and 50 per cent of Hitler's battle-fleet destroyed.'*

HMS *Manchester*   Arctic Circle and *Bismarck* Hunt
HMS *Excellent*   Portsmouth
1941 to 1942

COLIN helped. Even so, when we had explained our situation, the Director of Transport at South Africa House said: 'Captain Packer, you of all people must know only too well that the Battle of the Atlantic is on, and what that means in shipping losses. But if I can get your wife a passage, I will. She'll need to be at 48 hours' notice, and it must be understood that she goes *for the duration*. Now give me an address where I can find Mrs. Packer.'

Bertie gave him the name of an hotel in Newcastle-on-Tyne.

I wrote to Mother and Piet with my usual optimism. Peter's reply was even more optimistic. 'How wonderful! Do bring Jaggy out if you possibly can as the roads here are marvellous. It would be nice to have the car as well as you to be proud of. Arend is teaching me to drive. He has got over the habit of keeping the door open ready to jump for his life as he did when he taught you. . . .'

On the way to Newcastle we stopped off for two days at Liverpool to see Dorothy and Norman and Bertie's mother in her hotel at Heswall.

'She's had pneumonia,' said Norman, 'but you know what she is. She won't even discuss it.'

Dorothy smiled. 'And she refuses to move from her room when the Alert sounds. She says she's not going to be pushed around by that madman, *Schickelgruber*.'

When the time came for the old lady to bid her son goodbye she rose painfully from her chair by the fireside. She didn't falter as she embraced him, just said, 'God bless you, my son, and keep you safe.'

It was snowing hard when we reached Tyneside. The river was a shining guide to the dockyards and every day mobile smoke-belchers trundled round the area polluting the air with an oily artificial fog, a smoke-screen which concealed the ships from the raiders and – unfortunately – the raiders from the anti-aircraft batteries.

The *Luftwaffe* often called Bertie from his bed to attend to the safety of his ship immobilized in the dry dock.

One day he allowed me to go on board with him.

'She reminds me of the first time I ever saw the *Warspite*,' I said.

'Yes, before you went home to have Peter. Ships aren't at their most glamorous in dockyard hands.'

Stripped, unkempt, cluttered with weird paraphernalia, and echoing with the metallic shriek of riveters, the banging of hammers and noises beyond my ken, she looked and sounded to me as if she wouldn't be ready for sea for months.

'She will,' said Bertie. 'Three weeks today if she keeps to her schedule. 10 April.'

Shrapnel came charging along to greet his Captain and followed us to Bertie's quarters with his usual exuberance.

'He looks in splendid shape,' I said.

Bertie laughed. 'You should have seen him in Scapa! I court martialled him in the dinner hour in the presence of the ship's company.' He rummaged in a drawer of his desk. 'Here are his papers and the three charges.'

I read them ... 'For that he, Shrapnel, Able Dog First Class, Official Number 752, belonging to His Majesty's Ship *Manchester*, then being a dog subject to the Naval Discipline Act, did, on the eighth day of January, 1941, fight with Leading Cat Leslie, Official Number 751, also of His Majesty's Ship *Manchester*, on the Island of Flotta at Scapa Flow. ... Did improperly leave His Majesty's Ship *Manchester* thereby remaining absent without leave 48 hours ...

was guilty of an act to the prejudice of good order and naval discipline in returning on board the said Ship with his coat in a filthy condition, thereby bringing discredit on His Majesty's canine uniform.'

I patted Shrapnel. 'Good heavens! What was the sentence?'

'He was demoted to Ordinary Dog. When Admiral Holland saw the papers and the findings he broke into verse. I read the poem to the ship's company, but afterwards I told my Admiral that, with all respect, his poem could only be described as doggerel. So you see how ridiculously we amuse ourselves when we're out in the grey, not in active pursuit of the enemy.'

I followed him between decks to Leading-Cat Leslie's billet, and he showed me four miniature hammocks and one slightly larger neatly stowed away.

'The sailors made them for Leslie and her kittens and, believe it or not, taught them to sleep in them.'

Leading Cat Leslie appeared and snaked, purring, round my ankles, sleek and well-groomed, her kittens tagging along.

Bertie lifted one tiny black fellow with a white star on his forehead and put him in my hands.

'That's Sparty. He was born with his brothers and sisters while our guns were firing at the Italian fleet at Spartivento. He has no hammock.'

'Why ever not?'

'Corney decreed that Sparty was to be the Captain's personal rodent operative – that's the professional term for rat-catcher – so Sparty occupies the box you saw in my cabin.'

The *Manchester* kept to her schedule. Her full ship's company and some new officers were due to rejoin her and Bertie said I was to go back to London on 10 April.

On the morning of 9 April, while he was on board I received a wire from Colin.

ALL WELL BE ON STANDBY NEXT WEEK GOOD LUCK COLIN

So my passage to Cape Town had been arranged, and

maybe the *Manchester* would find herself in the South Atlantic! I could hardly wait to tell Bertie.

When he came back at dusk I ran out to meet him.

'I'll be with Piet and Mummy before long! Here's the wire.'

He didn't say anything, just went up to our room with his arm in mine. He shut the door and read the wire thoughtfully.

'Joy-Joy, I've had a note too. This morning.'

He handed me a small sheet of Admiralty notepaper.

'. . . I have much pleasure in informing you that the First Lord has approved your appointment to *Excellent* in command, in charge of the Gunnery School, Portsmouth, to date 15 June 1941'. It was signed by the Naval Secretary to the First Sea Lord.

'Whaley! That's a shore job! Will you be in the *Manchester* till June?'

'Yes. Then Whaley for perhaps a year, even 18 months. We could take a house somewhere near Fareham—'

'I could go home first and bring Piet back with me. We'll be together again.'

'You've forgotten something. If you go it's *for the duration*. That was a condition.'

After a while he said: 'This time I can't put any pressures on you. It's up to you to decide where you're needed most.'

That night Tyneside suffered a big raid. I left for the long drive back to London early next morning, my problem unsolved.

Philip Rhodes met me at Number Eleven and his first words made up my mind for me.

'So you won't be going to South Africa after all.'

'How do you know?'

'Colin told me you'd got a passage. Then I heard from John Godfrey that Bertie was going as Captain of Whaley, so I told Colin you'd be sure to cancel. Piet will naturally want to come back.'

Suddenly everything seemed simple.

Colin reckoned it could be arranged.

Bertie received my wire at Rosyth.

... I have been worrying about you so much and you can imagine how glad I was this morning to get your telegram to say you reckoned South Africa should be off. I just couldn't bear it if I were at Whaley and you in South Africa and not able to get back. And if we can get Piet back then the sun will shine.

Darling ... for the first time since I left you I am easier in my mind and heart. The thought of being ashore without you made me absolutely sick in the stomach.

Now I am looking forward to Whaley!

Early on Wednesday, 16 April, I was overjoyed to get a cable from Cape Town 'EXPECT MAKE SATISFACTORY ARRANGEMENT SEND PETER LOVE PETERSEN'

'It sounds as if everything's going to be all right,' I said to Bertie, who telephoned me from Rosyth that evening.

That night all hell broke loose.

Friday, 18 April 1941

... What a hell of a time you must have had! It shakes me to the core to think you should have to 'take it' without me.

After telephoning you on Wednesday night my wireless, curse its breath, told me on Thursday morning that London had had the biggest air raid of the War and that amongst other places Christie's had been totally destroyed. As that is next door to you I just gasped and gasped and my belly played squirrels, and until this morning, when the Lord and the GPO be praised, I got your telegram, the BBC went on and on about this 'Reprisal Raid' until I felt like an old rabbit skin the dog had taken out for the day.

But since getting your wire I am a different man, especially when I got another to say that, after weekending with Marion, you were moving back to Bedford and that you'd cabled to Mum to keep Piet. He *is* happy at 'Tees Lodge' and with his friends. His letters prove it.

Please give my love to Joy B. whose family are always stepping in to help.

Thank God you are safe, darling. I feel all different to-night now that I know you are unharmed. . . .

Weekending with Marion was a noisy affair as London took another blasting the following Saturday. But sleeping in her shelter was nothing new and every now and again we popped out like rabbits and smelt the spring freshness of her garden and watched the firework display with wonder at its glory and its terror.

'Unkie says the Aurora Borealis looks like that.' I said.

'Never mind the Northern Lights now,' she said. 'Come, Fritz! Joy-Joy you must write your letter to your Mother and Piet.'

In Marion's Shelter, Ruislip, 9.40 p.m. Saturday, 19 April 1941

My darlingest Mummy,
When you read this letter you and Piet will know that I am 'well and happy'. The enemy raiders are throbbing overhead but we are very snugly settled for the night, Marion and I and her dachshund, Fritz, who always lifts up his voice and sings when he hears the Alert or the All Clear.

Well, to go back to Wednesday night and Number Eleven King Street. The Alert sounded during the 9 o'clock News. . . . Earlier in the evening I had been at a cocktail party in the Boteler's flat on my floor – Norman knows it well. They were celebrating their seventh anniversary. Sheila B. drives for the Free French and is a grand girl. They went out later to Hungaria for dinner and were not in at about 11 when things really hotted up.

Cyril, the comical little porter-butler-and-everything-else, was on fire-watch duty on the roof. I'd gone to bed with my siren-suit over my pyjamas and was tucked up with a book. But sleep was out of the question. The blast from the anti-aircraft barrage kept billowing the black-out curtains in, and bombs seemed to be raining down. I went to the first floor landing where I found the Manageress, Miss Hillsom, and the two maids (Kate and Ellen), each over 70, and Miss Hutton the only other resident. She is very lame. The cook, who is old and crippled, was in her room in bed, undisturbed because she is stone deaf. Cyril was like a jack-in-the-box, *Whoooosh!* and he'd dart on to the roof and pop back to shout 'That was the Piccadilly Hotel and there's a gas main blazing by the Ritz!' *Wheeeee!* 'That was Victoria! A huge blaze started there—' and so on.

Presently John and Sheila and another young naval officer, 'Cocky' Cockburn, dashed in and shouted to me to come to their flat. At the same time there was a long screaming noise and *Crash!* Every window blew in. I was lying on my face on the stairs next to Miss Hillsom, pinned down by the window frame and covered by shattered glass. John and 'Cocky' fished us out and cleared the stairs. There was another *whoooosh* and the building reeled. Cyril shouted 'Christie's is on fire!' (Christie's shares a wall with Number Eleven and Sheila's flat.)

The bomb must have been a heavy oil fire-bomb because the place was a raging inferno in no time. Cookie, who had been blown out of bed, swooned and was revived with whisky. The two old maids were stunned and when I asked if they were all right they said, quietly and politely, 'Yes, thank you, madam.' Miss Hillsom's only thought was to rescue her canary, which she did. John said, 'Get what you can out of your flats now. In half an hour it'll be too late.'

We seized armfuls of our belongings and dumped them on the pavement or just chucked whole drawers out of the windows. 'Cocky' and I practically carried poor Cookie to the nearest shelter and then went back for Miss Hutton. It wasn't far to the shelter – about 100 yards – but it seemed an eternity.

What a sight! Christie's was a shell with a furnace roaring inside it, so lurid you couldn't look at it for more than a second at a time. The crackle and roar was terrific, the sky dull red, a roof of flying sparks. Most of Piccadilly and St. James's were on fire.

We then dashed to the garage in Duke Street to get out

Sheila's and my car before it was too late. John B. and 'Cocky' never stopped working, directing us all and taking complete charge. They were *magnificent*.

At last a beautiful rosy dawn broke and the All Clear sounded as the raiders made for home. There was a prowling taxi (how brave they are, these taxi drivers!) to take the old maids and Miss Hutton to the First Aid and Rest Centre.

We others drove our salved stuff to Gladys Hooper's flat in Bayswater, passing craters and wreckage everywhere. She had spent most of her time waiting for her last moment to come. When she saw us she was horrified at our condition – pitch black and red-eyed. Anyway we scrubbed ourselves and had coffee and sausages and went to bed. It was 6 a.m. At 9 I was up and cabling you and sending Unkie a wire. When I went to the Post Office it wasn't there – just a gigantic crater with a man digging in it.

'Where's the Post Office gone?' I asked, meaning where was it operating from. He laughed and said: 'Down the 'ole, Miss.'

When I got to Number Eleven the looters had already been through what was left of it.

Cyril and Frederick and old Cookie and the maids have lost everything. Cyril was a hero throughout. He was quite regardless of his own safety. The last I saw of him was going away in a taxi with his few belongings in an old hat-box – his total salvage. He peered out and grinned and said 'Goodbye, Mrs. Packer. I'm off to Berlin to see 'itler about this 'ere!' Pointing to King Street. Number Eleven was Cyril and Frederick's home and whole life for 30 years. They are First War pensioners.

In Berlin they are rejoicing and the flags are in the streets to celebrate. In London the dead and injured are being dragged from under the rubble in thousands.

Well, it's over now. But that night I knew what Hitler meant to do to us in this Island and realized that all my sentiments about Peter must stand aside. He might have come back to find his father at sea and no mother. And *this* is civilization!

I slept Thursday night at Bax's (was to have dined there anyway). He has Bill Mabane and three bomb victims there. They had been at the Ritz on Wednesday night and at 5 a.m. Bax had been outside Number Eleven. He said, 'I watched your place burn, and I said to myself, "Well, either Joy is in there and I can't get her out, or she's some place else and all right"!'

He was shaken but still philosophical.

Heaps and heaps of love – am dead tired and must get some sleep.

Later It was grand getting your understanding cable. Yes, one has to be resigned to many things these days.

The effect of those 'Reprisal Raids' was perverse. Instead of fear and despondency this concentrated devastation of the capital inflamed the wrath of the nation and made the whole country more than ever united and determined to fight on to the end whenever and wherever that might be.

I took Joy's Uncle Noel and Aunt Mabel Symonds at their word and arranged to return to Bedford and the Citizens' Advice Bureau which was once more inundated with the problems of evacuees and missing relations.

But first I went to Portsmouth and arranged to rent a house in Fareham, seven miles from Whale Island. The Captain of HMS *Excellent* and his wife were living there, and it was arranged that in June we should take occupation.

ON 11 May, the *Manchester* was guarding the Northern Approaches to the Atlantic, once more, based on Scapa.

. . . A fine packet of mails to greet me.

Piet is apparently in good form and resigned so perhaps it is as well he should be left in South Africa. My wireless tells me Westminster got it last night. The House of Commons!

Sparty follows Corney like a dog. He is an attractive little animal but unfortunately growing fast. You know what a big lusty chap Corney is with hands like hams. When I said how strange it was to see Sparty following him when he called, he said, 'Oh, that's easy enough, sir, all you've got to do is master 'em early.' Talking as if little Sparty was some great savage beast! I laughed my head off and couldn't tell him why.

Holland has taken over command of the battle cruisers and hoists his flag in the *Hood* tomorrow. We are all heartbroken that he is leaving us. He is a fine Admiral with a marvellous brain and is very human.

13 May How the Hess story must appeal to your journalistic instinct! The whole thing is fantastic beyond belief. Having heard the German version – that he's disappeared, mentally deranged, and jumped out of an aeroplane – on last night's 9 o'clock News, I sent for Coleby, my new Chief Engineer (late assistant Naval Attaché Washington). We discussed it and, said I, 'Next thing we'll hear is that he's arrived in England.' Of course he laughed. But he woke me at midnight to tell me it was so! Whatever the truth of it, it won't rebound to the credit of the Nazis. . . .

Hess, one of Hitler's intimate circle, secretly and on his own initiative, had stolen a *Messerschmidt 110* and, at enormous risk and with great audacity, had flown solo to Scotland and bailed out over Dungavel, the country seat of the Duke of Hamilton, through whom he hoped to negotiate peace terms with Churchill. He had no authority for this action. He was simply obsessed with a desire for peace and believed that if he could obtain favourable terms Hitler would be persuaded to agree. That he failed is history, but in Winston Churchill's *The Second World War, Vol. III*, he wrote: 'Whatever may be the moral guilt of a German who stood near to Hitler, Hess had, in my view, atoned for this by his completely devoted and frantic deed of lunatic benevolence. He came to us at his own free will and, though without authority, had something of the quality of an envoy. He was a medical and not a criminal case and should be so regarded.'

14 May I have a heartbreaking job dealing with my chaps whose homes and families are blasted. The letters they bring me are so brave and so pathetic. Not one complains, but many have lost all they have.

I fear for Dorothy and Norman. Liverpool has had a lousy week according to the news. 70,000 homeless and 3,000 killed and injured. Hull, Portsmouth and Plymouth too. Even Coventry. To starve us they must destroy our ports and win the Battle of the Atlantic.

Much as I dislike your going to London I'm glad you are doing canteen work at the docks with Alice twice a week. A 9d. lunch will be all the more acceptable to the east-enders if served by a pretty girl with a smile on her face.

Sparty, the cat, lives with me. You will laugh but I enjoy seeing him asleep in my chair. The attitudes he takes up are quite astonishing, very graceful, stretched out flat on his back. He is clean and well-behaved but his voice is breaking! *Thursday, 16 May* Once again you will be a sailor's wife for a bit and not hear from your old man of the sea.

At times I feel very low at the thought of leaving my lovely cruiser, but then I get all bucked up again at the thought of living in a house with you. That's how it goes.

Sparty is ill – is sick every time the bell strikes. He crouches on all fours, gives a hiccup and two miaows, and is sick on my carpet. As a change he wees in my bath-slippers which is not his habit when well. I think he has distemper. His sister came to visit him at his sickbed in my cabin, gave two hiccups and was sick on the carpet. At the same moment my man Jeeves asked me if I would like curried oxtail for lunch. I looked through the scuttle and my stomach was queasy and I could only mutter 'For God's sake, Crocker, look at that cat.'

Neville Syfret is relieving Holland as our cruiser Admiral.

Shrapnel has been invited to become a member of the Tail-Waggers' Club. He has personality – quite amazing – features in the *Sporting and Dramatic*!

I am reading Stefan Zweig's *Scott in the Antarctic* in the original German sent me by my Mother. . . . His last letter never fails to move me . . .

On 20 May the *Manchester* was in the Polar regions and

Bertie noted in his log. 'Snow storms for two days. When will spring come? Let alone summer!' On 22 May the *Manchester* and her sister cruiser *Birmingham*, reinforced by *Arethusa*, were ordered to guard the channel between Iceland and the Faroes, for on that day Germany's 'unsinkable' battleship *Bismarck* and the cruiser *Prinz Eugen* had been identified in Bergen Fjord. Instantly the Royal Navy prepared to guard the Atlantic Approaches, North and South. The North Sea was rough with cloud and rain and minimal visibility, but a naval aircraft managed to penetrate Bergen Fjord and reported the German warships gone.

The story of the hunt for the enemy raiders that would have wrought havoc in vital troop and supply convoys if they had got into the Atlantic is superbly told by Ludovic Kennedy in *Pursuit*.* The forces involved in the chase were many and relentless and the outcome of this great epic marked a turning point in the War at sea.

On 24 May the Yeoman of Signals handed Bertie a message that distressed everyone in the *Manchester* very greatly, as indeed it did the whole nation. The battle cruiser, HMS *Hood*, flying the flag of Vice-Admiral L. E. Holland, had blown up at 06.15. Sunk by the *Bismarck* in six minutes.

Bertie was, of course, plotting the action with every signal that came in.

On 26 May his log notes:

Am still very sad because I hear there are only three survivors from Hood *, so my kind clever Holland must be considered lost with his staff whom we all liked so well. And some 1,400 with them. This may seem bathos, but things close at hand affect one too. Little Sparty, my black kitten, born in battle and reared in* Manchester, *got sicker and weaker and yesterday could only just walk. He lay in his box in my sea-cabin and could only still give a feeble movement of his tail when I rubbed him under the ear.*

As I went on to the Bridge, Corney, whom Sparty adored,

---

* See page 12.

came up to me with a face as long as a sea-boot. 'Cat's dead,'
he said and went away. Sparty was wrapped in gay bunting
and, like a sailor should be, was committed to the deep. The
cold green waters of Hvaalfjord have him safe. He was such
a playful little chap and I miss him very much.
26 May No further reports. It must be getting dark. De-
stroyers should be able to shadow during the night. Pray
God we get Bismarck *down and avenge the* Hood.
27 May 4 a.m. The situation is developing beautifully and
classically. 11 a.m. Have just broadcast to the ship's
company that Bismarck *is being heavily engaged by* KGV
and Rodney *and that* Dorsetshire *has been ordered to tor-*
pedo the Bismarck *at close range. A cheer came up the*
hatches from between decks.

This must be the end. Thank the Lord Hood *is avenged*
and 50 per cent of Hitler's battle-fleet destroyed!

Far away in the Mediterranean, the Battle of Crete had
been lost. British warships, under heavy air-attack, were
evacuating British, Greek and Allied troops. Many ships
were damaged and six destroyers and three cruisers were
lost.

One of those cruisers was the *Calcutta*. For many days
and nights officers and men had been without rest and the
weary guns' crews were still at their posts when the enemy
dive bombers made their final attack. The last that was seen
of the 'Lucky *Calcutta*' was her mascot, 'Cocky', the white
cockatoo, like a battle ensign on the masthead. Yet he made
no attempt to fly away. He went down with his ship.

On 5 June Bertie said goodbye to his 'lovely cruiser', and
we spent a wonderful week in Devon at 'Farway', the beautiful Elizabethan manor house of Henry and Alice Hopkinson. I had never seen a grove of lilacs before or magnolia
espaliered against a mellow stone wall, and it seemed forever
since we had known what it was to be in a place of peace and
safety. That soft summer week's dream was a time of heal-
ing for us both.

On 15 June Bertie took command of HMS *Excellent*, the
Gunnery School, and we lived in 'Fareham Croft', a house

with a garden a few miles outside blitzed and battered Portsmouth. By the end of the summer Greece and Crete were overrun and Germany had swept deep into the heart of Soviet Russia. On 7 December the Japanese attack on Pearl Harbour brought America into the War and Japanese troops were landed in North Malaya. On 10 December Admiral Philips, flying his flag in the battleship *Prince of Wales*, took his Squadron close in shore, *without air cover*, to attack the landing forces. The following day we heard Churchill, his voice broken with emotion, broadcasting to the nation that the *Prince of Wales* and the battle cruiser *Repulse* had been sunk by Japanese bombers and torpedo planes.

We were glad when midnight closed the door on 1941.

For the first time in four years we saw the New Year in together. The night was sharp and cold, the garden frost spangled, but our thoughts were far away under the Southern Cross where church bells chimed and the Atlantic and Indian Oceans washed mid-summer shores.

23

'*Of all ships my old* Warspite!'

HMS *Excellent*   Portsmouth and 'Fareham Croft'
HMS *Warspite*   South Atlantic
1942 to 1943

OUR 18 months at Whale Island and 'Fareham Croft' were full of interest. We had friends to stay most weekends and occasionally VIPS. One of our favourite guests was Nancy Glover whose husband Philip – once flag lieutenant at Simon's Town – was not at sea. She was an even more brilliant tennis player than her naval champion husband and, as Nancy Lyle, had captained England's Women's teams in various parts of the world.

To our great pleasure, the King of Greece, now living in London, where the governments of our occupied Allies had their headquarters, honoured us by spending an informal weekend at 'Fareham Croft'. The garden swarmed with detectives who hid behind the hedges kept so carefully clipped by Able Seaman Foot, a gaunt retired pensioner brought back into the Navy for the duration. He was a barber in what he called 'the outside world'.

On Sunday morning we went to church at Whale Island and afterwards Bertie presented the Greek officers and ratings to their King who gave them words of brisk understanding encouragement. I know that Bertie was inwardly as moved as I was, for we could not bear to think of our beautiful friendly Greece once more under foreign domination – even though we fully believed it could only be temporary.

A few days later General de Gaulle paid a brief official visit to Whale Island to review the officers and men of his Fighting French Navy. Bertie told me afterwards that this austere formidable leader had seemed 'remote' with his men.

'He reviewed them and addressed them, but he didn't talk to any of them personally, and it must be hellish for them with their families in occupied France, totally out of touch, never knowing when they'll see them again – if ever.'

Then King George VI came, and the green lawns of Whale Island were vivid in the wintry sun, every bit of brasswork gleamed, and all hearts were lifted in ruined Portsmouth and in Nelson's old flagship *Victory*, which the Admiral used as his headquarters, where she lay in the dry dock, newly painted and polished. His modern offices had been blitzed, but the *Victory* seemed indestructible for she carried within her ancient timbers the magic of her name and that of England's best-loved sailor.

Meanwhile Bertie's *Manchester* had met a 'spot of bother' and been repaired in America where she was overwhelmed with kindness and hospitality. On her return to home waters she put in to Portsmouth for a few days and my husband became quite broody with longing to get back to sea and to grips with the enemy. The day she sailed he brought me a present. A small black kitten with outsize whiskers and a comic white blaze across half his nose.

'Corney persuaded Leslie to send him to you,' he said. 'His father is American and this little chap is named Franklin D.R. ....'

I seized Frankie eagerly and set him on the grass path fringed with Michaelmas daisies in full flower. If a street urchin were suddenly transported into thick jungle he could not have been more astonished than the latest son of Leading Cat Leslie, Chief Rodent Operative of HMS *Manchester*. The evening was still sunny and the spring-sweet grass was dry but Frankie high-stepped as if his paws were on cold wet sand. He sniffed at the tall daisies suspiciously, showed some interest in a mole-run and turned up his nose at the saucer of cow's milk I gave him.

Corney saw that both Frankie and I were puzzled.

'See, madam, the little fellow's never set paw on anything but a hard deck before. He can't make out the feel of grass, sort of.'

Able Seaman Foot removed the cow's milk and returned

237

with another full saucer. 'This is dried milk, sailor's milk, you might say.'

Frankie lapped it up and washed his face. He adapted himself to his new environment quickly but with reservations. He completely ignored the birds that sang among the flowers and trees.

'Ship's cats associate wings with seagulls – too big to tackle. They leave them alone and concentrate on rats and mice,' Bertie said.

Frankie did just that and added the vole family to his conquests.

Ordinary Dog Shrapnel, still smarting no doubt from the indignity of his court martial at Scapa, had seconded himself to the US Navy, so the *Manchester* had regretfully crossed her Free Frenchman, Official Number 752, from the ship's complement.

Then one day in the late summer Bertie brought me a copy of the London *Times* and showed me an official Admiralty communiqué issued at 2.30 p.m. on 14 August 1942.

Naval operations have been taking place in the Western and Central Mediterranean during the past few days. ... These operations have resulted in supplies and reinforcements reaching the fortress of Malta despite very heavy enemy concentrations designed to prevent their passage ... packs of U-boats, large numbers of torpedo-carrying and dive-bombing aircraft and strong forces of E-boats operating in the central narrows. ...

The Board of Admiralty regrets to announce that the cruiser HMS *Manchester*, Captain H. Drew, DSC, RN, was damaged and subsequently sank. Many survivors have been picked up and it is probable that others have reached the Tunisian Coast. ... Next of kin will be informed as soon as possible.

Among those who reached the Tunisian Coast, where he was imprisoned by the Vichy French till our invasion of North Africa, was Commander D. Hammersley Johnston who had served with Bertie in the *Manchester*. He was re-patriated on 24 November to Portsmouth, where his wife, Clare, was waiting for him at 'Fareham Croft'. It was there, with Frankie warm and content on his lap, that he told us the full story of the loss of the 'lovely cruiser' Bertie had left so reluctantly. The postscript was what we might have expected.

'Leslie? She absolutely refused to be saved. She'd never hurt a shipmate in her life, but she scratched and clawed furiously at the young seaman who tried to save her. Nothing would get her out of the boiler-room. You remember she always went there in battle or to have her kittens.'

So leading Cat Leslie First Class, Official Number 751, went down with her ship.

Off South Africa Japanese submarines were active in the Indian Ocean, as were their heavy naval forces in the East Indies and Pacific. Peter and his friends hoped for a 'scrap of some sort'.

Top House, Diocesan College, 18 August 1942

... We've been having a great time. Today we had an inspection of the Cadet Corps. It was good fun. We all march round and bluff ourselves we are soldiers. We, that is 'A' Company, have carbines from 1885 to drill with while the smaller ones in 'B' Company have wooden dummy rifles.

If there is a raid the whole school divides into sections as we do in Cadets with a Corporal over each. I'm in charge of one section with an officer.

The air-raid precautions are rather pathetic. We have been commanded to dig trenches 1 foot 6 inches deep and just wide enough to fit in so we won't get hit by quite so many splinters. These trenches are under the trees so the enemy won't see us and machine gun us.

This is what it said on the notice board concerning them. 'Some boys have lined the bottom of their trenches with leaves and pine-needles to make them comfortable. This is very silly because there are such things as incendiary bombs and to lie on such a combustible bed is pure foolishness.'

Well, I'm jolly sure I wouldn't stay long in my trench or know whether the leaves were burning if an incendiary bomb hit me in the guts! So it seems to me that our ARP* officer has seen our trenches without us in them and hasn't thought about us occupying the place the bomb would want to occupy. It's all quite fun. So let the fireworks begin!

What worries me is that the Russians are doing very well against the Germans. Will they fight us when they have finished with Germany? Let's hope they fight the Japs first.

Gran is getting some marvellous new things for the carpenter's shop. She has got us a lovely grindstone, a new vice about 5 inches across the jaws, and some new files and chisels. I haven't got the pulleys for my lathe yet 'cos of the War.

Among our weekend guests at 'Fareham Croft' was Bax who came as much for naval copy as for golf, tennis and bridge. Fortunately he was a most amusing speaker and was more than willing to give a talk to the sailors on the House of Commons or any other subject and answer the many questions fired at him. He was enthralled with some of the dramatic effects the Gunnery School used to train guns' crews. There was the Dome where an anti-aircraft pom-pom was mounted to shoot down shadow dive-bombers, and the Destroyer Dummy Deck. Of the latter 'night action' scene he wrote:

We watched while a destroyer gun crew was trained under War conditions similar to those in a destroyer at night.

'Action!' barked the instructor. Out went the lights. The deck heaved, the wind shrieked. Willing sailors in the wings hurled pails of water over the gun's crew.

'Enemy sighted!' Star shells flared as through the dark we spotted the shadow that represented a ship. The destroyer

---

* Air-Raid Precautions.

opened fire, the enemy retaliated. Burning iron castings fell upon the deck. . . . The noise of explosions nearly burst my eardrums. The enemy was duly sunk.

The lights went up. The crew dripping with sweat and water, looked at Captain Packer.

'Quite good,' he said. That was all.

On the way to his quarters we came on 15 more sailors peeling potatoes. They looked up but went on with their work. Packer stopped.

'Who is in command of this working party?' he asked. There was no answer. No one was in charge.

'Who is the man with the longest service here?' snapped Packer. A tall rugged fellow stepped forward.

'Didn't you know,' said Packer, 'there is always someone in charge of a working party? If there is no officer or non-commissioned officer then it is the man with the longest service. Why didn't you call your party to attention when your Captain passed? Carry on.'

Ten minutes later he suggested we return by the working party. At the sight of him the oldest serving sailor shouted 'Party'shun!' The Guards couldn't have done better.

'That's more like it. Carry on.'

Afterwards Packer said to me: 'That is a lesson they have to learn. Any time at sea those chaps might find themselves with every officer killed. There's always got to be someone in command.'

He had taught that lesson sharply but had purposely retraced his steps to show there was no hard feeling.

No wonder men like to sail under Bertie Packer.

About this time Noel Coward was preparing to make his fine film of the Royal Navy at War, *In Which We Serve*. It was based upon the exploits of the destroyer, HMS *Kelly*, which had been commanded by his close friend, Lord Louis Mountbatten.

Noel was determined to get every detail authentic and to portray the life of a ship from the day of her launching to the hour of her death on active service. He brought his team-producer, director and effects to Whale Island and received full co-operation from Bertie. He was our house-guest at different times during the production and borrowed gun's crews from HMS *Excellent* for his battle shots, and the Coldstream Guards lent him officers and men for the Dunkirk evacuation scenes. We went to Denham Studios to see the final stages of the production and met Bernard Miles, who was playing the Petty Officer, and John Mills, who was the Ordinary Seaman. Noel himself played the Captain.

Noel's heart and soul had gone into that film. It was his tribute to the Service upon which an Island race depends for her lifeline. His title was derived from the prayer used every day in the Royal Navy.

O Eternal Lord God, who alone spreadest out the heavens, and rulest the raging of the sea. .... Be pleased to receive into Thy Almighty and most gracious protection the persons of us Thy servants, and the Fleet in which we serve. Preserve us from the dangers of the sea and the violence of the enemy; that we may be a safeguard to our most gracious Sovereign ... and a security for such as pass on the seas upon their lawful occasions; that the inhabitants of our Island may live in peace and quietness and serve Thee our God; and that we may return in safety to enjoy the blessings of the land, and the fruits of our labours with a thankful remembrance of Thy mercies, to praise and glorify Thy Name; through Jesus Christ our Lord. Amen.

Early in the New Year of 1942 the severely blitzed King's Theatre in Portsmouth had been rebuilt and was opened once again with variety shows on three successive nights. Tommy Handley, the favourite comedian of that period, was the first guest artiste. The second was Robert Montgomery, the American film star who had played Noel Coward's part in the screen version of *Private Lives*, and the third night was Noel.

Robert Montgomery, who stayed the night at 'Fareham Croft', was a Lieutenant-Commander in the US Navy and Assistant Naval Attaché to the American Embassy in London. But he had left the screen long before his country declared War to drive an American Red Cross ambulance in the Battle of France. His wife had done War work in England and, when she had finally returned to America, she had taken with her several English children including those of the actor-playwright, Emlyn Williams. When I asked him if she was an actress his fine grey eyes turned heavenwards as he said, 'God forbid!'

When he spoke to his Pompey audience he was obviously deeply moved.

'I see your port and how terribly it has suffered, and I see all of you here tonight full of courage and the joy of life – patching up your Theatre, keeping up your hearts and spirits, and I can only tell you that I love you for it.'

Noel too received a warm welcome. He was nervous, which surprised me. 'Anyone would be with a voice like mine,' he said. 'When I open my trap I never have the least idea what noise is coming out!'

We had first seen him at that same Theatre with Gertrude Lawrence in the pre-London tour of *Private Lives* in the early days of our marriage.

In October *In Which We Serve* had its opening night in a West End cinema. It was a very special naval occasion and an enormous success. Bertie wrote to congratulate him and Noel answered his letter.

17 Gerald Road, SW1 – between Bristol and Nottingham
11 October 1942

My dear Bertie,
I can't just say 'thank you' for your letter, because it would be too inadequate. I think you know what it means to me that the Navy should think well of *In Which We Serve* – if they find it good nothing else is of any importance at all.

So now you realize why 'thank you' is inadequate for the things you say in your letter. . . .

My love to Joy. If I don't see you before the tour gets to Portsmouth I'll look forward to doing so then.

Yours,
Noel

A few days later Bertie heard that he was to be appointed Captain of HMS *Warspite*, Flagship of the East Indies Fleet and Admiral Sir James Somerville, the Commander-in-Chief.

'Of all ships, my old *Warspite*!' he said with a sort of wonder when he told me. If there was a scrap *Warspite* would be in it. She was a fighting ship if ever there was one.

Station Hotel, Hull, 18 November 1942
Dear Bertie

... I am both sad and pleased that you are going to sea again – sad because when I come to Portsmouth with the plays in February you won't be there and pleased because when I come to the Far East again, which I shall at the earliest possible moment, I shall make a bee line for you demanding nothing more than every attention, a comfortable cabin and a lot of mangoes.

What will Joy do and where will she go? I, who am going further and further north, salute you.

Love to you both,
Noel

On 21 October Trafalgar Day, Bertie addressed the men of HMS *Excellent*, many of whom were from the occupied countries of Europe.

They had mustered on the lawn and stood at ease as he spoke to them in the autumn light of a brisk fresh morning. He was a forceful and fiery speaker and said what he meant.

Today is the 137th Anniversary of the Battle of Trafalgar, the greatest naval victory we have ever had. It was one of the decisive battles of the world.

By 1805 Napoleon, who had tyrannized Europe, just as Hitler has today, had collected an enormous invasion force in the French Channel Ports to invade this country.

Only our weather-beaten ships stood between him and domination of the world.

On 21 October 1805 Nelson met the combined fleets of

France and Spain and, though heavily outnumbered, shattered them completely. Out of 33 enemy ships of the line, 22 were captured, and the remaining 11 bolted for Cadiz and were there for the rest of the War. Napoleon realized that invasion was off – just as Hitler did in 1940 – and gave the order for his invasion armies to turn about, and off they went to win more great victories in Austria.

But England was safe and able to rally the countries of Europe and finally they defeated Napoleon.

Perhaps the Battle of Britain in 1940 had done for Hitler what Trafalgar did to make an end of Napoleon.

We all know the great Lord Nelson was a remarkable tactician and fighter. He always seemed to know just when and how to strike. Like Drake he was the terror of his enemies. Yet all his life he suffered from the poorest health, and after the wound to his head at the Battle of the Nile he was seldom free from headaches. He was always seasick in bad weather. A year before Trafalgar he wrote 'Always tossed about and always seasick'.

He was a man of very great humanity, far ahead of his time in his treatment of officers and men. 'Brave as a lion and gentle as a lamb' his men said of him affectionately. His sense of duty was tremendous. Duty, as Nelson conceived it, consisted of an intense and passionate patriotism, which had the right to demand any sacrific. *This spirit lives today in our great Service.*

He was straight-thinking and downright. If anyone tried to tell him our enemies were not such bad chaps, Nelson's reply was '*Damn our enemies! Bless our friends. Amen. I am not such a hypocrite as to bless them that hate us, or if a man strike me on the cheek turn the other. No, knock him down, by God!*'

Let us then go forward to our tasks with Nelson's great patriotism, his high sense of duty, his burning spirit and his courage in battle and then indeed we shall be men.

For Bertie the Nelson tradition was very much alive in the crest and motto of his 'old ship', HMS *Warspite*. He longed to take her into battle.

My 18 months of freedom from anxiety were drawing to their close.

In the New Year we said goodbye to Portsmouth and our friends there and to Frankie D. R., who went to live in the Isle of Wight with an old shipmate of Chief Petty Officer Corney who understood cats born with a caul. We spent part of Bertie's short leave with his mother in Heswall, where we saw Dorothy and Norman, and then we took a tiny flat on the eighth floor in Athenaeum Court, Piccadilly, over-looking the wintry Green Park, for Hitler had temporarily decided to ignore London. Many of our friends were at the Admiralty where Bertie spent a great deal of time and was thrilled to find it a hive of activity working up plans for aggressive operations in many different directions. He played golf at Addington with Bax and his 'gang', saw much of John Godfrey, whose Intelligence Department was now fully extended, and of Philip Rhodes and Elspeth. In February he learned that he was to join the *Warspite* in Durban and was to take passage to South Africa in the cruiser *Sussex*, sailing from Scapa Flow.

'Then it won't be the Eastern Fleet?' I guessed.

'One never knows. Things change according to the needs of the time.'

They had already changed. As we had known would probably be the case, shipping was now closed to civilians. My chance of getting to South Africa had come and gone over a year ago. Only personnel required for special War jobs could be considered for transport priority. Every possible vessel had become a troop-ship. The great seaborne armies and supplies were on their way.

'Who on earth would *ask* for me except Piet and Mum?' I said desperately to Bertie.

His face was grimly set. 'I'll do all I can at that end, while you – here – must *make* – somehow manufacture – a job to get yourself to Cape Town. Propaganda is your line. You've been doing it all the War, unpaid and often unconsciously. Now find a wider purpose for your gift. Exploit it!'

'But how?'

'When you see the remotest chance, however unlikely –

246

and you'd see it in the blackest dark if it was there – spring at it, use it and twist its tail. I'll do the same.'

So, on a foggy February night, we met Corney at the barrier of platform 13 on Euston Station. For once the tall fresh-faced Isle of Wight man looked worried and his welcoming smile was uncertain. There wasn't much time to wonder about it. There was a great bustle on the blacked-out platform and the long troop train to Scotland was brimming over with high-spirited lads in uniform. They hung out of the windows and waved, laughing and singing, and the dim blue bulbs flashed by faster and faster, round the curve into the night and the fog towards battle.

It was the 18th anniversary of our wedding.

Central Hotel, Glasgow, Sunday, 21 February 1943

... Worn out and sleepy with golf, whisky and emotion, I had a very comfortable night leading a Commando Raid against the Japs on Shanghai Racecourse. Apart from that, the journey passed without incident and here I am having had breakfast and feeling as low as an alligator's ass ...

Naturally the whole of me is not a sad old suet pudding for I have the excitement of looking forward to seeing Pict and Mum and feeling the warmth of the sun and taking up an active sea job again. You have none of these. ...

His next note was from HMS *Sussex* at Scapa Flow

Sunday, 28 February 1943

... Just a word to say all is well. Corney has fetched up here and so have I and all my gear. An hour after he left his wife had a son, both doing fine. He is to be named Melvin Ernest. Corney is delighted as, owing to a delay of five days in our departure, he was able to go home again and see the boy!

The Captain is being very kind and helpful in every way but we are hideously crowded.

I keep thinking of you all the time and the horror of leaving you all in the air. You've been so plucky and enterprising over all this business, so persistently chasing up every possible line that you *must* succeed. If only I can hear that you've managed a passage I shall be happy. I say to myself it *will* be all right, it *must* be all right and all the time I have that horrid lurking fear it mayn't be....

In July Peter would be 17. He was working hard for his matric and he had a strong incentive to pass. He intended to 'get into the War' as fast as possible. There was no conscription in South Africa as there was in England with a systematic call up in age groups – boys under 18 pawing the ground in vain, men over 40 being drafted into administrative jobs when they longed for active service, women being put to work in factories or on the land or in whatever capacity the nation most needed them. In South Africa the volunteers were all ages from 17 to 50 and Piet and his schoolmates only needed the signature of a parent or guardian to walk from the schoolroom into the fighting forces.

If I didn't get home soon it might be too late for us to meet again.

Many people helped me as much as possible but it was up to me to prove my usefulness. Introductions were not enough and the fact of having strong personal reasons for wanting to get to South Africa told heavily against me. Bax introduced me to Beaverbrook. The 'Beaver' was not intentionally cruel but he was a Press Baron, self-made, a man who used people and did not intend to be used.

We met in his Leatherhead mansion with a view of England's green meadows in the blustery spring. He sat beside me, stared hard at me and summed up the situation. He was a gnome with eyes like Kemal Ataturk's – pale and fanatic. Bertie said of him once: 'He creates great opposition.' Therein lay his strength and his weakness.

'You're a good news reporter and feature writer, Joy Packer. That isn't in doubt. But you ask me to place you on one of my papers as a *War Correspondent*. You've been seasoned by the Blitz. You know the Far East, you know the Mediterranean. Greece, Turkey, Malta, China – you'll go anywhere, do anything. You aren't afraid, Right?'

I was more afraid of the 'Beaver' than the Blitz. He was preparing to shoot me down.

'But you stress the importance of the Indian Ocean, the Atlantic and the Cape route where both meet – and which also happens to be your home.'

'It's a good springboard. I could plug your creed. The Empire. And from the Cape I could go East, or to Cairo and the Mediterranean where Empire troops are fighting.' He let me have it then.

'You want one thing – to ride this job. It isn't on. A War Correspondent's family doesn't come into the picture. He's at instant notice – like a soldier. He doesn't choose his route. I'm sorry.'

He was right. I did want to ride a job. I'd done that once – with Imperial Airways. But first I'd had to create the demand.

South Africa House published syndicated articles on *Life in Wartime England*. I was a regular contributor.

The young woman in charge of Public Relations had sparkling black eyes and a quick brain. 'You could do more for us than this. Have you ever tried broadcasting?'

'Ages ago in Hong Kong. Women's programmes, stories for Children's Hour.'

'You must meet John Grenfell Williams, the BBC Director of the African Section.'

Grenfell Williams was South African, as warm and casual as his voice, reassuring to a stranger among the clinical offices and padded cells of the BBC.

'A lot of our young Servicemen are on leave in London or in transit,' he told me. 'We want to bring them to the microphone and let them talk to their folk at home.'

'A lovely idea. How can I help?'

'You know London, the good times and the bad. Take them around a bit – the City and so on. Then bring them back here and interview them off the cuff. Spontaneous stuff. Make them feel like it's a family 'phone call.'

Most of those boys were just a little older than Piet. From the top of London buses we looked down at the purple fireweed flourishing in the ruins and bombed basements turned into reservoirs, we talked to people in cafés and coffee stalls, and by the time we reached the studio we knew each other, and the boys were keen to tell their people – right now – what it was like over here in this scarred city that was still so very much alive. For me – as for the lads – it was talking to the 'folk at home'.

Grenfell Williams extended my scope. The legend of Leslie, the sea-going cat, went on the air. So did Shrapnel, the Fighting French dog from Dunkirk.

Somewhere, off the West Coast of Africa in the *Sussex*, Bertie made a note. 'Heard Joy last night interviewing two South African sailors. Good lads, but not enough Joy.'

It was then, at Free Town, that he was appalled to learn that the *Sussex* was *not* to call at Cape Town, but had received orders to continue round the southernmost tip of Africa to Durban without delay, thereby wrecking his hopes for a few days at 'Tees Lodge'. But his letter to me on 27 March 1943 was headed 'Tees Lodge'.

... When I found we were not to call here I got all steamed up and tried to keep calm, for it was vital to all our interests that this horror shouldn't happen. I thought of being shot off in the aircraft but it had bust, and of being hoisted out into a destroyer at 17 knots on the aircraft crane. The Captain wouldn't risk it. Finally this very nice Captain, with my assistance, thought up an acceptable reason for our vessel to nip in and out of this port and at the last moment it was allowed by the necessary authorities.

I was too excited and thrilled to keep still!

All the arrangements planned so long ago worked like magic. So, with Corney and very little gear, off we went to 'Tees Lodge'. Piet, who had been kidnapped from school by my 'agents', came galloping down the path with old Gyppy tottering after him, and then Mum. Mum had a nice cry and it was in all our minds, how could I be here without our Joy? ...

Mum is beautiful. A bit slower in 'hoisting things in' perhaps, but hers is a deliberate precise mind incapable of dancing from flower to flower with incredible speed like the blonde I am in love with.

Piet is a fine boy, lanky but not awkward. .... Nice deep voice, as frank and companionable as ever. We sit up late and have long talks about everything. Last night he said he'd like to be an engineer or a surgeon. Says that the idea of blood used to put him off but now he doesn't mind.

Old Fred breezed in to lunch, full of good cheer – a gust of fresh air and laughter.

In the afternoon Piet and I went to Bishop's to see his House Master (Payne) and the Head. Very helpful. He is to be entered for a good college at Oxford or Cambridge, but as soon as he matriculates will join up. Payne all for it. Said the boys at Bishop's were proud to join up the moment they left school.

I slept in your room. My God, Joy, I missed you terribly, thinking of all our years of happiness. . . .

Fred and Cecil gave a magnificent cocktail party for me at 'Barrymore' and invited all my friends. Charles te Water, and dear Maisie. I told them London had never been the same since they left. Little Freda had come in all the way from Stellenbosch as merry and naughty as ever. Princess Catherine of Greece full of fun and I could give her first-hand news of her brother. Sydney and Betty Waterson, Harry and Jean Lawrence – Jean very pretty, Harry now a Cabinet Minister – Gerda slim and more attractive than ever.

James Somerville has flown here to see Commander-in-Chief South Atlantic and I gather there might be a temporary unexpected change of my movements though not my appointment. This must not interfere with your movements *on any account* if you can get that much longed-for passage. I am flying with James S. and company on Wednesday and hope to see Molly and Norman for a week... :

He was going to join the *Warspite* in Durban where my brother Norman, now a Colonel SAMC, was in charge of the Military Hospital.

Peter wrote to me after his father had left. '... Dad has

251

fixed up everything so that I can join up when I've written matric. The day before he went we all listened to your Greek Independence Day broadcast from the BBC. It came through beautifully. Your slow elimination of the Foreign Ministers as the lights went down in Europe one by one was most effective.'

Bertie had told Harry Lawrence of my situation and that if the South African Bureau of Information would ask for me, I would be able to get a passage home and would be 'an asset in any propaganda job and do it 100 per cent'.

'Something may come of it,' Bertie wrote. 'Harry was very interested and sympathetic and Jean too. I'm hoping like mad. As Minister of the Interior he has a lot of say.'

But the trees in the Green Park were unfurling their young spring leaves and every day I'd watch them from my window and think, 'If I see them in full summer leaf I'll die of homesickness.'

Many weeks had passed since Bertie had sailed. Then one April day the telephone rang and the call was from South Africa House.

I sailed from Liverpool and saw Dorothy, Norman and my mother-in-law. The ship was very small and expendable and the convoy very large and precious. At its heart were the troop transports on the way to the Mediterranean. We waved them goodbye when they turned towards Gibraltar escorted by destroyers, busy as sheep-dogs. That strange voyage of zig-zagging ships and rats and six of us in a small cabin, three bunks against either wall, is described in *Grey Mistress*. But what I remember most was the awe and solitude of daybreak. There was a roster for submarine watch day and night – two hours at a stretch. I asked to be given the dawn watch. Alone in the anti-aircraft gun turret, watching for enemy periscopes that might feather the grey sea at first light, I understood why sailors have 'natural religion'. At that hour, between night and day, one is alone with nature and it is simple and right to say 'Preserve us from the dangers of the sea, and from the violence of the enemy ...

that we may return in safety to enjoy the blessings of the land
... with a thankful remembrance of Thy mercies ...'

On 30 May I looked up at the young man I had said
goodbye to nearly three years ago on Waterloo Station. He
had been a boy then, just 14. Now he was nearly 17, eager,
like his father, to be 'in the thick of it'.

As he drove me from the docks to 'Tees Lodge' I asked if
he knew where his father might be. It seemed a long time
before he answered.

'I'm pretty sure the *Warspite* passed your ship in the night
– homeward bound. Bad luck, Mom. But there's a letter
from Dad for you – came yesterday.'

24
'We shall not be out of things, wherever or whatever they may be.'

HMS *Warspite*
1943

Scapa
Mediterranean

OUR ships had indeed crossed in the night. Bertie guessed it might be so. I had no idea. But at Free Town, on the West Coast of Africa, he had managed to send me a welcome to 'Tees Lodge'.

HMS *Warspite, 18 April 1943*

. . . A word of welcome by courtesy of a chance ship.

You can imagine the tremendous thrill when I had your cable saying things had been arranged after such efforts in which you never let up and I like to think I helped. If it was H.L. who asked for you please thank him (and Jean) *very very much* for me, as well as for yourself.

I had a telegram on the 11th from Dorothy saying 'Joy very happy left us today' so now wait with great anxiety to hear you are at last safe with Mum and Piet. . . .

I am delighted with my new ship – or rather old ship. I have fine officers as far as I can see and a happy ship's company. At present I have her to myself so am thrilled with everything except my absence from you. Corney is in fine spirits and was very touched at your writing to Mrs. C. and sending Melvin a quid. He asked me to thank you most sincerely. He *is* a nice man. Able Seaman 'Knocker' White who helped Corney teach you to ride a bike is still with me.

I also have in my ship's company Able Dog Pluto. Born during the siege of Tobruk he came to this ship via a destroyer in which he was in many engagements. I will interview him, photograph him, and let you know more about him.

I see little chance, alas, of seeing you for very many months. Well, we can't complain in wartime. You will have a real job and you'll be with Mum and Piet. I have never admired Mum more. Apart from everything, never one word did I hear of complaint or disappointment, and heaven knows she's been disappointed often enough in expecting your arrival.

Piet will listen to you when you talk to him. He's not one of those chaps who just says 'Rot' either openly or in his mind. He turns things over and discusses them very intelligently and has many ideas. He takes very little for granted, but likes to convince himself of the truth of things, and of course he's the hell of a chap for getting his own way, but is 'supple in things immaterial'.

I'm holding thumbs for you like mad. What terrific determination you've shown. Most would have been beaten long ago. . . .

By mid-May the *Warspite* was in the Prince's Dock in the Clyde which she had guarded in the General Strike of 1926 when Bertie had been her Gunnery Officer. She was undergoing repairs for her steering gear which, even after her total reconstruction before the War, had still proved capricious on the way home from Durban.

United Services Club, Pall Mall, SW1, Tuesday, 18 May 1943

. . . If you deduce from my letters anything about the movements of my ship *keep them to yourself*. When last I saw James S. we were, for obvious reasons, moving behind such a cloud of camouflage that I wasn't quite sure whether I was coming, going or staying!

Anyway all is fine with me and my gallant lads and I expect thrilling times not too far ahead.

I've seen Vim at Craigholm* and Marion at Ruislip, both

---

* The Glasgow Girls' School of which Winifred Packer was Headmistress.

flourishing, and go to Dorothy, Norman and Mother next week.

Philip Rhodes met me in London where he'd fixed a room for me at Athenaeum Court. It's on the tenth floor with a raving pansy to look after me. He straight away asked me if I was your wife. (I mean husband, but with that chap one gets confused) and he told me what a charming lady you were and how he had found you in tears one morning, 'Just homesick, mind'.

Dined with Philip and Elspeth at 'Boodles' (patched up since your blitz in King Street). Yesterday played some tennis with Phil and Nancy Glover. Phil goes to a shore job in America tomorrow where Nancy may join him.

Fixed up a mass of things at the Admiralty but still unable to find out the whereabouts of your ship. This morning I rang up Bax who asked me to lunch at the House of Commons with him and Critchley. 'Critch' is just taking over as head of our Civil Aviation and 'Max and Bax' have teamed up again. After lunch 'Critch' went off and Bax and I sat in the sun on the terrace above the river and he told me everything about everything. I enjoyed myself, and he assured me that you were a girl with a three-track mind – your country, your son and your husband!!! Anyhow, he is, as you say, an *enfant terrible* and I told him so. I'm going down with him to the Anchor at Liphook from Friday to Monday, a gang of seven of us, taking the golf pro' Fred Robson from Addington and we are going to golf and gamble incessantly, God help me! We'll go in his car with my leave petrol. He's already betting the War will be over this year. I don't think so for a moment.

We are having lovely spring days and after all my seafaring the green trees and flowers simply leave one gasping. When days in England are warm and sunny it is staggeringly beautiful. We arrived a week ago in a succession of snow storms!

I don't know where to picture you. If only I could be sure you were safely at 'Tees Lodge'.

Have had tough tussles at the Admiralty about my ship –

or rather the folk in her – as of course the Admiralty want to take this opportunity to change everyone. I say *this is not the moment* and have scored a fair amount of success. Anyhow I am very happy in my job with my ship, officers and men, and would not be anywhere else these days, if I had the choice.

I am sure we shall not be out of things, wherever or whatever they may be.

Bertie was in high spirits, for he knew that the Invasion of Sicily had been planned as a prelude to invading Italy, and that the *Warspite* had been cast by Combined Allied Operations for an important role.

On 5 June he wrote from Scapa Flow where the *Warspite* was working up for her part in the great events to come, bombardment practices in particular, for it had been well proved that not only was air cover essential to troop landing, but also battleship bombardments of shore batteries and strong points before the actual assault.

... I am putting my old companion through her paces and thoroughly enjoying it. ... Once again I have developed an ardour for War and the more I set about perfecting the weapon the more I want to use it. ...

I am very happy with my *Warspite* and all in her. Yesterday for the first time I was able to walk around and talk to the officers and men at their jobs and learn something about them – establishing, I hope, a measure of confidence in their Captain. One can't hurry it. But this evening a Petty Officer asked to see me privately. He asked my advice. Here is the story. He has two sisters. One is married to a Merchant Service Officer who is a prisoner of war in Germany; the other, to a soldier in India. Both have two children between the ages of two and 11. The two wives and four children went to Withernsea on the Yorkshire coast to spend the weekend in a caravan they shared there. The boy of 11 crawled under some wire and came back with a grenade which he showed them proudly. It went off. Three of the four kids were killed outright, the fourth badly wounded.

One sister had her leg blown off and the other is seriously injured. The only relative at hand is their father aged 75. What was the Petty Officer to do? He was bewildered and his sister's artificial leg would cost £28. Was the War Office liable? Should he let her husband in Germany know? And so on. I gave him seven days' leave – couldn't give him more – told him to get a reliable solicitor from Hull to represent him and the interests of his sisters and furthermore to go and see his MP and tell him the whole story. To ask the MP to keep in touch with the solicitor and vice versa, and if the solicitor reckoned they were getting a raw deal he must ask the MP to intervene.

I also said I'd write at once and put the whole case before the MP.

Not an entrancing story, not easy or pleasant to deal with, but at the same time I was glad to be able to cope, for that is one of the obligations of one's position, after all. I only tell you this horror story because you know very well how these are the things that give one a common ground with one's officers and men.

Now for the lighter side.

Pluto the Dog is very impressive, his sturdy pugnacious form reminiscent of Geoffrey Layton. He is always the first on the scene when the Cable Party is piped to muster before anchoring. Straight away when the Cable Party Bugle sounds he dashes up forward, through the guard rails into the very eyes of the ship and stands there, strong and vigilant, until he is satisfied that the anchor has been cleared away and is all ready for letting go. Then he trots back and joins up with the common sailors until the anchor goes and the cable roars out. Then he trots aft sedately to the Quarterdeck to supervise the Marines lowering the after-gangway. Just about then, preceded by Corney, I arrive on the Quarterdeck on my way to my day-cabin. Pluto doesn't fawn, lick one's hand or jump about; on an even keel he approaches me with great dignity, cocks his head on one side with one ear up and one down, gives me a knowing look, winks his port eye, hesitates for a polite second, and off he goes to his next activity. He's a great dog – a dog of the world who doesn't work but superintends like hell and criticizes not a little.

My Navigator is a fine young chap called Blake – a Winchester boy with all the good manners associated with Winchester. He's great fun on the Bridge because he's a bird-watcher, he knows them all and keeps us interested and amused guessing what they are. I'm told he got so interested in his hobby that at the Cosmo and Stardust nightclubs in Durban he nearly died of insomnia, studying new specimens, their habits at night, including their flight and nesting-places!

Bax, your *enfant terrible*, is now the dramatic critic for Saturday's *Evening Standard*. So I wrote to the Editor and said how deeply interested I was in good writing and dramatic criticisms, and the new articles by B.B. in particular. The Editor is now posting me the paper weekly! I enclose Bax's article. Damn good too.

Monday 7 June Yesterday our old friend, Algy Willis (now *Sir* Willis!) arrived and sent for me and we had half an hour's heart to heart. He is to be my Admiral but will not fly his flag in my ship. I'm sorry. I'm sure that, like Holland, I should have been glad to have him, which is my highest compliment.

9 June There has been a heavy ball of suet sitting on my diaphragm for about five weeks, only partly relieved by Commander-in-Chief South Atlantic's bicarbonate to say you were 'safe', and now completely removed by Jacko's signal to say you really had fetched up on 30 May! Darling Joy-Joy, the thought that after all our continued struggles and nearly seven weeks' ocean going you are at last with our loved ones lightens my heart so much that I could, like the salvationist bandsman, 'just beat hell out of the bloody drum'. My manifestation will, I hope, take the form of tuning this ship up to such a degree that she can beat hell out of any 'Wop' or 'Nazi' she may meet. We are engaged on this at the moment. The 'burden' of being in command rests lightly on my shoulders for I have a good ship and good officers.

A week later the *Warspite* sailed in company with the huge Fleet massing in the Mediterranean to put Italy out of the War on land, sea and in the air. The *Warspite* was allocated to the 1st Battle Squadron, part of Force H now under the command of Vice-Admiral Sir Algernon Willis.* Bertie, always jealous of sharing his ship, wrote rather grudgingly when Rear-Admiral A. W. la T. Bissett hoisted his flag in the *Warspite* in Gibraltar.

... After some real stinking gales we have a lovely blue warm day with a hot sun. Most refreshing. Tomorrow I get my Admiral. I don't look forward to it – not because I don't like him, but because I've had my fine ship to myself for nearly three months. He is Rear-Admiral Bissett, just promoted.

I am simply living for your first letter. There are so many things I want to hear about that I expect your letter will have to come in a parcel! Heaven alone knows where it will find me or when. But it will somewhere sometime.

Tuesday To my great delight I had an airgraph today, but they are unsatisfactory – thoroughly read by everyone!

I'm thrilled you found all at home in cracking form and that you are already working with Information and the SABC.

Here we are all straining at the leash. We are a strong party under Admiral Willis and have the greatest confidence in his ability.

In fact I'm very happy about everything. May it continue so.

But I never stop thinking about you my kind, loyal, exciting Joy-Joy, and like the young men in last Sunday's lesson, which I read, 'I dream visions'.

Admiral Willis's Force H was operating from three different bases. The *Warspite* her sister *Valiant* and the aircraft carrier *Formidable* were allocated to Alexandria. They

---

* Later Admiral of the Fleet, Sir A. U. Willis, GCB, KBE, DSO.

were to cover the landings in Sicily on 10 July, to support the Army by bombarding targets ashore and of course to deal with the elusive Italian Fleet.

On 2 July, the Commander-in-Chief Mediterranean, Admiral of the Fleet, Sir Andrew B. Cunningham, sent a message to all those under his command in which he told them only what is was necessary for them to know about Operation Husky, *'the most momentous enterprise of the War – striking for the first time at the enemy in his own land'*. He also made every man aware of his own particular responsibility and importance.

Our object is clear and our primary duty is to place this vast expedition ashore in the minimum time and subsequently maintain our military and air forces as they drive relentlessly forward into enemy territory. In the light of this duty great risks must be, and are to be, accepted. The safety of our ships and all distracting considerations are to be relegated to second place or disregarded as the accomplishment of our main duty may require. On every commanding officer and rating rests the individual personal duty of ensuring that no flinching in determination or failure of effort on his own part will hamper this great enterprise.

The landings were set for 2.45 a.m. on 10 July. In the dark hours of the night of the 9th the great Armada set course for Sicily and Bertie's diary noted that 'the sailors on deck are all peering ahead and if they talk at all, it is in undertones. There is awe around us.' By the evening of 10 July, it seemed that all was going well while the *Warspite* and covering forces patrolled off Cape Passero on the southeast corner of Sicily. To everybody's disgust the Italian Fleet, except for a few submarines, quickly pounced on by our destroyers, failed to appear on the scene. However a U-boat attack damaged a British cruiser and the aircraft carrier *Indomitable* was struck by a German aerial torpedo and was escorted back to Malta by the *Warspite*. Bertie immediately called on the Commander-in-Chief. Captain S. W. Roskill in HMS *Warspite* gives an account of the exchange between them. The Captain 'vented his disappointment that no action had so far come the way of his ship. "Well," answered the Commander-in-Chief, "I can't get hold of the Italian Fleet, tie them down and let you have a go at them." "No," answered the *Warspite*'s Captain, "but I'm told Sicily is the biggest island in Europe, and I'm sure we could hit it if told to go and bombard." . . .'

Two days later the 8th Army's advance was held up at Catania, and at noon on 15 July, the *Warspite* and *Valiant* were ordered to sail immediately and bombard Catania from 18.30 to 19.00, not a second before or after.

Unfortunately the *Valiant* became snarled up with the anti-submarine defence and had to be left behind.

Bertie wrote to Peter on 21 July when the *Warspite* was back in Malta champing at the bit for her next active assignment.

21 July 1943

... If you happened to be listening to the wireless on 18 July you'll have heard that 'a famous British battleship' bombarded Catania. It was a lot more exciting than it sounds.

We raised steam like mad, but even if we averaged our maximum $22\frac{1}{2}$ knots we could not get to Catania till 19.00. Too late. We had to do more. Quickly worked up to 8 revs over our maximum. Suddenly our steering gear jammed and we went round in a savage circle and lost ten precious minutes getting our auxiliary steering connected. At 18.43 we were passing thro' the Open Fire Position at 16 knots and opened fire. A great mass of dust and smoke rose from the town right on target. We had exactly 20 minutes to do our dirty work.

Then everything happened at once. In those 20 minutes two submarines appeared and were quickly depth-charged by our destroyers. Three FW 190s got a load of oerlikon, pom-pom, 4-inch and 6-inch, but got away. They were moving at about 400 m.p.h. and machine-gunning like fury but with indifferent accuracy. The shore batteries opened up and the destroyers took them on as our big guns were pouring in the stuff. So it was a fine 20 minutes for the old *War-spite*.

When we got back Commander-in-Chief Andrew B. Cunningham signalled 'Operation well executed. When the Old Lady lifts her skirts she can run.' We are the only one of the big boys so far to have blazed at the enemy. The sailors now stick out their chests and are generally detested by the crews of the other ships of the Squadron.

By the way, I heard from a naval officer who'd been speaking to the Secretary of the Marsa that Mum's broadcast on Malta G.C. was a howling success. I have a very nice South African Lieutenant on board from Cape Town, called Curtis.

By the end of July Mussolini had fallen and Bertie wrote to me 'I think the change of régime is intended to make the path of peace simpler by eliminating the Fascists.' By the second week in August Sicily's resistance was nearing the end. The battle for the mainland of Italy would be a much tougher proposition for German reinforcements were pouring in from the north. Meanwhile the *Warspite* marked time in Malta and Bertie became enraged at getting no letters from South Africa.

9 August 1943

. . . I sent a cable yesterday to tell you all was well here and ask you to see someone about your letters. Here it is 9 August and my latest from you is your airgraph of 2 June. A South African on board has had two airletters delivered on board a fortnight after leaving Johannesburg. The Fleet Mail Office in Cape Town must find out what's happening. God knows where they're sending our mail.

My dear, poor Malta is a shambles. It's not fire which has done the damage but High Explosive so everything is *shattered*. And there's nothing to be bought ashore. Food is issued as if still besieged. I went to look for Richard Saguna. You would have wept to see his little hotel and the big room he had distempered for you in duck-egg green. All disembowelled, wide open to the street. They tell me he has gone to St. Paul's Bay. Outside my reach unfortunately.

Today my Rear-Admiral and I are lunching with the Governor, Lord Gort. So there's my silly news.

I miss you so frightfully and it makes you *so* far away not hearing from you. I am always thinking of you and Piet and Mum and wondering when we'll all be together again. And how is *Pack and Follow* getting on? I hope as well as the first half. Oh, dear. . . .

13 August When we lunched with Lord Gort, to my surprise and delight I found Noel Coward there! He was here for three days, entertaining the wounded brought back from Sicily, working like mad. None of my ship's company had seen *In Which We Serve*, so I sent a midshipman with a note to Noel to ask if he had a spare copy. He *had*! It is now on board and was shown last night for the first time. This morning Noel sent me a message to say his plane was delayed and could he spend the day with me. He came on board at noon, at 13.00 we lunched with the Admiral, at 14.00 put him to bed, at 15.00 took him in a boat to Tini to bathe, at 17.30 brought him back, at 18.00 got him to give us an impromptu open air show for half an hour. He had the sailors rocking with rude mirth, and I gained great face as no other ship had had a show from him. He's great fun and I enjoyed the day enormously. He enchanted 'Knocker' White by remembering him, and 'Knocker' is now the hero of the ship.

This evening I had a signal '*All well writing regularly Joy Packer.*' Hence I fancy my light heart tonight. I have written a stinker to Their Lordships about the delay in airmail from South Africa and have also kicked up a big stink here. Commander-in-Chief Mediterranean has sent a signal to Commander-in-Chief South Atlantic and the Admiralty. As I pointed out to him, in about AD 1600 when there was not even a Post Office in Cape Town letters were picked up from under a stone on Lion's Head and took about $2\frac{1}{2}$ months to reach their destination! I also pointed out that the average speed of an airmail from Cape Town now appeared to be three miles an hour, which seemed slow to me.

Last Sunday A.B.C. walked round my ship (his former Flagship) and made an excellent speech to the men. He's a dynamic little man. The Sicilian campaign is over *inside schedule* – so now what? A.B.C. does not reckon Italy will be out this year, and told us all so. At present the summer heat and inactivity are our worst enemies. I am very fit and do my best to keep everyone active. Corney takes crews away boat pulling and is his usual cheerful self and a great asset to me and to the ship. I am becoming quite attached to Bissett, my Admiral, who is behaving very well. I had a most amusing letter from Bax and quote one sentence. He says, 'I don't want to cause any trouble in the family but Joy says she misses me. This is sweet music. Personally I don't believe a word of it. It is London she misses – London and a sailor who thinks he can play golf.'

I hope he's right, darling.

25 August My sweetheart, I did a bold thing today and landed at Custom House and walked up Guarda Mangia to see if I could 'take it'. I couldn't, but that is neither here nor there. Not that it is knocked down. Only one house has been hit and it wasn't ours. But there were soldiers in 'Villa Diana' and there was no Joy or Peter or Nannie, and memory opened its door and the pleasanter the memories the more they turn one's innards over and over till they feel like spaghetti under the fork of a famished Sicilian. I continued over the brow of the hill and there were half a dozen Maltese children playing a game. They had built a 'house' of empty tins and cans and pieces of wood and this and that including some stones of sufficient weight. Presently the smallest child was carefully and unwillingly put in the 'house'. Then one lad became an aeroplane and rushed around twisting and turning his hands and zooming. As his fury reached its height all the children made frightful noises and pulled the 'house' down on top of the inmate. Then they sorrowfully dug him out and administered first aid with tears and lamentations. Somewhat macabre but quite exciting and I watched it out to the end. Some day, of course, they'll build a stronger 'house' of heavier stones, of which there are plenty lying about, pull it down on the child and kill or maim it for life and one more or less will hardly be noticed in the fecund life of Malta.

Able Dog Pluto is in disgrace. Just as the stately Marine Guard marched off for Colours this morning Pluto laid an enormous egg on the Quarterdeck right in their path. This mined the Sergeant in the lead and he skimmed down the deck like Donald Duck on skates. With a crash, as his rifle clattered to the ground, he fetched up on his enormous tail still moving South-South-West at 25 knots. It was unseemly and I believe, strictly between you and me, that Pluto and the Sergeant of Marine did not get on well! Anyhow the only thing smoothed over by this incident is the Quarterdeck. I swear I saw Pluto watching from behind the turret. What a lot of nonsense, but darling it's because I adore you and nonsense is better than tears.

30 August 1943

. . . I'm all dizzy and thrilled. Yesterday brought your bunch of letters – the first for three months. . . .

As I thought, your journey was a stinker but tho' you had no alarms and excursions, there were some in your neighbourhood at the time and I was very far from happy about you.

Don't let yourself get tied up in a clerical job. Stick with your Press Division and broadcasting. You'd be wasted in a steady office job, putting pins in the wrong places on a map, filing papers in the wrong docket and adding up figures incorrectly. It's not your line of country. English and history, yes, but method and 'rithmetic, *non*!

Things in the War are whizzing so fast that one ceases to comment. Sicily, Mussolini in the dirt bin, Boris in the bag, Churchill roaring round, Lord Louis let loose. Where the hell are we?

Anyway my 'old girl' is off for another roar. But where? As soon as we can get the south of Italy we could crack into Yugoslavia and Greece across the Adriatic. Hope I'm there! I promised Princess Catherine I'd be in the first British warship to steam into Athens Bay. So glad you've seen her. Give her my kind regards and suitably restrained affection.

I am right here in the middle of things. Corney is being splendid, his usual cheery self. My Admiral is very good, he's kind, intelligent and 'blimpish' and I find myself trying to shock him, which is stupid but I can't help it. The Secretary and Flags are very nice and very young. Like two Babes in the Wood.

Now I must leave you as we are off on the job tomorrow . . .

The 'job' wound up the Sicilian campaign and the *Warspite* and *Valiant* prepared the ground for the 8th Army to move across to the Italian mainland.

3 September 1943

. . . Just in from a good run up the Messina Straits. This has been released by the Censor and so I can write about it. Off we went, close up the Sicilian shore past Syracuse, Catania, Taormina and in to bombard near Reggio on the mainland where the Canadians were due to land the following morning at 04.30. We gave it a thorough plastering with our big guns and no one interfered, so we were not surprised to hear that the Canadians had got ashore without opposition and that there were white flags all over the place. Looking at our one-sided contest from the sea, if I'd been an Italian or a German soldier ashore I'd have taken to the hills as quickly as the Highlanders did when they heard Oscar Wilde had been released from Reading Gaol! We are, of course, very excited to know how our Army are getting on. It was great fun during our bombardment yesterday. We had a very young South African from Rondebosch called Webb spotting for us from an aeroplane and as we got on to the target, instead of the ordinary formal spotting reports, he started getting enthusiastic and saying 'O.K., O.K., give them all you've got. You're plastering them. Repeat, repeat. Give them the works!' Made us laugh.

It was odd passing Taormina and looking for our pub where we stayed when Etna was erupting and the railway covered with lava. Couldn't find it. The landing craft were drawn up in great rows on the beach waiting for zero hour and the Sicilian fishermen were out in their picturesque boats fishing as if there was not a War anywhere. They didn't cheer us or throw fish at us as we passed, nor did we swamp them with our wash. . . .

Afterwards Bertie and some of his officers flew from Malta to Reggio to land and see what their 15-inch guns had done to the gun emplacements near Reggio. There were 17 huge craters and every gun out of action. He wrote in his diary: 'We found an old farmer and a small boy who'd watched from a safe distance and they described it all with gestures and noises. "Marina – bom-bom-plonk-plonk," said the boy. "Soldati?" asked I. The boy did a running away pantomime. "Soldati refugio." Apparently the whole garrison refugioed fast. No wonder!'

Enclosed in his letter were two signals he knew would amuse me. They were from the destroyer *Gavotte* to the Medical Officer *Warspite*.

PET MONKEY DYING FROM EATING RED LEAD. REQUEST ANY HELP OR INSTRUCTIONS PLEASE.   13.00   31/8/43
REPLY: YOUR 13.00 GIVE ½ TEASPOONFUL EPSOM SALTS IN CUP OF WATER FOLLOWED BY COMMON SALT TILL MONKEY IS SICK. SMALL DOSES OF BRANDY DILUTED IN WATER MAY THEN BE GIVEN
14.20 P.M.O. WARSPITE   FROM GAVOTTE
V.M.T. FOR YOUR ASSISTANCE. REGRET THE POOR LITTLE FELLOW PASSED AWAY.   14.50   31/8/43.

Across the second signal he had written in his sharp hand which never bothered to dot the letter 'i'. 'This wartime tragedy explains itself but we have time for everything even in the middle of taking Sicily!'

25

'Biggish things have been happening.'

HMS *Warspite*   Salerno Landings
September to October 1943   Italian Fleet Surrender
                             Battle of Salerno

AFTER the Reggio bombardment and the unopposed Canadian landings on the mainland of Italy, the Allied plan was to capture Naples in readiness for the final advance up the boot of Italy which would certainly be hotly defended by German Forces. Meanwhile the terms of Italy's capitulation were being negotiated.

Force H, including the 1st Battle Squadron and her Flagship *Warspite*, was assigned the leading role in the operation. On 11 September, after returning to Malta, Bertie wrote to me of the greatest triumph the Allies had so far claimed in the course of four years at War.

HMS *Warspite, Saturday, 11 September 1943*

... Tonight I am writing you a story. ...

Well, biggish things have been happening. And so fast! Wait a bit. Today is Saturday. I must work back from there and then start off at the beginning.

Last Thursday, 9 September, was D-Day and 03.30 was zero hour for the landings in Salerno Bay. They were to be carried out by British and American Forces.

Not even *now* will the Censor permit me to give you all of the plan, for some of it failed and some was a 200 per cent success. Our job was to cover the landings and stick around in the Tyrrhenian Sea and stop anyone interfering with them. A nice maternal role.

So off we set on Tuesday evening not knowing our destination, west about Malta and Pantellaria, and so, with the great mass of invading forces, west of Sicily and east of

Sardinia into the Tyrrhenian Sea and 50 miles west of Salerno. Hot purple-blue Mediterranean summer weather and a three-quarter moon. (Three-quarter moons rise in daylight and sink about 1 a.m. growing roughly an hour later every night.)

For some time I had been as consistently expectant as any Maltese mother, so when 'Butch' arrived on board quite suddenly I smelt that there was something special in the wind. 'Butch' is Commander Butcher, USN, but he's not really a naval officer at all. He is something to do with Columbia Broadcasting and is General Eisenhower's right-hand man, sort of super *aide-de-camp* – keeps Eisenhower in touch with everything and looks after his publicity and so on. He's altogether charming and anything that passes him by could slip thro' the eye of a needle without slowing down. He was sent to us as 'official photographer' and knows less about loading a Leica than I do, so obviously something was on over and above the ordinary landings.

By Wednesday afternoon we were in the area, Capri not 50 miles away, and on Wednesday-Thursday nights we were all agog, for the Tyrrhenian Sea was thick with north-bound shipping. At 03.30 on Thursday morning the forces landed and there was stiff fighting on Salerno beaches. We, in the ships, had not been directly attacked. During that day we heard that Italy, as represented by the King and the Badoglio Government, had passed in their knife and fork. That didn't mean much because they hadn't anything left to fight with anyway. *But quite naturally we were interested in the Italian Fleet: Would they scuttle? Would they play with Germany? Would they come over to us?* The ship ran a sweepstake on it! We were all excitement wondering what next. Anyway Italy had caved in. But we didn't relax for a second. Every gun was manned.

At 21.30 it started.

We were relentlessly attacked by German aircraft with bombs and torpedoes – intensively until midnight and then sporadically. The moonlight is a gift for determined aircraft. They attack up moon. They can see us and we can't see them. So at first *sound* we crack off all we've got. We've

270

worked that up for about two months now, and for about five hours whenever we felt nervous we cracked off with all we had to give them. They couldn't take it. Of course they fired torpedoes and dropped bombs but as girlishly as a timid bean-fed mare.

The Gunnery Officer Hamilton, whom you will remember at Whaley because of his bright blue eyes, handled our considerable and varied gun armament magnificently. He was as cool as a cucumber and more effective.

I had one moment as bad as any this War. I heard (you may laugh but I *did*, in spite of our pom-poms and oerlikons and 4-inch and 6-inch guns), an aircraft roaring in. It skimmed down the safe edge of our barrage about 40° on the Port Bow. I rigged my eyes out like hat-pegs – so did the Navigator and the Officer of the Watch and Chief Yeoman of Signals. Suddenly there was a great shape down-moon about 100 feet up off the sea. Things happen terribly quickly – fractions of seconds are minutes. I saw this Ju. 88 drop his torpedo and I saw it splash and down the voice-pipe to the Quartermaster I roared 'Port 35!' I didn't think we had a hope of it missing us and it seemed about a thousand years before I saw the electric repeat from the rudderhead showing that the rudder was 35° to port. The torpedo – they travel 40 knots or so – had been dropped about 600 yards away, we were steaming 18 knots, Piet will tell you how long it takes before the torpedo hits or misses you. I can honestly say that I was holding on to things waiting for the bump and so was everyone else on the Bridge. I steadied up with my course parallel to the track of the torpedo and it literally missed my stern by feet (ship's stern I mean). The parallel track was so close that I had to climb up on the side of the Bridge and look over the edge to see it. Just then the Admiral roared out up the voice-pipe 'Good God, what are you doing? Can't you see you are broadside on to the moon?'

'Look over the Port side!' I sang out. 'You will see a torpedo track parallel to us. Can you see it?'

'Yes, I can,' he said. 'Well done.' So that was O.K.

There were shocks, explosions and rude noises all night,

and I said, 'Well, there's nothing like celebrating an armistice in the proper fashion.'

We were all very keyed-up and tired and very pleased, and dawn came and we settled down to whatever next. *And suddenly we were told to meet the Italian Spezia Fleet off Bône** (*North Africa*) *next morning and conduct them to Malta.*

So we set course to do so and we had the Greek destroyer *Queen Olga* with us, and our honour was great.

Meanwhile German aircraft had attacked the Spezia Squadron and sunk the battleship *Roma,* killing the Italian Commander-in-Chief. . . .

So at dawn on Friday, 10 September, we were off Bône, awaiting the Italians. We sighted them bows on at 30,000 yards just like we had in the *Manchester* three years ago off Spartivento and I said to Corney 'They look just the same.' He said he reckoned they did, sort of.

Well, they came on and it was about 08.00 and Captain Brownrigg from the Commander-in-Chief's staff went on board the Flagship to show them the way. We formed ahead of them and off we went towards Malta. It was a big moment. There they were, two 15-inch battleships, five cruisers and nine destroyers. It made one feel too important.

The 'old timers' were saying how they had seen the surrender of the German Fleet 25 years ago, and Curtis, a Lieutenant SANF from Rondebosch, who is my Acting Officer of the Watch, said 'To think I should be here to see this!' He had emotion in his voice and I felt just the same. The Padré, who is a grand chap and comes from Yorkshire, said, 'It all seems pathetic somehow,' and the Gunnery Officer who before he came to *Warspite* had been pushing convoys thro' to Malta with Philip Vian, said '*Mare nostrum*? We'll teach them *mare nostrum*!' and was as busy as a film star fan comparing their profiles in his book of words. Able Dog Pluto got terribly excited when he saw the Italians, rushed up and down, came up on to the Bridge, sat in my chair and then walked round on the edge of the Bridge

---

* Now Annaba.

barking at them. He has an uncanny knowledge of naval life, never misses anything that is going on.

So we roared down the North African coast to the eastward, and off Bizerta a destroyer, the *Hambledon* (Hunt class), flashed out and she was flying a Union Jack which was an Admiral of the Fleet. It was Admiral Sir Andrew B. Cunningham come out to see his old enemies go by. As he passed us at 25 knots and we at 21 knots he signalled to me. 'Glad to see my old Flagship in her proud and rightful position at the head of the line.' I had a minute to flash back 'The Old Lady will look after them all right.'

We led the way through the night and at daybreak there was Gozo and shortly Malta and we hauled out and let them go past to their anchorage off Ricasoli.

They were very smart with their ships' companies fallen in as they passed, and the cruiser *Eugene Savoia* couldn't drop her anchor for she had not used it for four years! She said she'd been alongside always. But what matter?

We went into the Grand Harbour where we are now. And A.B.C. has signalled to the Admiralty.

'*The Italian Fleet now lies at anchor under the guns of the fortress of Malta.*'

Sunday, 12 September We shifted berth early this morning and anchored off the breakwater and Admiral Bissett has shifted his flag to *Howe*. So once more I am alone in my glory. It is a great relief to be cock of one's own dunghill.

Our part in meeting the Italian Fleet and accepting its surrender is out on the BBC. I'm sure A.B.C. picked *Warspite* for the honour, she having been his old Flagship. After all, it is an historic occasion, but, like many memorable days, not really so different from any others. All the same, we are very proud of ourselves and if I can now take my ship's company home for some real leave my cup of joy will be as full as it can be. Personally I have no wish to go back and find no Joy-Joy in all those places which are linked so closely with her. It is sorrowful and I'd rather be out on the job in my own world.

I saw Charles Woodhouse yesterday. He is Captain of the *Howe* and had just got back from capturing Taranto – this will soon give us Brindisi and Bari and all the South of Italy, I hope.

If we are sent home I have thoughts of getting a temporary job to do with Greece should we invade there. I don't fancy hanging about a Home Port for two or three months' refitting.

The War is going so well that it won't be very long before Germany is out – she will be beset on all sides – shall we say a year? And then the Japs?

But it's hard to write sensibly about the War, for things are moving so fast and by the time you get this letter – in perhaps two months – all may be different. . . .

Much began to 'be different' almost immediately.

On 14 September, the *Warspite, Valiant* and the carrier *Illustrious* were on their way back to Britain to refit. But they hadn't gone far when a signal ordered the two battleships to Salerno Bay at full speed.

The first part of what happened next is contained in a letter from Malta to Peter and me.

20 September 1943

. . . Having just got back from a hazardous and successful enterprise, briefly put out on the BBC this morning, I can tell you as much as I'm allowed. The rest will follow. We were nearing Algiers* when we and the *Valiant* were sent off at 23 knots through the Straits of Messina to back up the 6th Corps of the American 5th Army at Salerno who were having the devil of a time. The Germans had counterattacked down the Sele River and were between the British and the Americans and were already announcing a second Dunkirk. So in we roared to within half a mile of the beaches – no place for battleships – but that was all right.

The fact was that our troops had bits of the beaches and the coastal plains, but the hills close inland were full of

---

* Now Alger.

German Artillery shelling our airstrips and beaches and further back in the mountains, out of reach of our shore artillery, were the heavy guns of the Germans. We had to put them out. A quick conference with the Americans and off went our Captain of Marines with a wireless set into the hinterland to observe and report whilst we fired our 15-inch guns. It went like clockwork and on Thursday 16th we knocked seven bells out of enemy troop concentrations, gun positions and road centres. About every two hours we got roared up by F.W. 190s and we knocked down quite a lot. The effect of our fire bucked up our troops ashore and un-bucked the Germans. You see, a 15-inch projectile passing over you makes a noise like an express train – and the thought of an express train full of high explosive rushing on its way towards the enemy, where it will explode with devas-tating violence, is pleasant. On the other hand the enemy, on whom those trains are converging, takes a poor view of the whole thing, which goes to show that it is hard to draw a firm line and say 'this is good' or 'this is bad'.

That night we went out to sea and the Germans kept at us with low-flying aircraft. Once more we stood them off, and at dawn we were in again in time to blot out back positions while the Americans counter attacked. The Germans clearly hated us! It was most encouraging to find they had a mass of wireless jamming our communications with the Forward Observation Officer – our Captain of Marines. We were pretty artful and skimmed around on pre-arranged waves so quickly that they never caught us up again. The American cruisers were firing like mad and we pounded away. I really believe it was the turning point, for our counter-attack went forward and still is going forward five days later.

The American Admiral Hewitt sent a signal when I with-drew. 'Am grateful for your efficient support which has aided so much the forces ashore. Hewitt.' We were being 'effing-wolved' the whole time and a touch of Swan Court*

---

* The block of Chelsea flats where I was in 1940 and which was damaged by High Explosive.

has made for us another story which is entirely for yourselves, even in its infancy. We are all on the crest of a wave. ...

On the following day, 21 September 1943, Winston Churchill addressed the House of Commons on the progress of the Italian campaign and the Navy's support in Salerno Bay during five desperate days and nights.

'From day three to day seven the issue hung in the balance and the possibility of a large-scale disaster could not be excluded. You have to run risks. There are no certainties in War. There is a precipice on either side of you – a precipice of caution and a precipice of over-daring. ... The battle swayed to and fro, and the Germans' hope of driving us into the sea after a bloody battle on the beaches must at times have risen high. ...

'*The British Battle Squadron, some of our finest battleships, joined the inshore Squadron in a heavy bombardment, running a great risk within close range and narrow waters from the enemy's aircraft, U-boats and the glider bombs which inflicted damage on some of our ships. They came straight in and stood up to it at close range, equalized and restored the artillery battle. ... It was right to risk capital ships in this manner in view of the improvement of naval balances.*'

The 'improvement of naval balances' was, of course, the elimination of the Italian Fleet. Bertie gladly lent his private records of this stirring and vital period to Captain S. W. Roskill who describes with authority what happened when the *Warspite* was struck by Hitler's newest secret weapon:*

'All the evening of the 15th and all the following night *Warspite*'s anti-aircraft guns were in action as she steamed up and down outside the bay. Very early on the 16th she moved right inshore again, to the position she had occupied on the previous day. Soon after she arrived the fighter direction ship signalled to ask if *Warspite* could provide a copy

* See p. 19.

of the Admiralty's report on the new type of German bomb. One of the secretaries at once typed the document and it was sent over by boat; but this prescient act was not to save the ship. ... Just after 1 p.m. fire was opened on enemy traffic concentrations and ammunition dumps. ... It must have been heartening to the hard-pressed soldiers to see the great ships steaming up and down only half a mile or so offshore, their guns belching flame, to hear the 15-inch shells screaming overhead, and then to see the heavy explosions in the enemy lines. ... At 2.30 p.m. only a few minutes after the fighter-bombers had disappeared, the ship's look-outs sighted what were at first thought to be three high level bombers at about 6,000 feet. They were actually wireless-controlled bombs, whose controlling aircraft was far away overhead at about 20,000 feet. Here is Captain Packer's account of what followed:

The three bombs when directly overhead looked like three very white mushrooms as they turned vertically down and dived for the ship at great speed. From the time of sighting to the time of the bomb's arrival was only some seven to ten seconds ... in the congested area avoiding action was not possible – and would in any case have been ineffective. One bomb came straight for the ship and penetrated to No. 4 boiler-room, where it burst. A second bomb was a near-miss amidships abreast the bulge on the starboard side. It burst under water. This bomb had looked like missing by 400 yards, but about two-thirds of its way down it curved in towards the ship. The third bomb was a near-miss on the starboard side aft.

'The 3,000 lb. bomb which scored the direct hit penetrated right through six decks ... to her double bottom before exploding, while the near-miss made a long gash in her starboard bulge compartments. One boiler-room was completely demolished, and four of the other five were soon flooded. ... "The situation," continues her Captain's report, "was unattractive. The ship was heavily damaged: she could not steam ... some 5,000 tons of flood-water had increased her draught by about 5 feet. She was only a few miles from

Salerno and liable to air attack at any moment: radar was out of action: it was known that there were submarines in the area and only four destroyers were in company: Malta was some 300 miles away and the Polish ship *Slazak* reported that she had overheard the Germans preparing another air attack." Never in all her long career had she been in such a predicament, and it called for all her own vitality and all the determination of her crew to save her. Yet astonishingly she had only nine men killed and 14 injured.'

Much later, when Bertie allowed me to see his own private diary, I borrowed extracts of the wounded ship's epic return to Malta, which I used in my wartime autobiography *Grey Mistress*.

[16 September 1943] *Dead overhead we suddenly sighted three new objects. Probably wireless-controlled bombs. It was clear they were going to hit us within seconds. . . . There was nothing to be done and I watched carefully.*

The first to arrive missed us by a few feet. A second later one hit us just abaft the funnel. The third near-missed the starboard side.

I was not thrown off my feet but for a fraction of a second had a kind of black-out like when you take a hard toss at football or off a horse. But I could see and think perfectly clearly all the time. Black smoke and dirt from the funnels and a hell of a noise. Thought the whole mast was coming down as it rocked, bent and whipped. For a moment I thought we were probably sunk and was quite prepared for the ship to break in two.

No one lost their heads or shouted or anything on the Bridge. They were all first class and the anti-aircraft guns which had opened fire kept firing. That was good.

Then there was calm after the storm. I found the ship would steer, the engines were going ahead. A fire was reported in the hangar. 'Put it out,' I said. Then to Guns. 'If we can steam and shoot we'll carry out our final bombardment.'

I set course up the swept channel.

Then reports began to come in, all very calm and accurate. The Principal Medical Officer reported some six killed and 20 wounded, three seriously. The Chief reported some 4,000 to 5,000 tons of water had come in. Water was dribbling into all sorts of places. . . .

I kept going at six knots. Then the ship would not steer. We were in the swept channel and we steered in a circle. I stopped engines. We were heading straight into the mines. A mine-sweeper sent us violent signals to get out of it. I couldn't, for the helm was hard over, and finally the starboard engine room died out too.

So there we were, once again, going round in circles with our way carrying us and quite helpless.

My husband told me, long afterwards, of the strange familiarity of that day when, as at Jutland, this same ship had waltzed towards what seemed like certain doom with her helm jammed and her guns still firing. Now, as then, Captain, officers and men united in the desperate endeavour to get their crippled *Warspite* back to port.

'Captain Packer prepared at once to be taken in tow,' wrote Captain Roskill, 'changed over to mechanical steering and called on the *Delhi* to provide anti-aircraft protection. The American tug *Hopi* had taken her in tow and she was moving slowly out of Salerno Bay. Two more American salvage tugs soon arrived and she then set course for the Straits of Messina at four knots, surrounded by screening destroyers. . . . With no lights except battery lamps, and no fans or machinery running, the silence inside the ship was eerie . . . with no forced ventilation the atmosphere . . resembled that in a long submerged submarine. There was no water to drink, only a strictly limited quantity of lemonade; and nothing but biscuit and corned beef to eat. The *Valiant* passed her during the night a few miles to the westward in a blaze of tracer. . . . '

At 2 a.m. she was only 15 miles from Salerno, 3 feet deeper in the water, listing heavily and 'the moon full bright'. Bertie's diary continues:

[17 September] *With the dawn the situation had worsened and there was much fatigue for no one had had much stand-off during the past few days, and since the hit everyone was on their feet, either at the guns, hauling in wires, bailing, pumping or shoring up. Men were beginning to sit down and rest and drop off to sleep as they sat. But they were all marvellously cheerful, willing and fatalistic. I said a few words to the sailors over the broadcaster. Ours was a common hazard of War, we had done what we set out to do and had been hit. We had scared hell out of the German Army and braced up our own soldiers. We might even have turned the scale. I admired their good humour and hard work. Between us we would get the Old Lady back to Malta.*

As I write Stromboli is abeam. The flooding has been checked and we are still float. I am still without sleep, but keyed-up, living on sandwiches and lemonade as the galleys are 'out'. And now on to the Bridge to get thro' the Messina Narrows. . . .

[18 September] *We had the hell of a night. . . . When we struck the tide-rips and whirlpools the ship became unmanageable. From midnight until 5 a.m. we were completely out of control and going through the Straits broadside on with all tow parted except one. However just as the tide turned off Reggio to take us back up the Straits again, I got a tug alongside each side aft and straightened her up sufficiently for the tugs forward to go ahead and get some way on the ship. Since getting through Messina all has gone well and now at 9 p.m. we are off Cape Pasero and should reach Malta tomorrow morning.*

Got two hours' sleep this afternoon and am completely refreshed. John May, the Physical Training Officer, was very thoughtful and had my sea cabin picketed, with instructions that no one should disturb me 'unless his journey was really necessary'.

Very busy making arrangements and reports so that immediate action can be taken as soon as we arrive.

The sailors are splendid, as they always are when things go wrong. I see them naked on the deck washing each other from buckets of salt water dipped over the side.

Bailing out compartments with buckets in this heat is hard work. About 200 men are at it all the time. . . .

So at last, on Sunday morning, with her dead committed to the deep, her weary sailors lined up on deck and her band playing, the Old Lady entered the Grand Harbour.

[19 September] *All the ship's companies turned out to see us go past and I got many signals. There is no doubt there was great anxiety that we should not get back. Well, we have. So, for the second time in 27 years, I have limped into port in the* Warspite *heavily damaged.*

Tremendous publicity hailed the *Warspite* and her sister ship *Valiant* for their part in averting the 'large-scale disaster' which Winston Churchill had told Parliament 'could not be excluded . . . it was right to risk capital ships in this manner. . . .'

On 22 September 1943, the *Times of Malta* (which, throughout the siege, had kept going) gave the two battleships a heartwarming welcome on their return to port. Desmond Tighe, *Reuter*'s Special Correspondent, must have interviewed everyone on board *Warspite* from Captain Bertie Packer to Able Dog Pluto. Lieutenant-Commander J. G. Hamilton, the Gunnery Officer, told him:

' "We were lying so close inshore that as the shells roared from our guns we could watch soldiers stripped to the waist unloading stores, supplies, lorries and tanks on the beaches. . . . Our forward observation officers who'd been landed on the beaches quickly put us on to good targets and we proceeded to plaster them. Our American colleagues were delighted. One signal came through saying 'Gee, I'd like to send my compliments to your Captain'. The whole time German planes made repeated attacks on us. At one time it was an incredible sight as practically all the heavy and light guns of *Warspite* and *Valiant* were firing at once." . . . Captain Crombie of the Royal Marines who went ashore acting as Forward Operation Officer for the bombardment gave me a very vivid description of the shoots. "I was lying with three ratings on a hilltop close to the enemy lines," he said.

"Below me on a plain I could see a tank battle going on. When our 15-inch shells rushed overhead it seemed like a sudden clap of thunder. Then I watched houses blown high into the sky and ammunition dumps going up with fearsome explosions, black smoke and debris flying into the air. I couldn't see the Germans themselves as they were concentrated in a deep ravine, but the ship's gunnery was extremely accurate and our shells were dropping clean on the target. The effect on the German morale must have been enormous." '

The *Sphere* and the *Illustrated London News* of 25 September gave the Italian Fleet Surrender and the Salerno Battle exciting pictured spreads with photographs of Captain H. A. ('Bertie') Packer inset and on Sunday, 17 October, the *New York Herald Tribune* saluted *'Warspite, Grand Old Lady of the British Fleet'*. The cutting was sent to Bertie by G. W. Alcock, who in his accompanying letter said: 'The *Warspite* has done such a grand job that you should well be proud of her accomplishment and it occurred to me that you might like to know that in the United States we are just as much interested in the *Warspite* as if she were one of our own ships.'

Our South African papers and radio, like the rest of the free world, gave the Navy full credit for its support of the Army, and Peter, Mum and I were as proud and excited as we were relieved that the Old Lady was safe – and, for the present, her Captain too.

Safe yes. But out of the game for some time to come. What would happen to Bertie now? Where would he go? He was back in Malta in his crippled ship receiving attention in the dry dock, and no home ashore.

HMS *Warspite, 30 September 1943*

... I am so delighted that you and Piet have picked up your close comradeship so unpleasantly interrupted. *We* haven't given him much of a home life, but we've done our best and he *has* had a home life. A background, many friends and a fine country for his future.

I am very keen you should buy a piece of land as you suggest, and don't make it too small! We want a garden one day between the mountains and the sea. I'm saving up for it and I know you are too. . . .

Here, we and the Old Lady have made quite a name for ourselves it seems. It's a matter of great luck. One goes on doing one's damn'dest and suddenly and unexpectedly picks up a bit of jam. Anyhow here we are in the same old haunt and will be for some weeks, I'm afraid.

The Mediterranean is certainly open – wide open – and Winston has said publicly that a big Fleet will be off to the East – not round the Cape, of course. At the same time the only dock, as far as I know in the Indian Ocean now that Singapore has gone, is Durban! I have already written asking to be considered for a big ship in the Eastern Fleet. . . .

9 October You will notice that I am writing this on my birthday. A quiet day.

When I turned out this morning at 07.00 to drink tea and listen to the news, I saw for the first time for months an enormous bunch of flowers crammed into a jug. Shortly afterwards Corney came in looking very self-conscious and smug and said 'Anything you want, Sir? Many happy returns of the day.'

'Well, Corney,' said I. 'How on earth did you remember it was my birthday? I was keeping it quiet!'

'I just come to remember, like,' said Corney.

'Where did these flowers come from?'

'Can't imagine,' said Corney, sweating all over. 'Nice, aren't they?'

'Lovely. It must be the Maltee in the Gopher (soda water) stall who brings me grapes. He's probably got a flower garden as well.'

'Reckon it must be, like,' said Corney, and went.

About 09.00, after breakfast, he came in again, as he often does.

'Have you any vases?' say I. 'These flowers are just crammed into the jug.'

No, he hadn't. Nor had the Wardroom.

'A pity Madam isn't here,' says Corney. 'She'd have a fine time like with them flowers.'

It was just what I was thinking and almost more than I could take, so I managed to say, 'Madam was much better at arranging flowers than growing them, wasn't she, Corney? Anyway, I must get on with the War – and thank you.'

Off he went, and so did I. So that was my birthday as far as birthdays go. Anyway, one thing I know for sure is that in 'Tees Lodge' I wasn't forgotten.

On 18 October we received a Night Letter Telegram 'via Overseas'.

PACKER TEES LODGE HOPESTREET CAPE
ADDRESS COMMODORE PACKER CARE C IN C MEDITERRANEAN
ALGIERS VIA CAIRO FIT AND WELL TEMPORARY APPOINTMENT
FEW MONTHS BEST LOVE PACKER

Soon afterwards the Old Lady was patched up and, under the temporary command of Commander the Hon. D. Edwardes, made her slow way home through the Straits of Gibraltar. In March 1944 she entered Rosyth Dockyard for the last extensive repairs that would enable her to play her part in the final invasion of Europe.

I know that when Bertie said goodbye to his brave mauled *Warspite* in the sunshine of Malta it hurt him as much, in its own way, as that other parting on a dark wintry night on Euston Station nine months ago. Their battles had been fought together and won together with a ship's company of which he had written at the time of greatest danger and exhaustion, 'The sailors are splendid as they always are when things go wrong'.

26

'Being ashore makes me seasick.'

| Allied Headquarters | Algiers |
| 1943 to 1944 | Caserta |

FOR once Bertie's natural buoyancy had deserted him.

c/o Commander-in-Chief, Mediterranean Station, Algiers via Cairo 17 October 1943

... Well here I am, and how! On Tuesday 12th Tim Sherwin* and I stepped into a plane and flew to Algiers. Piet will like to know that it was a Dakota troop-carrier. You sit on an aluminium bench along the side and it's hellishly hard-arse. We arrived in a thunderstorm and I've had the devil of a rush ever since. This place is packed. We have a small Naval Mess for Commanders and above in a hotel. I have a bedroom to myself which is more than most have.

I've never seen chaps work like the Commander-in-Chief's staff.

At 6.45 a.m. I get a great bundle of signals and go thro' them before breakfast, deal with them and a thousand other things in my office from 8.30 to 1 p.m., back at 2 and work thro' till 8 p.m. After dinner most go back. I won't. What's more, once I've got things organized, I'm damned if I'll work all those hours every day. If I have to, I'll reckon I can't organize myself. But it's one of those 'beginning jobs', and poor Tim went down with fever on the second day! I am Chief of Administration (Commodore second class) to the Commander-in-Chief Mediterranean, who is in the same gang and building as Eisenhower (Ike) and Co. This post

---

* Paymaster Commander T. Sherwin, Bertie's Secretary and right hand.

hasn't existed before and the fact is our Naval Administration, i.e. supplies of stores, repairs and maintenance of
fleets and bases nearly broke down thro' insufficient staff
organization. So I've been pulled out of my poor ship to
reorganize the whole thing. Someone ought to have been
here a year ago. It's a job I *loathe* but will of course do my
best. I don't know how long it will last and see no chance of
getting back to my dear *Warspite* and the good chaps in her.

In fact, my sweet, for once you find your Unk as low as a
boa-constrictor's belly button.

Anyhow, darling, anything may be round the corner, and
one is up one moment and down the next and sometimes it's
fun and sometimes not. At present being ashore makes me
seasick. I love you like hell. Something will happen. It
must.

His sister, Dorothy, sent him cuttings from the news-
papers and illustrated weeklies.

12 December 1943

My dear Dorothy,
Thank you and Norman very much for your combined
letter, cuttings and other letters forwarded.

I don't know why the papers went off half-cock about my
fine old ship. I hadn't seen them because I only get *The
Times*.

Out here in naval circles we don't think the *Warspite* did
anything very special and in fact behaved rather indecor-
ously, like an elderly spinster getting a ringside seat at an 'all
in' wrestling contest.

I am still working very long hours and have a whiff of the
Great from time to time as they whizz past going from here
to there and back again.

A happy Christmas to all of you.

Meanwhile Peter was swotting for his matriculation and
his House Master assured me that he would not fail. So the
day school broke up he and his friends rushed off to the

Recruiting Office to join up. They were 17. All they needed was parental consent.

I signed the form and memory flashed back to the first days of the War at Abingdon Bomber Station and a 13-year-old boy enviously watching the bombers take off and saying fervently, 'I hope this War lasts long enough for me to get in it!'

So the fourth wartime Christmas came and went. My own efforts had been diverted almost entirely to broadcasting and writing 'concealed propaganda' scripts and plays and taking part in them.

On 29 February (Leap Year) 1944, Bertie brought his sister, Dorothy, up to date on our news and his.

29 February 1944

My dear Dorothy,

I have been putting off writing to you from day to day and week to week. I knew you and Norman would want to hear about Piet. This is the latest.

He passed his matric first class and has joined up in the South African Naval Forces as an Ordinary Seaman and has written me a cheerful letter with a vivid description of cleaning out latrines on a hot day in mid-summer. . . . His idea is to get seconded into the RN Fleet Air Arm.

So there it is.

Meanwhile Joy cables excitedly (and with good reason) that Eyre & Spottiswoode have accepted her book *Pack and Follow*, have given her £125 advance royalties but cannot publish until 1945 thro' lack of paper. A great effort.

With me all goes well and I look like being here for ever.

A few of us had cocktails with the Duff-Coopers the other evening. The lights in their villa were dim and Lady Diana D-C* was wearing a golden tea-gown with the most magnificent jade bead necklace I have ever seen, even in China. She is a very beautiful woman and only smiles once

---

* The reigning beauty between the Wars.

287

every 20 minutes, so the thing is to time your joke 20 minutes after the last smile and you are obviously a successful humorist. We have formed an 'Admire Diana' club, and whenever she appears in public we admire her more than somewhat. It sounds as if we were insincere. I assure you of the contrary! Duff is quiet, pleasant, and obviously adores his Diana.

I have little news, for it is the same old nip, anything interesting is forbidden by the Censor.

The Frenchmen are very co-operative and I see a lot of the French Navy. There is, as you will have gathered, a 'hang over' from German Occupation days, and every now and then some 'collaborationists' are tried and bumped off.

And so it will continue, no doubt. No one worries except, I suppose, the prisoner at the bar.

I hope all goes well with you and Norman, Mother and 'les girls'. Joy's Norman was in Cairo but has been sent back to start a plastic unit in Cape Town and lecture at the University – which makes sense.

It was over a year since we had parted at Euston. It was no worse for me than for Mrs. Corney and the toddler her husband hadn't seen since he was new-born, or for many of my South African friends whose husbands were 'in the bag' in Germany or Italy and whose young children had been taught to call a photograph in uniform 'Daddy'. But with Bertie in a 'shore job' I became increasingly restless and, like my son, eager to be in the thick of things again.

My Mother recognized the symptoms in both of us.

'When Piet goes—' I began.

She finished the sentence. 'There'll be no holding you here. But people can't just go where they want these days as you know.'

By May, Bertie had the administrative post he detested fully organized, so when the Commander-in-Chief's Chief of Staff went on sick leave Bertie became Acting Chief of Staff as well as Commodore Administration. This interested him, so he was happier.

Mails too were more reliable.

Algiers, 5 May 1944

. . . I was delighted to have your letter of 24 April telling me, among other things, all about our Piet. He may have to hang around waiting for a passage for months. He will be impatient and you and Mum will be relieved. Oh, dear, I wish I could be with you all.

Well, I'm 'full out' at the moment. As Acting Chief of Staff I represent Commander-in-Chief Mediterranean at all the big high-level conferences, so I mix with the Mighty and have my hands and brain full. I must say that in the political meetings, where we discuss the political matters which affect the War in this theatre, I am glad of my Naval Attaché experience and knowledge of the Foreign Office way of tackling things.

I now live de luxe in the Commander-in-Chief's villa with his Secretary, Pat Miller, and drive about in magnificence in a car with a flag. Hoped to play tennis last Monday, which restores clear-thinking and chases away the cobwebs, but no luck as swarms of locusts everywhere were so thick that play was impossible. Country walks are out at the present as I have to be near a telephone always.

I see in my *Times* that Bill Mabane has married his lovely Stella Duggan. . . .

Piet, Mummy and I exchanged our letters as a rule. I was interested that Bertie had the temerity to offer his son advice on how to treat girlfriends. 'Unless you are the one to call the tune they will always push you around. They are made that way. So call the tune and they'll dance all right and like it. Of course it isn't necessary to call a tune on a foghorn or a loud-hailer any more than one goes after a butterfly with an elephant gun. A bit of sugar may work just as well. About myself? Well here I seem to be stuck. I've got a big job and someone has to do it and it happens to be me. But I do miss my *Warspite*. The great news today and the cause of this letter is a signal saying you have been recommended for Air

Branch Commission as pilot and are being discharged to RNB Portsmouth. The Barracks will be lousy and crowded but it will only be a stage in the game. Keep me advised of your movements for my big kick will come if I find you somewhere around and can get hold of you. It might happen ...'

It began to 'happen' when a letter, much mutilated by the Censor arrived at 'Tees Lodge' in the middle of May. It was addressed to 'Mrs. H. A. Packer and Mrs. Petersen' and on the back stated 'from Ordinary Seaman Peter Packer CPB 58 5881'. The grubby envelope was headed *On Active Service* and a gummed label told us it had been OPENED BY CENSOR/DEUR SENSOR OOOPGEMAAK. The date and name of ship were excised.

SS—— Durban

... We had a pleasant trip up here in a crowded troop train. We had to have seven sittings at meals but were only allowed to attend one!

When we got here yesterday we came straight aboard this trooper. She is (no, *was*) a lovely ship but has been filled everywhere with bunks. There are no smoking or writing rooms etc. All are stacked and lined with bunks. When we came on board the ship was already packed and we managed to squeeze in. We thought we were all set. Not a damn! This morning we saw the quay crowded with (a line snipped out by CENSOR). They started to come aboard. They are aboard. One can't move. We haven't got, nor will get, any leave ashore so the next time you hear from me will probably be UK. Hope so!

However an airletter card winged its way to me from a port unknown, stamped from HM Ships on 24 May 1944, and in it Piet said, 'I'm still hoping to see Dad but the trouble is we aren't allowed ashore anywhere. ... Well, Mom, you make merry for both of us till I get back or Dad does. Here's luck!'

By some means Bertie succeeded in extracting Peter from

his slow boat and arranged for him to rejoin it further along the coast of North Africa. This involved a week in a corvette as a 'look out' and a flight from Bizerta to Algiers.

Algiers, 11 June 1944

Piet has arrived! He flew in at midday. So tall and fit. He stepped out of the airplane in khaki shorts, shirt and a sailor cap and I was there to meet him with Corney. He shouldered his kitbag, and with his hammock in his hand like every sailor I have ever seen, we marched across the airfield to the car.

It was the hell of a moment. Soon we were at ease and I took him to the office and then to my room where he has a camp-bed and into the Senior Officers' Mess where he will eat. An ordeal for him, but he was easy and natural with everyone, so they were too. So kind, all of them. Then to my room where he got his dirty clothes ready for washing tomorrow and cleaned his shoes – very particular he is. And off we went for a swim. He's lithe, muscular and soaked in sun. Then back to the hotel at 5 p.m. where I am writing to you now after a couple of hours' work. Piet is with Corney borrowing a plain clothes outfit from one of my Lieutenant-Commanders so that he can go anywhere with me. When I am unable to be with him he will sail boats and swim with Corney. They are great friends. Tomorrow he is going out for the day on board a carrier to watch how things are done...
16 June ... I know you will want lots of news about Piet and me so I've managed to pinch a couple of spare letter-cards. We are having a fine time. He gets on well with everybody whatever their rank or station, and is mixed up in sailing and swimming. Last night I gave a dinner party for six in a 'Taverna' in the woods. Countess de Breteuil (the 'Queen' of the French Auxiliary Transport Service), big cheerful and sophisticated, her pretty Adjutant, and the little 19-year-old Princess Anne de Bourbon Parme,* her Personal Aide, who is attractive and amusing and got on

---

* Later married King Michael of Rumania, since dethroned.

with Piet like a house on fire. Our sixth was Teddy Phillips, a Lieutenant RNVR, who is of the French Liaison Section. Next week we hope to go for 24 hours to a mountain chalet I have borrowed. Oh, if only you could be with us it would be heaven. But, even if some miracle brought you here, wives are absolutely forbidden. . . .

The 24 hours in the mountain chalet sounded wonderful, 'the air glorious', and the company too! My restless longing to share it all was torment. The pattern of the War was widening, 'very fluid', Bertie wrote. 'Everything is moving fast and well in Italy. Let's hope it will increase its impetus and bust the enemy wide open. My future movements are more clouded than ever. I shall find you somehow when this job allows. It's hell without you.'

26 June 1944

. . . Our Piet left me at 07.30 this morning cockahoop and on top of the world. He should join a draft and the Chief Petty Officer in charge is the Chief Steward of our Mess who is a great friend of his. Last night he was ironing and packing till 1 a.m. and no longer is my small room full of damp clothes hanging on lines, ironing board, shoes, chocolate, belts, knives, whet-stones, bathing trunks, towels, books, letters, etc., in fact a Widow Twankey's kitchen at its worst. But of course I miss them, however much I blasted and damned them. He is now as keen on his kit as he used to be on electric trains, working models and explosives. He knows no half measures. Well, we've had a fine time. On Saturday he had lunch out at the camp where Anne de Bourbon lives and works. They swam in the afternoon and in the evening I got out there and we had a kouss-kouss in an Arab cottage. It is rice (or semolina cooked like rice) with meat and hot sauce. A curry really. During the meal cats, dogs, chickens and goats wandered in and out and it was all very simple and picturesque. The Moroccan *garde champêtre* to whom it belonged talked to the goat just like a dog. And the goat stood on the man's head like a chamois on a peak and it was all fun. Then Piet went off with Anne to a party and arrived in my room at 3 a.m. Incidentally, he is very strict about spirits and quite firmly declines the many offers he has made.

The War goes well everywhere. My only depression besides Piet's departure is your absence. I can't bear it – but must.

I couldn't bear it either, especially when someone 'in the know' hinted to me that it was quite probable that my husband would be at least another year in the Mediterranean! Everything always seems blackest in the small hours before the dawn and on 30 June Bertie received a letter from me, written after a sleepless night and reflecting my despair at the prospect of a parting which was likely to be extended from months into years. I couldn't have chosen a crueller moment to send it.

94-General Hospital, Algiers, 30 June, 1944

. . . This has been one hell of a week. The night Piet left, last Monday, I was brought here and was operated on for a double rupture on Wednesday. Today it is Friday and I am lying flat on my back, as you can imagine, in some discomfort. It seems I'll be helpless for a fortnight at best. Not serious but a ruddy nuisance. This place is an ex-workhouse at the back of Algiers turned temporarily into a military hospital. The heat is breathless and I lie and sweat. There are no fans, no ice, no fly-netting, no bell for the night nurse and I can't move to switch a light on or off. The radio blares all day and my room is part of a ward – a sort of alcove. On the other hand the doctors, sisters, etc., are all very nice and kind, and so are the other patients – all young soldiers, so one can't complain.

Yesterday your letter arrived (written at 4 a.m.!). It could hardly have come at a more unsuitable moment and I realize you are 'in a state'. I agree with all you said, except that one dreadful sentence that lay on my brain all night 'that you are beginning to fear I could do without you'. You must *never* say such a thing again. Ever. It was an awful thing even to think!

The horror is that wives simply are not allowed here. Vice-Admiral Burrough at Gibraltar, Moore at Naples, Morgan at Taranto, Hamilton at Malta, Poland at Alex. – all in two-year jobs ashore – are definitely not allowed to have their wives with them. *No one is* – except the Commander-in-Chief in a shore job and Heads of Diplomatic Missions like Duff-Cooper. And no one in our Armed Forces is allowed to employ civilians in any capacity. So that's that.

But I believe staff may soon be wanted for UNRRA* and various other Welfare organizations and that Cairo is the best recruiting centre. If you are prepared to leave Mum and can get to Cairo somehow, on some pretext, and take a chance we *will* some way manage to see each other again. We must.

The whole thing is that I am to relieve Dundas as Chief of Staff in October whatever happens. *That means another year at least in the Mediterranean.* C-C has told me so. I am incoherent. Forgive me. . . .

When I read this letter, so close on the heels of Bertie's happy reunion with Peter, I was shocked and stricken with remorse. I had had no idea he was in hospital.

The beautiful Cape – always generous – was a wartime Paradise for ships or troops on their way to battle via the Cape route. The organization for their welfare, comfort and entertainment, under the leadership of Lucy Bean, head of the SAWAS (South African Women's Auxiliary Service), was comprehensive. South Africa had plunged heart and soul into every form of War effort. Her fighting forces had campaigned through Africa, liberated Abyssinia, shared the hardships of desert warfare and the Allied advance into Europe. General Smuts was universally acclaimed as one of the greatest soldier-statesmen of his time. But although many South African homes were bereaved they had not

---

* United Nations Refugee Rehabilitation Association.

suffered the devastation of enemy attack nor any invasion other than that of a vast flood of refugees from the Far, Middle and Near East. All in all, the Cape was the best place anyone could wish to be in under the circumstances. My mother pointed these things out to me patiently, but I had made up my mind to get to Cairo, and from there 'into the War' again and if possible into Bertie's theatre of it.

On 6 July I made my first application to be considered for a War job in Egypt – War Correspondent, welfare, propaganda or information services – through the South African Bureau of Information.

A few days later Peter arrived in England, and he saw the Packer family and Hillie before going to Portsmouth Barracks.

94-General Hospital, Algiers, 17 July 1944

... Your 29 June airletter has just arrived. Of course I understand the problems. Our Chief Wren here tells me you should apply for a Cairo job thro' the British High Commissioner's Office in Cape Town. Give it a go, darling. Soon. These things take time.

I was thrilled to get your cable of Piet's safe arrival and of Philip's marriage to his Elspeth and have written to congratulate him. Any day now we should hear about Piet and I do hope he will be successful, tho' I hate flying. Let us be thankful that they don't send half-trained boys out in awful old crates these days. He will have full training and the finest aircraft and can be proud for ever after.

I'm still flat on my back and have had a bellyful of heat, flies and staring at a white wall. But the op has been perfect, I'm told, and no longer will an old cat claw at my guts. Today is Monday and on Thursday I'll be allowed up for the first time. My relief has been appointed and I must be 100 per cent fit and in Italy by the beginning of August. Admiral John Cunningham (no relation to A.B.C. who is going to be First Sea Lord) will be my boss. ...

These things take time. My application of 6 July was

getting me nowhere. Bertie's letter arrived on the 24th and I instantly went to the High Commissioner's Office, filled in a long form, produced proofs of my ability to be useful, a covering letter, references, and the requisite 'recent photograph' which I hoped looked responsible and honest. Weeks passed. Bertie was in Italy, Peter was accepted for the Fleet Air Arm and would soon be drafted to Texas USA for his training as a pilot (part of the lease-lend agreement between Britain and America), and I complained to my young friend, Gerda Syfret, that I was 'going slowly mad'. Gerda was the secretary of Lady (Eileen) Graaff who, among her many other welfare activities, was Head of the Red Cross in South Africa. Her son, Sir de Villiers Graaff,* like Gerda's husband, was a prisoner of war. Lady Graaff was also a great friend of my Mother's, and when she heard about my unproductive efforts to get a War job in Cairo, she decided to give matters a push. So, on one unbelievable day at the end of August, Gerda came to 'Tees Lodge' to see me.

'I have a copy of a telegram which concerns you. Here it is.'

From: Ambassador, Cairo.
To: High Commissioner for the United Kingdom, Pretoria.
      27 August 1944. Received 28 August.
      No. 24.

I have received a (1 group omitted) dated 30 July, from Lady Graaff of South African Women's Auxiliary Services Command No. 13 Cape Peninsula recommending services of Mrs. Packer who has applied for a post in Cairo. Can you please inform Lady Graaff that we are anxious to find something suitable for Mrs. Packer and think we shall be able to do so once she has arrived in Egypt. There is however nothing immediately except a job as assistant Feature Editor in News Division of Minis-

---

* The present Leader of the Opposition in the South African Parliament.

try of Information here at £240 a year. It would be necessary for Mrs. Packer to pay her own passage. Please telegraph whether Mrs. Packer would accept this post in which case Ministry of Information will make formal appointment. I realize this post is beneath Mrs. Packer's qualifications but I would emphasize that there is a good chance of finding something better for her after her arrival here, so I trust she will not be too much discouraged by terms offered.

I couldn't believe it.

'You're not dreaming,' Gerda smiled. 'D'you take the job?'

'Do I take it? I grab it this minute! How do I say thank you?'

Within a week I was on board a trooper bound for Alexandria.

'We know you have to go,' said Nannie, when she and Mummy said goodbye to me on Cape Town Station. 'We understand.'

They didn't wait to see the Durban train go. Like Piet's, four months earlier, it was packed with troops.

In Cairo I lived in a hostel for women in various war jobs and every day at 6 o'clock, in the golden light of early morning, buses collected us, dumped us at our offices, brought us back at 1 p.m. and collected us again at 5 p.m. when we worked till 8 p.m. These hours seemed odd at first but the desert midday heat was still considerable and the arrangement was sensible. The Gezireh Sports Club was not far from the hostel and those who cared to arrange tennis or swimming instead of a siesta could do so. My job at the Cairo branch of MOI consisted mainly of writing articles – many of them about the Far East – and working for magazines with a wide distribution among the Forces. The Naval Officer in Charge, Commodore Barry Stevens, was helpful in every way, and so were several diplomats who had known us both in the Balkans. It might have been a delightful assignment for the duration but to me it was a stepping-stone. All my antennae were directed towards Italy.

How I got there was through a series of coincidences already covered in *Grey Mistress*. I believe very strongly in coincidence but I also believe it can only be turned to account when every force of mind, initiative and instinct is on the hunt like a hungry animal. One senses any opportunity, however improbable, and follows it up with supernormal determination and cunning.

At last the unbelievable happened and a Colonel whose name I did not know decided that I could be useful in an organization known as PWB. On 30 October, I received confirmation of the appointment, above an illegible signature.

SECRET & PERSONAL PWBC/69 *PWB (EMC) MEF*
30 October 1944

Mrs. J. Packer c/o MIME CAIRO
This is to confirm that you have been engaged for a position with this Organization in Italy w.e.f. 1 November 1944. A condition of this engagement is that you are prepared to work with PWB anywhere in Italy.

You will be given one month's notice of our intention to terminate your services, after which we undertake to repatriate you to Egypt.

In Italy you will receive a basic salary of £300.12.0 per annum, which will be paid into your account in London with the Standard Bank of South Africa, Northumberland Avenue, WC2, plus local subsistence alowance of £182.10.0 (equivalent), making your total emoluments £483.2.0 per annum.

(signed) Chief Administrative Officer.
CHE/KJ
Copy to Principal F & FAO (British).
      AFHQ

Nearly four months had elapsed since 6 July, when I had made my first tentative assault on my final objective.

Commodore Stevens sent Bertie a signal to Allied Headquarters in Caserta and gave me a number at which to telephone him on arrival.

Never was a desert dawn more wonderful than on the day I took my place in the Dakota troop-carrier and strapped myself into the aluminium seat. Vesuvius flew her delicate white pennant, Salerno Bay sparkled beneath us and we landed at Capodichino Airport. An American Sergeant checked our papers at the transport office.

'PWB? You'll want transport to the PWB HQ in Naples.'

'Where is Caserta?'

'The opposite way. About 20 minutes in a jeep.'

'Is a jeep going there?'

'There's always a jeep going to Caserta. Want a ride?'

'Yes, please. Have I time to make a telephone call?'

'If you make it snappy.'

I gave the Freedom Number of the Naval Headquarters and was put through to Commander Tim Sherwin, Bertie's Secretary.

'Joy! The Chief of Staff is out of his room. I'll find him.'

'No, Tim. I'm hitching a ride in a jeep from the airport right now. Just tell him.'

'Come to Archway Eight. Corney will be there to meet you.'

The green plain of Naples, an avenue of sycamores, a huge palace, Archway Eight and Corney with his beaming smile.

'We knew you'd make it somehow, Madam.'

He drew a snapshot from his pocket.

'Your little Melvin! It must be. He's exactly like you.'

'The wife says so – and very old-fashioned in his ways.'

He took back the snapshot and picked up my suitcase. I followed him up a wide staircase and along a stone corridor. 'TO OFFICES OF COMMANDER-IN-CHIEF MEDITERRANEAN, ROYAL NAVY.'

Corney tapped on a door marked SECRETARY TO CHIEF OF STAFF.

'Here we are, Madam.'

Tim sprang to his feet. On his desk were photographs of Kathie, his young blonde wife, and the little son he had not seen. Corney put down my suitcase and disappeared.

'This is a great effort, Joy. Very exciting. You'll find the Chief of Staff alone.'

He opened the door between his offices and the one marked CHIEF OF STAFF. I was dimly aware of a large map-lined conference room and a screen dividing it from a huge desk covered with papers and an elaborate system of telephones. An open window framed the plain of Naples and the shining Volturno River. It silhouetted the familiar figure crossing the room towards me.

27
'We have got together and are incredibly happy.'

Allied Headquarters	Caserta
1944 to New Year 1946	German Surrender in Italy
	V.E. and V.J.
	Peace. Malta

AHQ Italy, 10 November 1944

Dearest Mum,

You are the first person I quickly write to tell that my Joy-Joy arrived by air last Saturday. Don't let's go into the struggle to get her here, or even the kindness of the Commander-in-Chief who I thought would be furious but instead invited us both to stay at his 'Villa Emma' overlooking Naples Bay and Capri, and gave us the Royal Suite where the King slept last July on his visit here. So it was all just wonderful. The day was the first sunny day for two months!

Our honeymoon stopped this morning when Joy went off to her new job in Rome. She will save up her days off and visit me from time to time so my life is full of happiness. I cannot get away at all. My work is persistent, no half days or holidays, but Joy will be near. We are still trying to make up lost time by talk and have got quite a long way towards covering *almost two years apart*.

Anyhow, our Joy is quite unperturbed by her travels past or ahead of her. I only hope that now you know we have got together and are incredibly happy, it will make up to you a little for her absence.

Your very happy
Bertie.

'Villa Emma' was the official house requisitioned for the use of the Commander-in-Chief Mediterranean, Admiral Sir John Cunningham, who had a quizzical smile, an administrative brain and a sentimental heart which made 'Villa Emma' specially dear to him. Not only was the house luxurious with terraced gardens leading down to a private beach, but it was reputed to have been occupied by Ambassador Hamilton and his Emma, whose love affair with Nelson was a story as indestructible as the *Victory* herself – a story that began in Naples. For Bertie and me our brief stay at 'Villa Emma' was sheer enchantment, a haven of refuge in a beautiful over-civilized land under the harrow of a War more terrible than anything we had known in England. Italy had been taken over by her ex-ally and became everybody's battlefield. She had been shelled, bombed, fought through house by house and her ports, roads, bridges and fields mined and demolished by the retreating German armies. Her domestic situation was as complex as it was catastrophic. She had lost a War and turned against Fascism. Her puppet King had abdicated in favour of his son, Umberto, sponsored by the Allies and distrusted by his own people. In the North a few Fascist regiments continued to fight with the Germans, while in the mountains the anti-Fascist Partisans were waging guerrilla warfare aided by the allies. Their fate when captured was dreadful and included their families. Mussolini was in hiding.

Rome, however, had suffered comparatively little damage because the 'Eternal City' had enjoyed international immunity.

I was billeted in the PWB requisitioned hotel near the Via Veneto where we had our headquarters in a huge ice-cold building which had recently been occupied by the dreaded SS officers.

I reported to my boss, Captain Kenneth Carrick, a wartime officer in the Royal Artillery, who was Head of the PWB Publications Section. He was quick, concise, a born improviser who knew what he wanted and got it. He was approachable yet very much a 'loner'. From him I learned that PWB stood for Psychological Warfare Branch of Allied

Headquarters at Caserta, a combined Anglo-American organization with many ramifications, some strictly secret and military and others propaganda. Many of its personnel were refugees from the Occupied Countries of Europe who monitored news from underground movements.

'The term *Psychological Warfare* is *never* to be used,' said Captain Carrick. 'We are simply a unit of PWB. Every unit minds its own business. Ours, in Publications, is to project the Democratic principles of freedom and to encourage the Italians to help themselves to rehabilitate their shattered country. We are an information service. At first you'll be writing pamphlets and you'll be given directives. Our operation is flexible. As situations alter so must our methods. You'll find they alter constantly.'

It was a crazy outfit and I enjoyed the variety of our activities and those of my foreign colleagues.

Rome that winter swarmed with soldiers on leave preparing for the next big offensive and wherever they went a half-starved cloud of children surrounded them like mosquitoes, pleading for *caramele, cigarette*. Candy and cigarettes. Cigarettes were the only currency that year when the lira was not worth a song. Emaciated *signorinas* beckoned the troops too, hoping to hear the three whispered words that promised food in exchange for favours, '*Buona sera, Signorina!*'

Most nights I went back to the unheated office where Bertie could telephone me when the line was reasonably clear. Then I'd return to the small room I shared with British–French Suzanne and Italian–American Jane.

'You're mad to go out alone at night,' said Suzanne who worked in *Basic News*. 'Don't you know about the pack of prowling children who hunt like wild dogs and kill for the sake of a pair of fur gloves and fleece-lined boots, to say nothing of your coat and sweater? They're driven by cold and hunger. You can't blame them.'

I didn't believe her. But next morning I read about the child-killers in *Basic News* – after that Bertie telephoned me in our Mess. There was no longer any need for us to write to each other.

But I typed letters to my Mother and Peter in duplicate. Mother kept hers. They were stamped *Field Post – Passed by Censor*.

12 Polindep Unit CMF*, 4 January 1945

My darling Mummy and Piet,
This is a great day. Bertie has just phoned me from Naples to tell me that he has been promoted to Rear-Admiral! It seems he was wakened in the middle of the night to receive a message from Their Lordships (the Admiralty) to say that he had been promoted and confirmed in his present appointment as Chief of Staff to Commander-in-Chief Mediterranean. That means his job will continue for approximately a year and I shall have the lovely safe feeling that he is ashore and we are in the same theatre of War. So all in the garden is most beautiful. I must say I don't feel at all like Mrs. Admiral – at most Mrs. Commander – but how proud I am of Bertie all the same!

He is coming here 'on business' this next weekend. I have never spent a weekend with an Admiral before!

By February the South Africans had liberated Florence and PWB Publications and Displays moved north into a strictly military zone. I now wore khaki battledress – trousers and jacket with PWB tabs on the shoulders. The Medici Palace on the banks of the swift-flowing Arno was the Army Headquarters and every Piazza was plastered with huge signboards indicating Welfare Centres, Clubs and various amenities. A curfew was imposed at 10 p.m.

All the graceful historic bridges had been destroyed by the retreating Germans except the Ponte Vecchio which had been blocked and mined at either end. The waterfront was a mass of rubble where children with legs thin as toothpicks played and jumped and were occasionally blown up by un-exploded mines. After the more or less unharmed grandeur

---

* Combined Military Forces.

of Rome, this intimate heart of Italy's mediaeval culture, violated by War, was sad and stirring, Its art treasures had been hidden when possible, but many had been looted by Goering and carried off to Germany.

After four months of dormitory life I was thrilled to be allocated an attic bedroom to myself, tiny but with a view across red-tiled rooftops to spires, domes and the green hills already touched with early blossom.

My work had changed its character and I was now in charge of all displays in our Information Centres throughout the newly liberated area – panels showing the progress of the War, rehabilitation and reconstruction in Italy, beautiful features of the 'American Scene', indifferent ones of Britain, and medical and scientific advances in the Democracies. They were received hungrily by a people subjected for years to a Fascist-controlled Press and Radio.

14 Polindep Unit CMF, 8 April 1945

... Note new number Mum and Piet! *14*. We are the 'tail of the dragon' and follow our successful armies up the boot of Italy.

A wonderful thing happened last week! Into my office, which I share with Emmanuela, my Italian caption writer, came a tall rangy American General with a wicked gleam in his eye. He is a Mormon from Salt Lake City – very funny about it.

'Nice to meet you, Mrs. Packer,' said he. 'Your husband sends his love. He's dining with me in the Generals' Mess at Caserta tomorrow night and we thought it would be nice to have you with us. My name's McChrystal.'

I nearly fainted! General McChrystal is the Big Boss of our outfit and many others in PWB.

'Wonderful,' I gasped. 'But Caserta is an awfully long way from here.'

'I have a plane,' said he. 'Your boss tells me you're well ahead with your work and that you aim to do a feature on Royal Navy reconstruction in Naples and Leghorn.'

So there I was in Caserta next day with Tim Sherwin

organizing an official photographer to go with me to get the story, and Bertie putting me up in 'Villa Masoni' which he shares with the Commander-in-Chief's Secretary and the Commodore Administration. Bertie looks well and is in great form and we could hardly believe in our good luck.

The Generals' Mess is a sort of super camp on the hill above Caserta, with luxurious prefab army huts in a glade that smells deliciously of spring and overlooks the Palace and the vineyards away to the sea. We dined in a log cabin, very comfortably furnished and a blazing fire in an open hearth. General McChrystal introduced me to a slight sleepy-looking fair man, Major-General Airey, who is Field-Marshal Alexander's Intelligence Officer. He'd just come off leave and had brought a very well bred miniature dachshund with him. The little animal seemed mournful and General Airey said, 'He's not used to communal life yet and he's homesick.'

'Where did you get him?' I asked, but his master just looked vague. 'Oh, he's a Swiss breed – rather special. We call him Fritzel.'

Then Bertie brought General Lyman Lemnitzer along; American, vital and very amusing. Bertie said 'Lem is Deputy Chief to Field-Marshal Alexander and the greatest possible help to us. He has a way with foreigners.' Lem laughed and said 'I wish you could see this guy of yours at our staff meetings. He brings everything back to essentials. You should hear him pull them back when they get away from the point. He has a great sense of proportion.'

After dinner we talked a while and Fritzel sat on my lap and looked sad. I told General Airey I knew a Fritz-dog who joined in every conversation (Marion's). He shook his head. 'Not this chap. He knows that dogs should be seen and not heard.'

I was only away from Florence for four days but in that short time much had happened. In America President Roosevelt had died and Truman took his place. In Florence the night sky blazed with flashes of white light and the hill reverberated with the long sombre boom of heavy guns.

General Mark Clark's great offensive had been launched and the final battle of Italy had begun. In Germany the Russians were closing in on Berlin. Himmler's death camps were opened by the Allies to reveal their inhuman horrors. And within three weeks the little Swiss dachshund Fritzel made the headlines.

Fritzel was the 'cover plan' for Generals Airey and Lemnitzer who, disguised as American civilians anxious to buy a dog of his famous breed, had gone to Switzerland to conduct secret negotiations for a German Surrender in Italy.

The negotiations succeeded and the Instrument of Local Surrender was signed on 29 April, at Caserta Palace in the office of General Morgan, Chief of Staff to the Supreme Allied Commander, Field-Marshal Alexander. Bertie, representing the Naval Commander-in-Chief, was one of the signatories and was also present at preliminary meetings in a secret army hut in the Generals' Camp. He gave me his impression afterwards.

'The two German envoys were Lieutenant-Colonel von Schweinitz representing von Wietinghoff-Scheel, Commander-in-Chief of the German Forces in Italy, and Major Wenner acting for the Waffen SS General Wolff. They wore civilian clothes and clearly disliked each other intensely. Morgan, Airey and I were all German interpreters so we understood their asides, but of course we didn't let on. Everything was done through the official interpreter. The two German emissaries were typical of what they represented. Wietinghoff's Colonel was tall and very correct, an officer of the old school, whereas the SS Major was a dark hard-faced little Nazi thug. Whenever he tried to take the lead the Colonel shut him up with a sharp *"Halt dein Maul!"* Our General "Monkey" Morgan was splendid and when either of them raised an objection he said: "We are not here to argue. Unless you accept our terms unconditionally *as they are* negotiations will cease at once." And so it was.'

The Surrender came into effect on 2 May, at Rheims.

... It's unbelievably exciting! Total Victory in Europe. One thing follows another in an avalanche of drama. Hitler and Eva Braun, Himmler, Goebbels and his beautiful wife and young family all dead! Suicides and executions in all directions. Mussolini and his mistress, la Petacci, hanged upside down by the Partisans who have taken Milan. Our Information Centres are besieged day and night by crowds crazy to see the evidence of the end of Fascism. For me, of course, it's extra thrilling because Bertie was one of those who witnessed the signing of the first German Surrender at Caserta – and that after leading the Italian Fleet into Malta in the *Warspite*! It only remains for him to do the hat trick and take a Surrender in the Far East!

So now it's Japan.

Well, I've been asked to go on to the Far East with this organization and as it looks as if both my men will be fighting in that theatre I have of course jumped at the prospect – but on condition that Bertie does not need me somewhere else.

Our bomb-happy soldier is waiting to pack my typewriter as we move further north today ...

... At last I have breathing space to write to you both – the Censor now permits me to say where we are. It is Milan and I occupy a little room high above the city. Right now the sky is pink with sunset and the Cathedral stands against it in a pattern of lace with the gleaming gold Madonna at the top. When the Partisans liberated Milan she was unveiled after four years and the whole populace went mad with excitement at seeing her again. I think it says marvels for the Allied bombing that the area around the Cathedral is laid waste right to the doorway and the Cathedral itself untouched! Hundreds of birds nest in the niches of the saints. It's lovely to watch the Martins swoop and circle.

My boss is trying to arrange for me to go on to Trieste with a small section of this unit, but at present women are not allowed there as it is a 'flash point'. So, as usual, I have no idea 'what next?' ...

20 Polindep AIS, 15 July 1945

... A very memorable date – 19 today, my Piet!

Ten days ago the embargo on women employees was suddenly lifted and we packed up the Milan operation in 48 hours and set off with all our office and personal gear in three 3-tonners. We spent the night in Venice and next day took turns riding in the cab with the driver. I really enjoyed it. The country looked fertile and it was wonderful to come through the mountains and see the sea again with RN mine-sweepers in the harbour!

Trieste is sweltering hot but beautifully situated. It is temporarily under the control of an Allied Military Government.

We now call ourselves AIS (Allied Information Services) and are subject to military regulations as we are part of the 8th Army and are billeted in the hotel requisitioned for Army and AMG officers.

I have to plan our displays in three languages, Italian, Croat and Slovene and have a whole new bunch of artists and translators to train. They are all very temperamental and politically-minded and only agree on one point – that Fascism stinks. There are often riots and shootings in our outposts.

Very exciting! Bertie is coming to inspect the ports around here, Fiume, Pola, etc., as Venezia Giulia is far from peaceful. I hope to go with him, as AIS serves that area, which Tito wants to keep and expand for Yugoslavia. ... It'll be a long time before 'who gets what where' is sorted out!

20 Polindep, 24 July 1945

Bertie came here for the weekend and we had a wonderful

time. He told me that the Commander-in-Chief Mediterranean is going to remain on in Italy for another six months. So, about September, Bertie is to go to Malta where, as Chief of Staff, he will be acting C-in-C entitled to an official house and domestic staff. This morning he telephoned to say that the C-in-C had received permission from the Governor for me to live in the island!! This afternoon I told my boss, Major Carrick, that I wanted to resign in six weeks' time. He seemed really sorry because we've all been a very enthusiastic team but he quite understood how marvellous it is for me to contemplate a reasonable married life again.

Bertie is on the crest of a wave and *so* happy about Malta.

Two days later Japan received a dramatic ultimatum from the Big Three – USA, Britain and Russia. *Surrender or be destroyed!* She ignored it. On 5 August the first atom bomb was dropped on Hiroshima followed by another on Nagasaki on 9 August. In Hiroshima alone that one bomb devastated an area of 14 square miles, killed 60,000 people outright and thousands more by slow radiation. The following day the Japanese Government agreed to surrender providing the sovereignty of the Emperor remained intact. The Allies replied that the Emperor would be subject to the Allied Commander-in-Chief. On Tuesday, 15 August 1945 the Japanese War Minister committed ritual suicide, and the final capitulation of the last enemy in the Berlin–Rome–Tokyo Axis was announced. On Friday 17 August the Formal Document was signed in Manila and accepted by United States General Douglas MacArthur, now appointed the Supreme Allied Commander.

World War Two was over. And the terrible threat of nuclear power had been demonstrated to all mankind.

On 3 September, I wrote my last letter from Trieste to Mummy and Piet.

... Well, my dears, I have just had the happiest possible weekend with my Unkie who flew here from Caserta on Friday and left this morning. He is very well and full of pep and naturally we spent a great part of our time discussing Piet's future. That's why I've come back to the office tonight to write to you peacefully about it all. But first, and before I forget it, you'll be glad to know that Bertie has just been awarded another decoration. He now has the CB as well as the CBE. The CBE is Commander of the British Empire and he got it for Salerno and organizing the naval part of the invasion of Italy, but this new decoration (which is senior to the CBE) is for being Chief of Staff through all this successful stuff in Italy and also includes his war service at sea and ashore throughout, and I reckon he thoroughly deserves it. Oh, by the way, it stands for the 'something-something' Order of the Bath, which sounds ridiculous, but it's a dark rose-coloured ribbon with a lovely medal. He now has a real array of them and lives up to the good old name Fred gave him all those years ago when he called him 'Joy's war-horse'. But most of all, I love the two little oak leaves on his ribbon which stand for Mentions in Despatches both in the *same* ship and yet in two different Wars, the *Warspite* at Jutland as a Sub-Lieutenant and the *Warspite* at Salerno as Captain.

Now to Piet's future . . . after great discussions Bertie suddenly said, 'What would *you* want to do if you were a lad?' And I only knew one thing – I wouldn't want to be or do anything that had a ceiling. I still believe the limit in life should be the sky. Whatever job he takes up should hold no limiting factor. The goal must be in the mists. That's not advice I'd give *anyone*. But it *is* advice I'd give Piet. When you know your own limitations go for an objective within them. If you are not prepared to admit to your limitations, because you have not yet decided what they are, you can take a chance and fly wide and high. I tried to express something of this feeling to Bertie, but he kept my feet on the earth. 'The law is the way to anywhere,' he said.

My instant reaction was hostile, and then in a flash I knew what he meant. If you know the law you are good for anything under the sun. You can take off in any direction.

But I have a feeling we will get together somehow and throw our ideas back and forth. We'll still be in Malta when

Piet gets back to England and if we don't find *some* means of meeting I'll be very astonished.

Bertie and I are like a couple of ecstatic kids about going to Malta and having a house again. He flew over to the island the other day and saw one that's just right – 'Casa Rohan' – a large villa in Guarda Mangia overlooking St. Julian's Bay. We'll have a Maltese steward (Cianta who is at present in charge of the 'Villa Masoni' Mess and is superb), a second steward, a naval cook and assistant and a maid for me, and we'll be expected to entertain and give dances and dinners for about 16. There'll be Wrens working in Malta, of course, but wives will have to wait till the transport and accommodation situation improves. The island has been restored, even unto the goats, but the rebuilding of homes will take longer. I want to buy a horse and ride a lot. Think of having a horse after wanting one all my life!

That's the absurd part of the Navy. One moment one is living like a slut in a pig's hole and the next one is queening it somewhere. There's no sense in it but a lot of fun.

You'll have to hitch a passage to Malta Piet!

Peter did just that, though I never achieved my dream of owning a horse.

One bright November morning Bertie telephoned me from his headquarters in Lascaris above the Grand Harbour.

'There's a chap just arrived in a destroyer from Portsmouth. I'll be bringing him back to lunch and we'll be putting him up for a couple of weeks.'

The 'chap' was tall and bronzed with a slight American accent.

'Piet!'

'Mom, I wanted to surprise you and Dad, so here I am.'

At last the three of us were together and safe after five years of War.

During the sunny fortnight Peter spent at 'Casa Rohan', Admiral Glassford, in charge of the United States Naval Forces in the Mediterranean, flew to Malta to confer the Legion of Merit, Degree of Officer on my husband. Peter

312

and I were proud of the Citation read by Admiral Glassford, but Bertie thought it 'a bit much'.

For exceptionally meritorious conduct in the performance of outstanding services to the Government of the United States as Commanding Officer of HMS *Warspite*, and subsequently as Commodore Administration and Chief of Staff to Commander-in-Chief Mediterranean during the period of almost continuous offensive operations against the enemy in the Central and Western Mediterranean in 1943 and 1944. A forceful leader and skilled seaman, Rear-Admiral (then Captain) Packer, fought his ship gallantly in the face of tremendous opposition during the Allied invasion of the Italian mainland, carrying out three brilliantly executed bombardment missions against the enemy at Salerno to provide excellent support for the advancing United States 6th Army Corps before his vessel was put out of action by several hostile bombing attacks. By his keen initiative and meticulous attention to detail the varied and complex duties of his vital assignment while serving on the Staff of the Commander-in-Chief Mediterranean, he ably assisted in formulating comprehensive plans for the subsequent invasion of southern France. Rear-Admiral Packer's sound judgement, superb tactical ability and loyal devotion to duty throughout were contributing factors in the successes achieved by the Allied Forces in this vital theatre of War.

Peter returned to England by warship and joined a draft of young South Africans due to go home by trooper. They arrived in Cape Town on Christmas Eve.

A few months later we too sailed for South Africa in a troopship and spent Bertie's accumulated leave at 'Tees Lodge',

Part Five: Sailor in Peace
1947 to 1962

28
'*You know that my heart lies in South Africa.*'

Commanding 2nd Cruiser Squadron	Home Waters and
Flagship HMS *Superb*	Mediterranean
Fourth Sea Lord Board of Admiralty	London
Commander-in-Chief South Atlantic	Atlantic and Indian
Flagship HMS *Bermuda*	Oceans
1947 to 1952	

BERTIE'S mother died in 1946 while we were still in Malta and Peter in Cape Town where he had decided to study medicine. We were glad that she had known the War was over and her son and grandson safe. Yet Dorothy wrote: 'It was sad that Bertie's letter came too late for her to read about Peter's decision. But a curious thing happened. The day before the end she was lying peacefully in bed smiling at her thoughts altho' so terribly ill. Then her doctor came in to pay her his usual evening visit. He is a tall dark young man, always very gentle with her, and he has that "born to heal" look that my Norman has. Mother opened her eyes and gave him a most welcoming smile, took his hand between both of hers and said "my big grandson!" That night she became unconscious and Bertie's letter arrived next morning. Almost as though she had second sight and knew and was happy about Peter.'

We were on leave in South Africa when Bertie heard that he was to go as Rear-Admiral commanding the 2nd Cruiser Squadron in the Home Fleet, hoisting his flag in HMS *Superb*. So plans were made for Peter to join us in London where he could continue his studies at Guy's Hospital. Meanwhile we had bought a two-acre plot in the Cape Peninsula so dear to our hearts. One day we would build our first and last home there.

At that period the seas and oceans were being swept for mines, passenger ships were few and waiting-lists long. Britain was still strictly rationed for food, fuel and luxuries, while Europe convalesced from the ravages of War.

The Royal Navy – reduced by five years of loss in unremitting warfare but not yet by the politicians at home – 'showed the flag' in strength and amity in the liberated ports of the world.

The *Superb* and her sister cruisers paid a strenuous series of goodwill visits from the Channel ports to Scandinavia, and also in the Mediterranean.

For once I made no attempt to follow. Bertie's programme was exacting and official and I was content in our Chelsea flat shared by Peter and a cherished skeleton known as 'Bones' who left limp extremities dangling over our sitting-room chairs. My book *Pack and Follow* had been surprisingly well received and I was contemplating a follow-up and was writing articles for magazines in the meantime.

Bertie's letters echoed the relief of peace and some sad reminders of the brutality of War. His notepaper was stamped in red with the flag of a Rear-Admiral on the left.

Flag Officer Commanding, 2nd Cruiser Squadron, c/o GPO London, Antwerp, 23 November 1946

... This morning about 30 reporters came on board. I'm sending you some of the French and Flemish cuttings. Piet will have no difficulty reading the Flemish which is a close relation to Afrikaans. This afternoon we entertained all the groups of the Resistance Movement, about 100. Six chaps had been crippled by the attentions of the Gestapo. ...

I must tell you that an elderly Commander RNR came up to me yesterday and said he and his wife were thrilled by *Pack and Follow*, couldn't put it down and his wife was 'swooning to meet' me! So he brought her along. You wouldn't enjoy this visit. Too official. Yesterday I went to call on the Belgian Artillery, then to Brussels for a quick lunch with the Ambassador, and layed a wreath on the tomb of the Unknown Warrior, then back to Antwerp to watch a football match, *Superb* v Belgian Navy – we lost 3–2 – and on to the Town Hall for 'beating the retreat' (an excellent setting in the Cathedral Square and the Marine Band first class). Finally a Reception on board for the Provincial Governor. . . .

At the end of February, the Squadron went on the spring cruise to the Mediterranean doing combined exercises and firings on the way.

Casablanca, 17 February 1947

. . . At 8 a.m local time I listened to the South African commentary on the arrival of the *Vanguard* in Cape Town and the King and Queen landing with Princesses Elizabeth and Margaret. The commentator talked about South Africa's blue sky and sunshine and the old Mountain and so on and brought my heart to my eyes. Darling, it is our wedding anniversary on Thursday, the day we sail for Gib. I've tried to arrange for flowers to reach you on that day – 22 years! I shall be thinking of you then as I do every day, but very specially. . . .

Yesterday we had a presentation of British decorations on board to French officers. Officers' children and relations present and glowing with pride. The French are all most forthcoming and amiable and you would think they had all fought like tigers all the War. Some have, of course, including the General who never once wavered and is a great man.

317

... Your two lettercards arrived. It was sweet of you to go and see old Lady Cunningham. They always seem rather a lonely pair somehow. Your talk with Admiral J.C. (sounds very religious) was interesting. I expect he has Fourth Sea Lord in view for me, God help me! You know that my heart lies in South Africa and our plans have never attracted me more. Every time I see the Spanish houses here I think of our plot of land and the home we mean to build and don't want to be too old to enjoy it. Well, the next year will tell us, and I know from 22 years' experience that wherever it leads me I shall have you by my side.

That year and the next were brim-full of work and play for all three of us. I joined him in Scandinavia under the midnight sun and then in Cowes where the *Superb* was Guard Ship and the finest yachts in the world spread their sails to compete in classic races. For Bertie there was a memorable visit to the Isle of Arran off the Irish coast with the King and Queen, the two Princesses and Prince Philip as his guests on board his Flagship. Prince Philip was then engaged to the future Queen who Bertie said 'looked so happy and so lovely with her young glowing skin and pretty ankles'.

When he returned to London we went to the French Embassy to an Investiture Ceremony at which Bertie was given the rank of *Commandeur* and the *Croix de Guerre avec Palme*. To Mummy I wrote: 'We teased him no end because the French Ambassador kissed him on both cheeks when he pinned the decoration on his uniform and Bertie is the last person to be kissed by an Ambassador, French or not! But he sustained the ordeal with his usual fortitude.'

In 1948, Admiral Sir John Cunningham's prediction became fact and Bertie was appointed a Lord Commissioner of the Admiralty and Chief of Supplies and Transport. So dreams of 'the home we mean to build' had to wait, as far as we were concerned. Peter, on the other hand, had nesting ideas of his own and in May 1949 he married South African

Glendyr Orr at Holy Trinity, Brompton, and they moved into a pretty mews house just behind the Church. In 'Tees Lodge' too there was rejoicing. Mummy gave a family party for the occasion and Nannie arranged 'celebration cakes and presents' for Cookie, Teena, Arend and their families.

Towards the end of July, Bertie had to go to Malta in the course of duty. He took passage in a naval supply ship and to my delight I was allowed to accompany him. Although our life together had been so disjointed, many unbreakable human bonds lent it permanence and continuity. A letter from Nannie, now widowed and living with my mother at 'Tees Lodge', bridged the gaps of time and distance in her angular German handwriting, with significant words in capital letters.

'Tees Lodge', 27 June 1949

My darling Girlie, you and your dear Admiral will be on your way to Malta soon. Very often my thoughts go back to the Island, and to that first morning when you called to me to go on deck and the early Morning Mist parted and there was Malta in front of us like a Picture out of a Fairy Tale. The Wonder of that I can never forget. I do hope you will both enjoy your time there and have some REST. . . .

If you see Angela and Carrie, you can tell them I still have some of the hankies they embroidered for me. Perhaps you will see Jessie, the lace woman, too. My best Regards to your Admiral.

We were able to pass on Nannie's messages and already we saw the increasing resurgence of the Fortress of Malta, George Cross. The lean years had been rewarded and we could take back many things still unobtainable in England.

Early in 1950 Peter and Glendyr returned to South Africa so that he could complete his studies at the University of Cape Town and at Groote Schuur Hospital, as they intended to settle at the Cape.

For once the parting was painless, for we knew that in September, Bertie would be Commander-in-Chief South

Atlantic, based at Admiralty House, Simon's Town, and flying the flag of a full Admiral in HMS *Bermuda*. His Chief of Staff and Flag Captain was to be Philip Currey, who belongs to a well-known Cape family, and whose attractive wife, Rona, was a great asset to all of us.

I wrote my last London letter to my mother on her birthday.

195 Cranmer Court, Sloane Avenue, SW3, 6 July 1950

My darling Mummy, many happy returns and all our love! What a lucky year this is – the year of our Silver Wedding. To think that it will bring us back to the Cape where we first met and where we mean to live is a sort of 'full circle' for us all, and before 1950 is out we will see our first grandchild and you your first greatgrandbaby!

We have had big excitements during the past few days. On Tuesday Marion and I went to Buckingham Palace for the Investiture which entitles Bertie to be called 'Sir Herbert'. This accolade is a sort of endorsement of the KCB he received in the Honours List.

There were a great number of decorations of the various Orders to be bestowed and it takes about an hour. We had to be at the Palace at 10 a.m. and didn't leave till 12.30.

One goes up the marble stairs with the crimson carpets and is almost immediately separated from the relation to be invested. So, while Bertie went his way, Marion and I walked through the beautiful apartments that lead one out of the other till we reached the magnificent Throne Room. Back of the raised stage is the Throne, two carved chairs under crimson hangings, in an elaborate alcove with columns on either side and indirect but effective lighting. Facing this stage were rows of little gilt chairs and it was a case of take your place in order of arrival and not of distinction. The only people given preference were the children who, with their mothers, were ranged round the raised galleries at the sides of the room. The room is as lovely as anything you could imagine, white and gilt, immensely lofty, glorious chandeliers, mirrors, columns, tapestries. Soft music played in the Minstrel's Gallery, Beefeaters in their red Tudor uniforms stood around and the Equerries showed the audience to their places and told them how to behave. 'Do not sit down till the King tells you to do so, keep silent during the Ceremony' and so on.

Well then, the King appeared with the Chamberlains and various court officials, and the names were called, and, each in turn, those to be decorated entered by one door, received their Medal or their Order and went on and out. When the Knights were accoladed they had to go down on one knee and the King touched them on each shoulder with a sword, and though he did not actually say 'Arise, Sir Knight!' that was the effect. Bertie told us afterwards that they were told, 'You will probably find it easier to go down on your right knee but, if you have difficulty, the left will do.' Some of the new Knights were pretty ancient and rheumaticky and creaked on any knee, but they had a sort of knee-rest wheeled in for the Knight-making which made it a good deal easier for all of them. They knelt on a step.

Bertie's KCB is magnificent. A petunia ribbon goes round his neck with a sort of cross which hangs just under his collar and tie and on his right pocket he wears a glittering star and I was very impressed last night when we went to an Evening Party at the Palace and he was covered in so much glamour!

Last night we again found ourselves in the Throne Room for the Dance. Before it, we dined in a party of about 18 given by Lady Annaly who is a dear and used to be Lady-in-Waiting to the Queen when she was Duchess of York. She is a personal friend of the whole Royal Family.

At the dinner I sat beside General Lord Ismay who, during the War, was Military Adviser to Churchill and then to Mountbatten in India. He is still a power in the land, as wise a bird as you could find and nice and easy too. He is a close friend of Smuts whose world knowledge he very much admires and he treasures a long Xmas letter in Smuts' own hand which he received last year. But he did say to me, 'The only time I can say Smuts was definitely wrong was before the Battle of Britain. He urged us *not* to withdraw our aircraft from France. He said "Hurl it all in!" If we had, the Battle of Britain must have been lost – and perhaps the War with it'. That's interesting, isn't it?

Peter Fleming was there too with a sad cynical monkey face, and Lady Peel (Beatrice Lillie, the actress) looking uncomfortable in a tiara she had 'borrowed' from her jeweller. It kept slipping about. I had no tiara, but wore your diamond star in my hair, and my dress was slate blue slipper satin, very full, an extravagance from Worth. You'll be seeing it soon. Bertie said, 'You look very lovely and I'm proud of you,' but it's hard work to look lovely when one's 'getting on' and I think his heart was in his eyes.

These Evening Parties at the Palace are less formal than most and the stage was also represented by Douglas Fairbanks Jr. who is very attractive and danced with the Queen, and exquisite Moira Shearer, the ballet dancer, was there looking as if she might leave the dance floor and float to the ceiling any minute. She has an enchanting face as if a shy red fox had been turned into a lovely girl.

The Queen was in white satin and tulle, a crinoline embroidered with crystal and rubies and when she danced there was always a little clearing around her. The King didn't dance. Princess Elizabeth was absent owing to the imminent arrival of her second. We talked to the Geyers (South African High Commissioner and Mrs.), he, much impressed by the lovely state apartments, and she, small and timid with a glass of orangeade in her hand while the rest of the glittering assembly lapped up bubbly galore. We also had a chat to Babs Wemyss looking so distinguished with the jewels of the Wemyss and March family sparkling round her neck and in her hair.

Heavens! This has turned into a Snob's Diary!

Our two years based on Admiralty House, Simon's Town, were a wonderful climax to Bertie's naval career. We were surrounded with old friends both South African and English. Dorothy and Norman came to stay with us, so did Philip and Elspeth Rhodes and Phil and Nancy Glover and many others both personal and official. Bertie's Secretary,

Commander Tim Sherwin, and his wife Kathie and their young family, lived close to us in the Admiralty House Compound on the seashore. Chief Petty Officer Corney and his wife and son Melvin were there too and Corney drove the big Humber flying the flag of the Commander-in-Chief. I shared Bertie's travels which took us deep into the heart of Africa as far as northern Nigeria, the French and Belgian Congo, the East and West Coast, Zanzibar and Madagascar, South-West Africa, and the many African territories that are now independent countries and were then on the launching pad of emergence. I kept diaries of our varied and fascinating journeys with all their beauty and savagery – there was plenty of that too – and they formed the basis of my African travel book *Apes and Ivory* and influenced many of the novels that came later.

Most of all we loved those quiet family times when Mummy, Piet and Glen and baby Ronnie came to stay with us between the mountains and the sea, and on summer evenings when False Bay turned from violet to rose, we had our sundowners out of doors. Then the long shadows of the trees fell across the wide lawns of the sea garden, the red-winged starlings uttered their melodious calls, the moonflowers poured their scent into the approaching night, and the Southern Cross glimmered among the constellations wakening in a luminous Madonna blue sky.

There were many great occasions in those two years and many homely ones. There was happiness and some sorrow. Our whole community was saddened when King George VI died and the young Elizabeth, then on holiday in Kenya with Prince Philip, was called home to assume the heavy responsibility of the Crown. Even the children in the compound were aware of that time of mourning.

We had planned our house and we looked forward to the day when we could build it, but as the sands ran out I knew that my husband was preparing to meet the hardest of many hard partings. He never spoke of it, nor did I, and since it had to happen there was comfort in the knowledge that he would face it here where his heart lay and what remained of our future.

So one warm November evening, when the sun sank behind the hills and the old white house lay in shadow, we stood together and watched the ships in the bay still tinged with pink and gold. The notes of the sunset bugle carried across the water as HMS *Bermuda* lowered the flag of the Commander-in-Chief, Admiral Sir Herbert Packer, for the last time. My hand was in his as he bade his silent farewell to the Royal Navy which he had loved and served so faithfully for 45 years.

29

'He was the happiest man I've ever known.'

'Cressage'	Cape Peninsula
S.A.S. *Good Hope*	The meeting place of the
1954 to September 1962	Indian and Atlantic Oceans

WE called our home 'Cressage' after Bertie's birthplace in Shropshire, with its wide view across the Severn to the Wrekin and the hazy Welsh Hills.

Our view from the Kirstenbosch Ridge was magnificent too. We looked towards the granite bastions and deep gorges of the southern flank of Table Mountain where the waterfalls cascaded in winter with a song that carried across the wooded valley between the Mountain and our home. Northwards lay the Cape Flats and the coastal range of the Drakenstein, snow-crowned in winter, especially the highest peak, Die Matroosberg (the Sailor's Mountain). Beyond that was the hinterland rising from the arid plateau of the Karoo to the gold-bearing, grain-growing uplands of the highveld 6,000 feet above sea level and 1,000 miles inland from the Cape Peninsula. The sea was not quite visible but it was near, and at night from our terrace we looked down upon the lights of Table Bay and the network of roads and towns spreading north beneath the stardusted sky.

A rose garden and a vegetable garden were Bertie's care and my delight. Climbing Peace wrapped her strong thornless beauty round the rough mountain-stone pillars that marked the entrance of our drive and bloomed profusely. We found it good that Peace should bless the threshold of our home. Indigenous flowering trees and shrubs hid 'Cressage' from the road, tempting the brilliant sunbirds and the long-tailed sugar birds with their nectar. Their calls filled the air and we knew and loved all the wild birds skimming in and out of our garden. Their song and twittering were music to me, so was the throaty cooing of the quarrelsome greedy doves who occasionally fell victim to our cats or even to our little white dog, Snowy. A white squirrel lived among the pines, and there were, too, grey squirrels who stole the doves' eggs and borrowed the untidy nests of our pretty Cape sparrows to use as a maternity ward, which was silly because the squirrel families were too heavy and down would 'come cradle and baby and all'.

Piet and Glen lived near us and soon Ron was joined by Chris, then by Tony and some years later by Willie. Mummy came often to stay for a few days and Nannie too. My brothers and their families were close by. We had many friends and Bertie's philosophy enabled him to 'live in peace and quietness and . . . enjoy the blessings of the land. . . .' He became Federal President of the Navy League and did all in his power to promote the 'fellowship of the sea' and to encourage the young South African Navy which modelled itself upon the Royal Navy and bought its ships from Britain, and paid for them promptly, bringing prosperity and employment to British shipyards. A subsequent British Government rejected these valuable contracts and South Africa was reluctantly forced to trade elsewhere which was less of a problem to her than it was to Britain's economy.

With Bertie's encouragement, I wrote my first novel, *Valley of the Vines*, which became a Literary Guild Selection in America. This was followed by *Nor the Moon by Night* which was also a Literary Guild Selection and a Dollar Book Club Choice. It was filmed by the Rank Organization in the beautiful Valley of a Thousand Hills in Natal. The wild beasts in my fictional sanctuary fortunately stole the picture. When I took Mummy to see it, she whispered in bewilderment 'We've come to the wrong cinema, Joy. This isn't your picture.'

'No darling,' I said. 'Just enjoy the animals and the scenery and forget the story!'

She sighed and murmured, 'A lot of things muddle me these days.'

Not long afterwards in June 1959, she died peacefully in her sleep. She was in her 88th year. She hadn't been ill – only increasingly tired and deaf. She must have had some premonition the night before because when Teena brought her usual glass of warm milk at 9 o'clock and waited for her to finish it, her gentle dark eyes resting tenderly on *die ou nooi* – 'the old mistress' – Mummy took her hand and thanked her for her long faithful service. 'Kiss me, Teena,' she said, '—and goodbye.'

Nannie wrote to comfort me afterwards. '. . . You and your dear Husband will know how I feel for you all. It just seems that a Higher Mind arranged everything perfectly. It has been before us for a long time. The dear Lady quietly slipped away and is at Rest. We have all lost Somebody who will always be missed. Everything will be different now, but that is the way of Life and one has to make the Best of it. All my love to you Darling and your Admiral, from your old Nan.'

Nannie moved to the Arcadia Home for the Aged where she had good friends, and she was pleased when she found her room overlooked the cemetery!

'It's peaceful and beautiful under the Mountain,' she said. 'And I can see where your mother and father lie and remember the happy days at Tees Lodge.'

She lived a great deal in her memories but she was never allowed to feel lonely or abandoned and continued to share our lives and the little boys, who were like 'great grandchildren' to her.

We were granted nine years in 'Cressage'. It held great contentment for us and when traumatic events in South Africa produced severe repercussions in our own personal lives we sought comfort in the wild beauty of our surroundings and the permanence of our Mountain.

On 22 March 1960, after a very special dinner party to celebrate Nannie's 80th birthday, we saw on the Cape Flats the dull red glow of the African townships, Langa and Nyanga, against the night sky and heard that in Johannesburg simultaneous riots had caused serious loss of life in

Sharpeville. The powerful 'wind of change' was fanning the flames of African nationalism throughout the land, even here at the Cape where the African was neither indigenous nor deep-rooted as were the coloured people who shared a blood heritage with the whites, and the Moslem Malays imported from the Far East by the Dutch East India Company 300 years ago.

On 18 September, Bertie wrote to his sister, Dorothy.

... Since we live in an atmosphere of threats these days, this letter is a threat and a warning that we hope to visit you next year sometime. Perhaps for Christmas.

Joy has nearly finished her new novel, *The Glass Barrier*, again with a Cape background. Although she hasn't made it an apartheid story, she hasn't been dumb enough to pretend such things don't exist in this lovely country and has dipped into these thorny subjects boldly. In fact, it has more 'meat' in it than any of her others.

Nobody bothers much about the coming Republic. So long as South Africa can stay in the Commonwealth I really don't see that it makes much difference if we have a President or a Governor General. What we hope is that the government will develop a kinder and more liberal outlook on such matters as giving real opportunity to the black and brown inhabitants of the new Republic of South Africa.

Our severe personal shock at present is that Piet and Glen are bent on settling in Australia. Piet, in partnership with Fred, is doing very well as an ENT Surgeon here, but reckons there are good openings for his special type of surgery – microscopic ear operations – in Australia.

They both hate the racial tensions here, are very progressive in their outlook and don't want to bring up a young family in an atmosphere that they think may deteriorate. I don't agree. But we give them our blessing and what help we can and wish them the best of luck. It is their business and they must live their lives as they think best. What worries us is that Glen will not have domestic help and will have to cope with all the chores for four young children, but she is undaunted and is already teaching them to make their own beds, breakfast, etc. We shall miss them very much indeed, but there it is, and, after a shaky start, Joy has settled down to a fatalistic and sporting view on the whole enterprise.

On 28 August 1961, our young family came to 'Cressage' to bid us goodbye. We had all decided it was best that way. It was a good date for a new beginning, I told the little boys, because it was the anniversary of their great grandparents' wedding day – a day that had led to a wonderful life for all of us.

When they had gone with a flutter of small hands from the car windows, Bertie and I went on to the terrace in the sunset. It was chilly. The sky above the western peaks was pink herringbone, and in the gap of Constantia Nek the late afternoon light was concentrated in a golden goblet.

'Like the cup-of-gold on our creeper,' I said.

Bertie looked up at the rich green leaves above our big landscape window.

'Too early for the cup-of-gold – not yet spring. But something's going on in the mossies' nest.'

There was always something 'going on' in the big untidy home of our Cape sparrows.

'I think it's an earthquake,' he added.

I shook my head. 'It's Mrs. Squirrel who's using it as a maternity ward. She's always doing that.'

We watched as the 'mossies' flew round the invaded nest with frantic high pitched protests. Mrs. Squirrel, in some final convulsion, tore it from its moorings and the cats watched, inexorable as fate, to welcome the new-born infants.

'Oh,' I gasped. 'How awful! The bottom's dropped right out of Mrs. Squirrel's world.'

Bertie's arm was about my shoulders.

'Yes,' he said gently. 'That makes two of you.'

Towards the end of the year he wrote again to his sister Dorothy: 'Things have been too difficult lately and we must cancel our trip to the UK this year, a decision which has cost us much moaning and groaning. I haven't been well, having migraine-type headaches that leave me rather mauled and with a foul nausea. We hope to make it next year instead. Joy is writing to Winifred and Marion. I find myself very busy with the Navy League and ex-servicemen's associations of all sorts but still have time for my garden which is a delight to us both. We are happy to say that Piet and Glen write cheerfully from Perth, Western Australia, which they love.'

By the middle of 1962 there was no longer any talk of our going to England. Bertie was fighting his last long battle with failing health. The headaches increased in intensity and he was no longer able to enjoy walking round his garden, dearly as he loved it.

Spring came early that year and in September I brought him the roses he had grown with such pleasure, bowls of sturdy Peace and delicate Queen Elizabeths. At night he dreamed of ships and battles and I had the feeling that already he was returning to the element that had dominated his whole life.

Peter flew from Australia to be at my side on the soft silver-grey day when the *Good Hope*, Flagship of the Commander-in-Chief of the South African Navy, put to sea with all the South African Naval Captains on board to do honour to the memory of a 'great sailor' who had never failed to support and encourage them.

Somewhere off the coast near Cape Point, where they say the two great oceans meet, his ashes were consigned to the deep as he would have wished, and the rocky cliffs, so wild and lonely, echoed the bugle calls of the 'Last Post' and the 'Reveille'.

In the weeks that followed I received hundreds of wonderful letters, but perhaps it was his friend and Secretary, Captain Tim Sherwin, RN, who touched my heart most deeply.

. . . I have never known anyone with a greater capacity for

330

living and enjoying his life to the full, but so unselfish and with so many natural gifts that, to everyone with whom he came in contact, he always gave more than he took.

He was certainly the *happiest* man I've ever known. . . .

Cape Peninsula 1973–5

THE END

VERONICA BY JOY PACKER

Derek Symes, newly arrived in South Africa, had a brief affair with Veronica, a beautiful coloured girl – but their love led to unforeseen complications when a child was born, even though the affair was over. For Veronica was determined that their child should cross the colour line and be brought up with all the opportunities open to white children. Only Derek, and his new wife Lindy, could give him that chance, but their attempts to help him led them into blackmail and tragedy.

0 552 10444 2   65p

THE MAN IN THE MEWS BY JOY PACKER

Ravenswood was the country estate of the Fleet family. It had its own quiet magic, that old Queen Anne manor house set in the soft Sussex countryside. Ann Olivier knew that this graceful and dignified home would belong to her daughter Rachel one day . . . if nothing occurred to upset the plans for Rachel's wedding to Jim Fleet. Ann was intelligent enough to know that there were serious gaps in her own past, unaccounted for by a sojourn of twenty years in South Africa. Jim's father, Sir Jasper, was disconcertingly shrewd . . . he watched every move she made on her first visit to Ravenswood. He's dangerous, she thought, I must go carefully . . .

0 552 10173 7   65p

JUDY GARLAND BY ANNE EDWARDS

In this brilliant, deeply human and glittering book – the definitive biography of Garland the star, Judy the woman – Anne Edwards has re-created the life, the loves, the sorrows, the joys, the disasters of a legendary woman. Drawing on a wealth of previously unavailable material, on the intimate revelations of those who knew and loved Judy, on her own meeting with Judy Garland, on the memories of friends, fans, strangers and contemporaries, she has written a book that is sensational in its revelations of the truth behind the Garland legend and the Garland headlines, and at the same time hauntingly, heartbreakingly moving and compassionate; at last, the great, major book that Judy Garland's life deserved.

0 552 10063 3   75p

I, TOM HORN BY WILL HENRY

. . . I must leave this truth where it will be found. The story is all told, all written down, waiting only to be passed to the one who will get it from me tonight when he comes for the last time. No one could have told this story but me. I rode that trail in Wyoming alone. From the first day, it was Tom Horn against the pack . . .

The Old West that Tom Horn knew lived and died with him. When he was gone, the West was gone. In I, TOM HORN, Will Henry recreates the man and his times through a first-person narrative, as a possible lost autobiography of the legendary cowboy. Those who read it will always wonder . . . was this man guilty, or did his enemies kill him to make innocents of themselves?

0 552 10105 2   65p

VALLEY OF THE VINES BY JOY PACKER

Dieu Donné had been the de Valois home for generations, and elderly Constance de Valois was determined that the historic homestead, set in a beautiful South African valley, should remain in the family forever. Roxanne, a war orphan she had adopted as a child, shared this determination. But Merle, the estate's rightful heir, had other plans ... The changing fortunes of the de Valois family and their dramatic battle over the fate of Dieu Donné are the background for Roxanne's search for her true parents, her forbidden love for a famous journalist, and her desperate bid to save Dieu Donné from disaster ...

0 552 10442 6   80p

BORSTAL BOY BY BRENDAN BEHAN

'If the English hoard words like misers, the Irish spend them like sailors; and Brendan Behan, Dublin's obstreperous poet-playwright, is one of the biggest spenders in this line since the young Sean O'Casey. Behan sends language out on a swaggering spree, ribald, flushed and spoiling for a fight.' – KENNETH TYNAN

0 552 09864 7   75p

DIANE DE POITIERS BY BARBARA CARTLAND

When Diane de Poitiers was born to joyful parents in the little town of Saint-Vallier, in the valley of the Rhone, an old crone prophesied 'she will cause tears to fall and joys to be known. And those who weep and those who rejoice she will be greater than them all.' Diane was indeed destined to be great – she was a descendant of Louis XI and related by marriage to Charles VII. As she grew up she displayed formidable qualities of intelligence – and her beauty was just as remarkable. When her lover, Henri, was crowned King, she skilfully piloted him through the first difficult months of his reign. She was an important member of the King's Privy Council, controlling its members as well as its master.

Barbara Cartland's biography of Diane de Poitiers is a glowing tale of the achievements of the King's mistress. Today she and Henri are still remembered for their unchanging, indivisible and eternal love . . .

0 552 10065 X   45p

METTERNICH BY BARBARA CARTLAND

Barbara Cartland's study of Clement Metternich, architect of the Congress of Vienna, and during his lifetime the saviour of Austria, concentrates on his personal rather than his political life. Born in Koblenz in 1773, Metternich was the second son of Count Franz Georg, a high official in the Imperial Court, and Countess Beatrice, an intelligent and beautiful woman. It was Beatrice who trained her son to grasp the importance of power.

Metternich's life was a series of amorous episodes. His Mistresses included Constance de la Force, a high-born refugee from the French Revolution, Caroline Murat, Napoleon's sister, and Princess Katherina Bagration, mistress of the Tsar of Russia. And despite this philandering, Metternich inspired devoted love in his three wives . . .

0 552 10064 1   45p

A SELECTED LIST OF CORGI AUTOBIOGRAPHIES AND BIOGRAPHIES FOR YOUR READING PLEASURE